THE CONTEMPORARY FRENCH THEATRE
The Flight from Naturalism

BY THE SAME AUTHOR

France and the War
France and the Problems of Peace
Impressions of People and Literature
White Temple by the Sea (poems)
Contemporary French Poetry
The Eagle of Prometheus (poems)
The Poetic Drama of Paul Claudel
Mary Stuart (a verse play)
Symbolisme from Poe to Mallarmé
The Harrap Anthology of French Poetry

The
Contemporary
French
Theatre

THE FLIGHT FROM NATURALISM

by

JOSEPH CHIARI

D.-ès-L.

GORDIAN PRESS

NEW YORK

1970

Originally Published 1958
Reprinted 1970

Library of Congress Catalog Card Number - 76-128187
SBN 87752-126-3

AUTHOR'S NOTE

THIS is neither a thesis nor an attempt at writing the literary history of a period; it is a selective study of a generalized attitude towards drama in France, which began to hold sway at the end of the nineteenth century and has, from then on, affected most important playwrights. This attitude could best be described as anti-naturalistic, although of course one must bear in mind the facts that anything alive is never clear-cut enough to be categorized, that there is no watertight separation between naturalism and anti-naturalism, and that the latter is never a single-minded creed.

The writers included in this study are predominantly anti-naturalistic, yet it must be noted that there are important writers like Gabriel Marcel, Salacrou and Julien Green, in whom the blend between naturalism and anti-naturalism is such that they could not be listed under this heading.

The plays of André Obey and Albert Camus belong, in climate, to this study, yet a searching analysis of these authors' works would seem to be rather out of proportion with their dramatic stature. Obey achieved world-wide fame with his play *Noé*. Albert Camus, to whom I shall return in the conclusion, has not yet overcome certain difficulties inherent in his moralistic outlook, and for the moment his plays suffer from the weakness which could be best suggested by Gide's remark: "C'est avec de bons sentiments qu'on fait de la mauvaise littérature."

CONTENTS

Preface to New Edition

THIS book was written fifteen years ago, and it was published before the emergence of what is now called, "the avant-garde theatre", the "New Theatre" or worse still, "the theatre of the absurd". One can easily imagine Beckett's wry smile or Genet's laughter if either were to be described as an absurdist, or as members of the "theatre of the absurd". As for Ionesco, another willy-nilly member of the Absurdist club, he has uttered disclaimers clear-cut enough to discourage any but the most persistent label-makers and foisterers. "For me", he said "inside existence, everything is logical, there is no absurd", or, "the absurd is nothing but the denunciation of the derisory character of a language which has been emptied of its substance".* I have endeavored to deal with the problems of the absurd as well as with the work of Beckett, Genet and Ionesco, in my book entitled *The Landmarks of the Contemporary Theatre* which came out in 1965, and which will be reprinted in this current series. It is sufficient to say that the absurd is, outside the specific domains of philosophy, a very inane notion, totally meaningless when applied to writers. None of those who are called avant gardists, or absurdists, like Genet, Beckett, Ionesco, Adamov, Arrabal, or others, lay any claim to being possessed with a philosophical mind. The only one who obviously has a philosophic mind, and who is pre-

* Ionesco, Notes et Contre-Notes, pp. 32 and 102.

occupied with metaphysical questions is Beckett, and he disclaims any labels, and would not dream of trying to reconcile his obsessive ontological preoccupations with the motion of the absurd. Both Sartre and Camus have each, according to his respective philosophic gift, attempted to explain the philosophic notion of the absurb, and both have come to the conclusion that it is a purely relativistic notion, which is only meaningful, as Camus put it, as part of man's response to the ontological incomprehensibility of life and the cosmos. But neither Sartre nor Camus has been honoured with the label of avant garde, or absurdist, and if they have attempted sometimes, not very successfully, particularly Camus, to dramatize their philosophic notions and beliefs, none of those unwilling members of these two much publicized categories would ever subscribe to the notion that plays should be or could be dramatizations of the philosophic beliefs of their authors.

As for the notion of *Avant-garde,* Baudelaire, who was considerably irritated by the application of military terminology to literature and art, has given the most apt, and still valid castigation of such a deplorable habit: "This use of military metaphors, implies minds, made not for militancy, but for discipline, that is to say, for conformism, minds born for servitude, and only able to think in society."* To me, these oversimplifications, and love of simple categories and nomenclatures are part of a grocer's mind, but have nothing, or very little, to do with art and literature. First of all, if one wishes to use such terms, one must realize that one is always the avant-garde in relation to somebody else. Diderot and Beaumarchais were avant-garde compared with Voltaire who was only the rear-guard of Racine. Hugo, Theophile, Gautier with his red waistcoat, were avant-garde compared with Delille

* Baudelaire, *Mon coeur mis a nu*   N.R.F. "La Pleiade, p. 1285.

and Nepomucene, Lemercier, and later, Maeterlinck was as much avant-garde compared with Zola, as Copeau, Lugné-Poe, Jarry, Appia, are avant-garde compared with Antoine and his naturalism, and so on, and so on, so that every avant-garde is continually absorbed in the main body of the troops, left lying dead in a ditch, or turned into a rear-guard. Nothing is more futile than the translation of art into movements or into military forces, marching forward against imaginary foes, or towards some new Jerusalem.

The artist belongs to his time and either positively or negatively, reflects aspects of his time, but art is above all, individualism, and Genet is as different from Beckett or Ionesco as Sartre is different from Giraudoux or Claudel. What is therefore the sense, or rather, the nonsense of grouping them under the same label or of trying to force upon them the same straight or loose jacket? It does not fit, and it only casts ridicule on its maker. All these writers, walk each his own way, and say each his own say, though admittedly they all share in contemporaneity and they use with varying degrees of skill, the same French language.

The word poet is a much bandied about word and it is applied to all and sundry. Beckett and Genet are both poets and masters of language — two qualities which necessarily lift their work on to a high level of art. Ionesco's poetic vein is more limited and he is not a master of language, whatever else he is; yet, he is notwithstanding these shortcomings, a master of the stage, a most fertile fantasist, and a creator of suspense and unease, particularly in his short one act plays, above all he is a significant revealer of the obsessions, anxieties, conformism and deliquescence of the personality, which afflicts his age. Yet, though he may have kicked out psychology through the front door, it has returned disguised as psychiatry through the window, or the back door, and though he may have replaced plot by situation, and deep emotions by allegories, these are no advantage to drama. Still, he has produced, by now, a corpus of work which assures him a reasonable place in the contemporary French theatre, and a niche in the Academic Francaise.

The problem is different with Beckett and Genet; not that either of them ought not to be if he wishes, a member of that august assembly. Though it is certainly difficult to imagine in spite of its greatest liberalism, how an ex-goal bird, pimp, thief, ex or not homosexual, could be elected as a member of the green uniformed fortica. But the differences between Beckett and Genet on one side, and Ionesco on the other, are not confined to being or not being of the Academy. Both Beckett and Genet are in their own respective ways religious writers, endowed in each case with remarkable vision and profoundity, and intent in exploring the truth and the purpose of the human condition.

Beckett's work, best represented by his masterly play "Waiting for Godot", is a concrete image of existential and metaphysical aspects of the human condition, seen through dramatic characters part of our God-forsaken, catastrophe-obsessed twentieth century. He has neither invented the form which he uses, nor the questions which he asks, for these questions are old, and from Shakespeare to Pirandello, they have been asked over and over again; and as for the form, Maeterlinck had already explored it. But what is original and particularly Beckettian, is the extraordinary bleakness and poignancy which the poor formed animals of Beckett move, caught between two infinities, half-dumb through suffering, aware of what has been and above all of the fact that Godot, light, or hope which are not quite dead could turn up, or revive and thus make life worth while. Therefore these formed animals who are waiting and suffering, go on nobly bearing their misfortunes, and thus they are the greatest encouragement to their fellow beings who see in them fellow creatures who are greater than the fate and sorrows which plague them.

Genet's theatre is also religious. His characters seem to be stained by some kind of original sin. They are by some strange fate criminals, prostitutes, blacks or coloured people, and they are condemned to carry the burden of their guilt, which only death can lift and transform into an apollerois. Genet is Dostoevskian. For him, evil transforms, transfigures and can obviously be the last rung on the "ladder towards sanctity: O Evil, marvellous Evil, the only thing that remains with us, when everything else has us." But Genet's protest is not only a protest against the human condition; it is also a social and political protest in the name of all the oppressed. Maids and servants are oppressed by their bosses and colonial people — black or arab — by their masters, and they will only be one in harmony once they have passed through the screen of death.

After Beckett, Ionesco and Genet, other writers, like Vauthier, Schéhadé, Arrabal, have come to show that the French theatre is very much alive and that it continues to explore in dramatic turns, the significant aspects of the human condition. Yet, the landmarks of the French Theatre are still what they were when I wrote a book bearing that title, five years ago.

JOSEPH CHIARI
London, October 1970.

Introductory

ART is illusion and not imitation, creativeness or revelation through the fusing force of individual genius which is what it reveals, and not pure and simple representation. If the artist holds up any mirror to nature, it is the mirror of his own individual mind which, in its individuations, is as unlike other mirrors as his fingerprints are unlike those of other men. In fact, one should not talk of a mirror, but rather of a prism with an unknowable formula, which is used in an attempt to decompose the phenomenal and perceptual world into its essential components so that they may be apprehensible to man. A dramatic action is an illusion, a "game" played according to rules; it is a fable or a story which, when it blends true creativeness with a stage production which is faithful to it, is a more rewarding experience than any so-called surface or sectional realism. The only realism which has meaning is that of Rembrandt, Dante or Shakespeare, and of the few great artists who can suggest beyond the phenomenon—whether it be a wrinkle, the crease of a dress or the emotional surface of words—the perennial force which informs all these appearances. This kind of realism is not conveyed by perfect histrionic imitation of reality or by faithful reproduction of life's properties on the stage; it rests on truly imaginative creations and on productions conceived as architectural devices meant to blend with the whole, and not as photographic imitations of reality or as set pieces of pictorial or architectural excellence.

The reality which we see on the stage is the reality of the author, actor and producer; it is not in fact reality, but a synthesis of creativeness which will be the starting point of the spectator's reality. A play is a means of illustrating a theme or an otherwise inapprehensible truth; its aim is to create, in the infinity of space and time, instants and figures which, if they are endowed with essential truth, lay claims to eternity. A good play has many

I

levels of meaning—social, historical and universal (that is to say, belonging to all men at all times)—and it has all these meanings by being faithful to its own inner laws, and not by attempting to be a means of moralising or of imparting political or religious truths. Although there are good plays with an explicit message, they are good plays in spite of it and not because of it, for the greatest plays are those in which morality is an integral part of the aesthetic experience involved in witnessing or in reading them, and not something explicitly put forth by any one of the characters. The theatre is a social art, and directly or indirectly it has an essentially moralising effect. If it merely aims at being a means of tickling the epigastrium and of making one laugh at incongruous situations or expressions, or a means of whiling away a few digestive hours, then it is an instrument for an end, which is superficial and vulgar, and not an end in itself, which is the aim of all art. Art unrelated to any profoundly human experience is not art, it is only craft; it merely satisfies a biological urge, and is to life what pornography or prostitution are to true love; it may delude or give pleasure for a few brief moments, but it always leaves behind a sour taste in the mouth and an ineradicable feeling of degradation. Such a superficial, rootless pleasure indicates decay and a society dangerously intent on turning itself into an epicurean flock. A theatre which is no longer an integral part of a living culture indicates a debased society, a society which only dreams of *panem et circenses*, and has lost the kind of centre which made the *Oresteia* or the conflicts of *Lear* part of the very life of the people who witnessed the performance of these plays.

Without probing too deeply into the old academic debate implicitly suggested by Hamlet's advice to the players, and explicitly stated by Diderot, as to whether the action on the stage is an imitation of reality or conventional illusion, and whether the actor should live the action or consciously use all his skill and alertness to make his audience feel and believe what he wants them to believe, it might be apposite at this juncture to say a few words on these problems and on the general problem of realism.

Johnson's famous statement in his preface to Shakespeare in 1765 can be accepted as a fair summing-up of the average playgoer's attitude in the Elizabethan age: "The spectators are always in their senses, and know, from the first act to the last, that the stage is only a stage and that the players are only players. They come to hear a certain number of lines recited with just gestures and elegant modulation." It is obvious from such a statement that a Shakespearian play was more of a literary experience than many critics, intent on reducing dramatic speech to interjections or silences, are prepared to admit. An actor well trained in rhetoric, as was the case in that period, made full use of every word; he aimed less at re-creating in terms of naturalistic behaviour the characters which the dramatist had imagined, than at delivering effectively by skilful use of movement, gesture and voice, the words which the dramatist had written. He would make full use of the rules of rhetorical delivery taught in every grammar school and university, and the playgoers, who had a direct or indirect knowledge of these rules, were in a position to appreciate the finer points of stage performances.

In the Elizabethan age or in Molière's time actors "acted" their parts according to the rules of the profession; they did not believe in the Stanislavsky method, or in the kind of cinematic realism so prevalent in our time, and which consists in filming scenes of everyday life in which the protagonists are not actors or actresses, but average people doing or experiencing things which are part of their lives. The cinema is a synthetic art, and it can make use of such *disjecta membra*, the theatre is an organic art and it cannot do that; its actions are not natural but "unnatural", co-ordinated not in the studio but alive and by the creative minds of the author and the performers. Any actor who, before or after Stanislavsky, believes to the full in the part that he plays runs the risk of leaving the three walls of the stage for the four walls of the asylum. Molière did not choke himself to death in the part of the *Malade imaginaire* because he was in deadly earnest; he had been ill for some time, and should not have been on the stage at that moment.

Whatever method an actor uses, he is never completely the part in which he plays. He is moved, if emotion is involved, but his emotion is artistic emotion: "Nous ne devons éprouver l'émotion que pour mieux l'imiter, pour mieux en saisir les caractères par l'étude et la réflexion," said Talma, who had once been called to order by a beautiful actress, with whom he was playing, with the words: "Take care, Talma; you are moved." Molé, an actor contemporary with Talma, said one night at the end of a performance: "Je ne suis pas content de moi; je me suis trop livré, je ne suis pas resté mon maître; j'étais entré trop vivement dans la situation, j'étais le personnage même, je n'étais plus l'acteur qui le joue. J'ai été vrai comme je le serais chez moi; pour l'optique du théâtre il faut l'être autrement."

L'optique du théâtre—and of art in general—requires that the man who plays Lear be no more Lear than the man who wrote the play. For how could Shakespeare have become Lear without ending, not at the foot of the imaginary Dover cliff, as his creation does, but in Bedlam? However distraught the poet may have been by the blows which wrenched Lear's soul, he obviously retained his inner core or identity, which is genius imaginatively projecting itself in visions which epitomize and transfer certain aspects of existence on to the woof of eternity. The poet was Lear, or the very essence of Lear, when he was putting his words on paper, but he was also Cordelia, Regan, Goneril and all in turns: this implies the existence of an axle, a central seeing eye or listening ear which unobtrusively records the cosmic collisions of these plasmic, yet more real than life, figures. Any actor who attempts to tread the depth that Shakespeare trod, though he does not require to embrace with his imagination the various aspects of the dramatic symphony of which he is only a part, must nevertheless be able to grasp something of the core of the part that he is playing, its relationship with the other parts, and through natural and trained mimetic gifts, he must be able to give the audience a display of all the phenomenal aspects of the emotions and thoughts which he successively receives from and tries to convey through

4

words, to which he adds action. But in order to do that, whether he chooses to give the impression that he lives the part, or on the contrary the impression that he knows full well that he is merely putting it across with the connivance of the audience, he must always retain a core of individual consciousness or identity which controls whatever he is doing. If, for instance, he identified himself to the full with Lear, there would be no reason why he should pay any attention to the notion of playing in harmony with the other characters, or why he should not completely forget his words and rant and rave in earnest in the way any Lear not created by Shakespeare's genius would do, and by so doing he would cause real terror and not aesthetic excitement, and chaos instead of harmony.

How often have we read that Sarah Bernhardt was always the same Sarah, that Olivier is always Olivier, and Gielgud always Gielgud, whatever parts they play, in the same way as Shakespeare, Racine or any other great dramatist retains a core of easily recognizable individuality, whatever the theme or character he is bringing to life? Nobody would confuse Turner with Cézanne, or Beethoven with Wagner or Debussy, whatever the themes they deal with, for art is individual, though, of course, not personal. No actor or author can ever annihilate his inner individuality into any single creation without destroying himself, as, for instance, Hölderlin and Nietzsche did. He must, and he generally does, keep an inner centre of radiation, and the greater the genius, the wider the range and the greater also the illusion of the absence of any set core. That is why, to the sage of Weimar or the pilgrim of the Lake District we oppose the protean, chameleon-like Shakespeare; there was indeed the man who knew, before Diderot, Goethe or Brecht, the necessity of never being fully committed to any given idea or emotion, and the true meaning of "alienation". For what else does the irony of the fool in *Lear* or that of the grave-diggers in *Hamlet* tell us, except that life, as these two great characters, Lear and Hamlet, see it, is unbalanced, incomplete and self-destroying, and that in order for it to be what it ought to be and run its normal course to old age and decay, it must be tempered by the wisdom of the fool and the knowingness of those who have prolonged contacts with skulls and bones? The audience may, and does, live and suffer with Hamlet or Lear, but it does so as the actors do, as part of the great fiction which begins once the lights are switched off in the auditorium and the stage becomes its concrete imagination. For the author the fiction begins the moment he takes his pen and closes his five senses to concentrate on "unheard melodies".

The identification of actor with part and spectators with characters is greatest in plays of a tragic nature and in which the pathos is unredeemed either by grotesque or by comic scenes, and the identification depends essentially on a community of beliefs between actors and characters, and between spectators and characters: the highest peak of identification is reached with mystery plays or episodes of the life of Christ enacted by Christian actors for Christian audiences. In such cases, all involved re-live, according to their imaginative empathy, the actions portrayed on the stage; the same identification must have taken place with Greek plays in ages when they were truly part of religious rituals and festivals. As far as modern audiences are concerned, these plays have no doubt lost a certain amount of their force; the awe-inspiring power of the gods and of Fate, and the hubris which brought divine wrath on to earth have disappeared, though the power of myth as embodiment of an affective knot of perennial significance remains. The Oedipus complex has for the moment been explained in terms of psychology which shifts compulsions from the external to the internal plane, but the ontological relationship of the forces involved is as valid as when this myth first emerged in human consciousness. Scientific explanations which only apply to the phenomenal aspects of reality do not invalidate the metaphysical speculations and conclusions about inner reality and man's relationship with it. A modern pseudo-Greek tragedy like *Phèdre*, in which the springs of action are psychological and Christian, should call forth identifications varying according to the religious beliefs and the experience of the participants; and I do not mean identification with Phèdre as character, but only with the feelings and the situation involved. In Shakespearian tragedies, in which the mythical and purely elemental aspects play a greater part than in the tragedies of Racine, the distance between actor and character, and also between character and spectators, is bound to be much greater than that involved in the plays of Racine; the comic and grotesque scenes add to the tendency towards a dissociation which is increased further by the universality of the action; besides that, such features as the play within the play in *Hamlet*, the soliloquies, as in the case of *Richard III*, in which the hero shows clearsightedness about himself, all work against identification and tend to isolate the action within its own domain preventing it from being absorbed into the life of the actor or of the spectator. While it is possible to reduce the plight of Phèdre to the level of everyday life which makes identification easy, it is impossible to bring any one of Shakespeare's great plays to such a level. Therefore the distance between actors and characters, and characters and spectators is much greater and can only be bridged by people who, unfortunately for them, are no longer subject to the control of reason. Therefore one can infer that it is far more difficult and a far greater achievement to play to perfection Hamlet, Macbeth or Lear, than to play Andromaque or Phèdre; the demand made upon imagination in order to reconcile opposites and to maintain a synthesis of conflicting forces being much greater than the empathy required in order to feel Phèdre's or Andromaque's plight and the mimetic gifts to exteriorize it. There is, of course, no possibility of identification in comedy, comedy being essentially based upon contrasts, whether in situation or in characters or between characters and their speech, and upon the continuous irruption of the abnormal and incongruous into the normal and congruent; in order to apprehend these irruptions the intellect must constantly be on the *qui vive*. In comedy the audience is generally completely dissociated from the characters on the stage, and most of the time laughs at them; what counts in the comic action is not so much the feelings, which are secondary, but the behaviour, the speech and actions of the characters, and in order to convey these three aspects the actor must concentrate not on identification with the part, but on acting it so as to obtain the effects he is aiming at.

Art is essentially symbolization, separation from the object which engages the artist's attention and only acquires significance through this transmutation. This separation from the object is not conceptualization or abstraction, though that comes into play also, but above all an absorption of the essential structure of an object by an individual sensibility which permeates it and creates out of it an organic entity, source of intuitive knowledge or wisdom. Unless this symbolization takes place the object remains a sign or a gesture calling for an immediate response, not in terms of imagination, but in terms of kinetic human reactions. If there has been no transmutation of reality by the artist, there will be no transmutation by the reader or the listener who will respond to it as if the whole thing were real, and as if his emotions were directly involved. Busoni put this case of "distance" or "alienation" aptly: "Just as an artist, if he is to move his audience, must never be moved himself—lest he lose at that moment his mastery over the material—so the listener who wants to get the full operatic effect must never regard it as real, if his artistic appreciation is not to be degraded to mere human sympathy."

Here we have a hint of the kind of emotions which go into the making of art, and of the kind of reality art is aiming at. The emotions are never actual emotions directly described, but emotions imaginatively recreated, and therefore they are not something perceptual and fragmented, but something organic which has passed through the webs of an artistic imagination. The reality of art is this final entity or symbol born from an artistic sensibility and embodying relationships between the feelings expressed and the perceptual shapes that they are given, which are new and bear the imprint of the creative mind. The artist can only express himself in symbolic forms which cannot be replaced by discursive language or representational reality; these aspects of knowledge are neither interchangeable nor co-extensive.

Realism, that is to say the use of reality or of the image of an object to convey emotions and thoughts, did not begin in the 1850s; it is as old as man's first attempts to express himself through art and through words. Realism is a word with a very fluid meaning; the realism of Dante, Chaucer, the Middle Ages, or that of Rembrandt, is neither that of Zola nor, on the whole, that of our time, except in the case of a few outstanding creative minds. The reality of the Middle Ages is that of Thomas Aquinas, that is to say it is the phenomenal aspect of creation fully integrated and informed with the Divine. Nature and the human body are as much part of God as soul and spirit; the realism of the second half of the nineteenth century is conscious post-Cartesian realism, that is to say the fragments of a broken mould the spirit of which has fled; it is concentration on details for their own sake as part of the picture of the mediocrity of a life strictly confined to space and time and lived with blinkers. Angels and daemons are either dead or part of a pre-Raphaelite imagery. Baudelaire was the last to struggle with Satan; Flaubert's St. Anthony merely entertains, in the course of a nightmarish night, the visions despatched to him by Breughel. Life is Emma Bovary or Thérèse Raquin, the sordid pleasures of warped, simpering ideals produced by a schizophrenic society, leading either to arsenic or to the Seine. After Flaubert, whose insistence on art as being its own end and having its own implicit morality led him to the same dock as the author of *Les Fleurs du Mal*, art becomes with Dumas fils, Zola and others the prostituted instrument of morality and social utility. "Art is a criticism of life", they said, and the artist must play his part appointed by a society which takes art as it takes medicine—to flush the system—and pretends that vice is merely the creation of the author's perverted mind. Molière's motto, *instruire en amusant*, is split into two; the artist must instruct, that is all, and men can enjoy themselves on the quiet with their five and more senses, in Gargantuan or gallant backstair exploits, in pursuit of long hair and scented skin. Yet Molière did not mean by *amuser* to entertain the attention superficially in order to distract it from the unbearable contemplation of the inner reality described by Pascal or T. S. Eliot, but rather to cause aesthetic pleasure and to provoke an experience which, satisfying our innate sense of proportion, harmony and truth imaginatively apprehended, leaves us spiritually enriched and with greater inspiration and love of truth than all the preaching and sermonizing of characters who are all too obviously the mouthpieces of their authors. The moralizing, realistic theatre of Scribe, Dumas, Augier, Becque, the heirs of the *comédie larmoyante* of Lillo and Diderot, ends in *pièces à thèse* and melodrama. We had to wait for Ibsen, who used realism as Rembrandt had done, that is to say by giving each pigment, each gesture its prolongation of eternity, its essential individuation; every detail seized and described is not the mechanical reproduction of the camera or mirror which, whether one likes it or not, always distorts, but the one deliberately selected from among others so as to show in its singularity and intense life the whole complex of subterranean forces which go into its making. It is, in short, the result of the work of the imagination expressing through perceptual images the life which informs them; it is creativity through phenomena and not scissors-and-paste work or quotations and concepts skilfully arrayed so as to compose a picture; it is objective, that is to say universal and religious or transcendental; it is in fact true realism. On the contrary, late nineteenth-century realism is scientific and rhetorical; the object is apprehended as a phenomenon which is nothing more than the data which it offers through the senses and the rationalizing faculties, and it is used didactically as part of a demonstration or as an instrument of social redress and reformatory zeal, and that is not realism but the fragmented naturalism which, as far as the theatre is concerned, has nowadays taken a new turn.

We often find ourselves confronted with statements to the

effect that life is chaotic and meaningless and that therefore art cannot fail to be so. The fallacy of such assertions does not stand the briefest examination. The statement that life is chaotic or meaningless is not an objective statement endowed with universal value, but a subjective statement which is only valid for a subject or for a given number of subjects at a given time. Things, events and situations have in themselves no other meaning than that of being what they are meant to be, owing to their component forces and elements. The only meaning of a stone is to be a stone, something which can be analysed and decomposed into its elements, but the causality of which cannot be explained without involving oneself into an infinite regression. The meaning of life is to be life, and mechanistically and metaphysically that meaning is inseparable from life itself. This is not a tautology but merely the acceptance of a form of ontological or idealistic phenomenalism which recognizes that the real meaning of a thing is to be what it is and to be known as such, as a phenomenon or thing in itself whose real meaning, for those who posit the possibility of such a real meaning, transcends, and yet can only be glimpsed at through individual subjectivity. The human mind, which partakes of the reality or essence which informs the phenomenal world and is endowed with varying degrees of self-awareness, can, through the phenomena which are the objects of sense-perceptions, obtain glimpses of the structure of things and their true relationships.

Meaningfulness, meaninglessness and chaos are essentially human concepts which cannot be conveyed by mimetism or by the representation of scenes or events which seem to be chaotic and meaningless. First of all, as things in themselves, these events or scenes are neither; they are organized, that is to say they are the result of causes, and they are meaningful in the sense that their causality is ultimately realized and offers a concrete embodiment of meaning which, although inapprehensible for some, is not so for all men. Secondly, both chaos and meaninglessness are meaningful human concepts, but their meaning can only be derived from their concretization and not from abstractions, at least not from abstractions which are not based on concrete, perceptual manifestations of chaos or of meaninglessness. That means that these concepts are like other concepts, the result of mental organizations which must rest on particulars. Chaos can no more be conveyed by a chaotic conglomeration of phrases purporting to be a work of art, than meaninglessness can be conveyed by meaningless phrases, lack of action or unredeemed silence. In such cases there is no experience of chaos or of meaninglessness, for the subject has not been given means by which he could, through his perceptions starting from actions and words, rise to these two concepts. A chaotic work could be either the result of surrealistic outpourings of the subconscious which could be used as material for psychoanalysis, or a form of wilfulness which could be meaningful for its author only. Silence is as much defined and suggested by words as space is by the objects which it contains. These two concepts do not exist in themselves, they are attributes of mind based on particulars—words or things. If an artist wishes to convey the idea of chaos, metaphysical or temporal, he must organize his composition, whatever medium he uses, in a way which will make some kind of communication possible.

A play is, as is well known, amongst other things the result of a communion between actors and audience, and a playwright does not convey an idea of frustration or boredom by frustrating and boring the audience. Nevertheless, there is a new school of dramatists flourishing in France and much acclaimed in this country, whose motto seems to be: *twitches, whispers and silence*, and who seem more and more inclined to think that a frustrated and baffled audience will come out of the theatre illumined about the meaning of the frustration and the boredom of life. Yet the audience did not come to the theatre to be bored or frustrated, but to experience human emotions, including boredom and frustration, at one remove from life. These emotions are not kinetically felt; they have been imaginatively lived by author and actors, and they are apprehended by the audience in a similar way. The believers in fragmented naturalism confined to superficial religious debates and social documents little removed from the journalistic level will probably soon join forces with those Parisian dramatists who believe in the stage as the place for twitches, whispers and silence, to represent the slice of life which they call reality, as an empty stage.

Yet the only true reality is that of man apprehending himself in the act of experiencing intense moments of awareness of his separation from, or union with, his fellow-beings and with the universe to which he belongs. This kind of reality, fleetingly grasped and not easily conveyed, can only be suggested by works in which the shapes, colours and volumes or the words are like crystal, equally reflecting everywhere the informing glow of the creative vision.

PART I

The Poets

CHAPTER I

The Background to the Flight from Naturalism

THE second half of the nineteenth century was the age of scientific discoveries, industrial progress, and profound belief in reason and scientific methods. By the middle of the nineteenth century people were tired of the exuberance and of the much-heralded individualism of the romantics, and they were ready to welcome the application of scientific methods of control and close observation of facts to the arts. So we had the parnassians, the lovers of impassive beauty, and the realists, who, like Zola, could apply to art the same clinical detachment and keen observation of facts which characterize the scientist at work in his laboratory. But in art as well as in life there are no complete divisions into black and white; the various genres whose separation is strongly stressed in texts of literary analysis, intermingle and overlap continuously in life, and, strange as it may seem, Victor Hugo, Hérédia, Zola, Rimbaud and Baudelaire were contemporaries. Yet literary criticism gives each one, and with a wide enough amount of truth, different labels—Victor Hugo is labelled a romantic, Hérédia a parnassian, Zola a realist, Rimbaud and Baudelaire symbolists; one could add Flaubert, who is generally described both as a realist and as a romantic. One can see at once the insuperable difficulties which arise when juggling with labels and when trying to affix them to something as complex as life or its expression—art. Each one of these descriptive words has a residuum of truth which compels a quasi-general acceptance, yet we cannot but find ourselves on the verge of untruth if we try to force upon them very definite categorical meanings which are valueless without the context of history. All the various meanings of these words can easily be present in the same man; it is only a matter of degree. Baudelaire, for instance, could rightly stand all those epithets in turn, in a way which proves the co-existence of all these attributes of art in the same man, yet he is described, and with sound reasons, as a symbolist.

Symbolism is not new, it is at least as old as literary expression; it ranges from the apocalyptic symbolism of the Bible to the crystalline, sparingly used symbols of the classical age; it is part of the process of conveying suggestions of a sometimes unapprehensible reality, yet a reality which is neither accepted as being nothing but rational nor beyond the final grasp of the conscious. But if we mean by symbolism a new way of conveying through the arts experiences of inner and outer reality, a conscious attempt not to describe what cannot be described, but rather to convey the totality of an experience which fuses subject and object, something which involves the whole being in a timeless moment and implies a new attitude to language, then symbolism began with Baudelaire and Rimbaud and soon became the self-conscious artistic creed which since the 1880s has dominated modern art. Whether they were described as classic, romantic, parnassian, or realist, all the writers who come under these headings had on the whole been concerned with describing reality, physical or psychical, in clear, rather representational language. None of them could be labelled obscure. The symbolists proclaimed their desire to remain faithful to reality, but took different roads. They felt, with Baudelaire and Rimbaud, that reality was so complex, so intricately interwoven with the world of mind and imagination, that it could no longer be described, but merely hinted at, suggested through means which would enable the reader, the listener, or the spectator to recapture the image of that reality. That was symbolism in literature, and impressionism in music and painting —both, in a way, refinements of realism in the arts.

By the end of the eighteenth century, the importance of the

mystery and the impenetrability of its core had come to light through the great mind of Kant, who showed the limitations of Cartesianism and the fact that man's sensorial apparatus could only apprehend the phenomenon, but not the "noumenon", which could only be hinted at, or apprehended intuitively through imagination. That was the attitude which underlay in various degrees the whole of the English romantic movement from Blake to Shelley; in France there was Rousseau, but we had to wait till the symbolists, Rimbaud and Baudelaire, for its complete emergence.

In France, by the end of the nineteenth century, artists and thinkers realized that the attempt to seize reality in its essence and to fix it in artistic creations was vain. They realized that the noumenon eluded the grasp of the mind compelled to content itself with the phenomenon, for in the end pure thought is non-thought, the mystical experience of the void, an experience which can only be mnemonic, secondary not primary, phenomeno-logical and not ontological. In the end they came to realize that the only reality which man can grasp is not that of the external world subject to scientific laws, but that which lies in man's consciousness of that external world and in psychological time, the meeting point of being and non-being, the ever-moving present. The long descriptions of Flaubert or of Balzac limited reality, deformed it in the same way as Courbet or Millet limited it with their solid lines and their ethical connotations. The exact word, the precise image, the clear-cut line, killed true reality, and put in its place a picture of it reduced to proportions which everybody could apprehend. Symbolists and impressionists re-tained their sense of mystery towards reality, and they realized that they could convey an impression of that reality only with colours, sensuous words or images brought together according to psychological affinities, and not according to the logical laws of language or of factual observation. So, with them, we enter a period of coloured phenomenalism and musical and pictorial impressions of the words in an art in which the eyes and the mind, deprived of concrete lines and points to hold on to, rose steadily like the flames of a fire to fade away into the ecstasy of the atmosphere or the void which surrounds them. That was the Mallarméan journey, the flight from reality whose only worth was as material for art. Tired of the hollow eighteenth-century rationalism which had developed into fruitless positivism and materialism, realizing that the millennium was anything but just round the corner, men began to reassert their faith in the ideal world and in the mystery of man and the universe. The end of the nineteenth century was not a religious age, in spite of the strong figures of Newman and Hopkins, but it was an age of great searches in pseudo-religious worlds, such as illuminism, psychic processes, spiritualism and all other aspects of non-material reality. The supremacy of the ideal world, of the world of the mind of Hegel, Berkeley and Schopenhauer, over the mechanistic world of Descartes or the sensuous world of Condillac is reasserted once more and is echoed in art by artists from Keats to Wagner and Yeats. The only true reality for these artists is that of art, and the phenomenal world is merely an illusion of the senses or the transient material which the artist chisels into perennial gold. This world of "Grecian urns", "hammered gold", or "musicienne de silence" belongs not to the world of logic and rational speech, but to experiences resulting from art whose essence aspires to the condition of music. By the end of the nineteenth century, art tends more and more towards abstraction. In this connection one must bear in mind two things; first, the fact that music is the most abstract of the arts, thence the notion that they all aspire to its condition; and secondly, the fact that abstracting is an essentially imaginative process and is therefore central to the artist's tasks.

The latter part of the nineteenth century is overshadowed by the powerful figure of Wagner, whose influence was acknowledged by all symbolist writers. Verlaine said, "De la musique avant toute chose"; poetry was for Baudelaire the rhythmic creation of beauty; Mallarmé said, "the poet must see with his ears", while for Valéry the poets' task consisted in attempting "de reprendre à la musique leur bien".

The Wagnerian theory implies that feelings and emotive states which are beyond the realm of words can only be suggested by music, which is, in contradistinction with poetry, a "vague" art. This was the cardinal belief of the symbolist school of poetry, yet not of Mallarmé, who knew better and who outlined very clearly the distinction between heard and unheard music, and who maintained the supremacy of the word over music—heard music, of course: "La poésie proche l'idée, est Musique par excellence—ne consent pas d'infériorité." Mallarmé's journey was that of Beethoven in the Ninth Symphony: for Beethoven, it was from music to the words, and for Mallarmé, from the contingent to the essence. In the balcony scene of *Romeo and Juliet*—an example quoted by Mr. Eliot so as to show the "mirage of verse drama which presents at once the two aspects of dramatic and musical order"—the poetry is song, the revelation of two enchanted souls filled with the sublime passion which makes heavenly joy: the substance not so much as Wagner's as of Mozart's music, which is, above all, joy. In Wagner, music takes over where words leave off, in order to express emotions which overflow them. To be precise, this music tries to express not so much the depths or the heights of the human soul as an excess of feelings over words and means of verbal expression, a longing for something indefinable, the something which was so widely felt and misinterpreted by the romantics. But, excess of feelings does not necessarily imply depth or supra human sensibility: it may only imply the lack of the necessary genius to coalesce these feelings into form: for, paraphrasing Coleridge, we might say that no truly essential feeling or thought can lack its form without, by so doing, denying its very existence. This, then, is not music tending towards the Essence or the Idea—the pure music of Plato, source of all things —but music as a vague art. It is not music as an ontological means of expressing or conveying the essential truth, but music designed to convey the state of turgidity and indefinable agitation which

21

hides the great calm and the perennial quality of the depths. We are left half-way in a vagueness favourable to relative subjectivity and apt to satisfy the creative itch of the masses, but incompatible with the pursuits of the mind interested in the Goethean journey towards "greater and greater light". I do not mean that great art reveals and solves all mystery, for mystery is part of great art, and Goethe's urge was perhaps too strong in that direction. I mean rather that in great art the phenomenal world, the world of the senses, which is our only means of apprehending the essence, must be clearly conveyed, whether through words, pigments, lines or notes, in images, objects, symbols, and sensations which have both interaction and suggestiveness, but are not themselves vague. Reality, in order to be transcended into its timelessness, must not be wrapped up in a haze or drowned in vague sounds, but clearly outlined, so that it may radiate clearly towards the sun which we cannot see, but which gives it life. Vagueness can suggest emotive states favourable to dreams or phantasmagoria, but cannot provoke experiences informed by truth.

The first symbolist poets, Baudelaire, Rimbaud, Mallarmé, did not write for the theatre; it is only the post-symbolists Maeterlinck, Verhaeren, Dujardin, Paul Fort, W. B. Yeats, Claudel, Eliot and others who have turned their attention to the stage. Between what are generally described as the two waves of symbolism lies a renewed upsurge of the conflict between realism and idealism, and at the same time a great revival of the theatre. That revival centres round two main names, Ibsen and Wagner. Ibsen, whose influence was soon going to supplant that of Scribe, was no doubt conversant with the French theatre, since during his career as director of the Bergen Theatre he had produced well over fifty French plays, including twenty-one by Scribe. Like his great contemporary Wagner, he greatly admired Scribe, and they both derived profit from him. But Wagner and Ibsen had gifts unknown to Scribe, and each in his own way was going to introduce into the theatre changes which are altogether the most striking we have seen since the last great age of drama, the seventeenth century. Ibsen, a poet convinced that "verse had been injudicious to dramatic art", wrote the greater part of his dramatic work in prose and sought to give a naturalistic background to problems which pertain to the realm of mysticism and symbolism. His search for the true inner life of the soul led him to one of the main tenets of symbolism as a literary creed, which is that the deepest emotions cannot be expressed but can only be suggested by music, silence or symbolism. The supremacy of music as a means of suggesting depths of emotions beyond words rejoins the point of view of Wagner who, with his new approach to opera, had in mind the same public as Ibsen—the rapidly increasing middle-class. The differences between Ibsen and Wagner are of course much greater than the similarities: Ibsen was intent on the discovery of the inner life, Wagner on grandiose projects, such as the restoration of a national psyche and the achievement of a synthesis of music and poetry, with music as the dominant element. But the poets of that period who were intent on writing for the stage were also conscious of Ibsen's wisdom, and they too tried to blend naturalism and symbolism. Probably none of them was more conscious of that wisdom than Maeterlinck, who admired Ibsen, and in his own way tried to reconcile poetry and popular success, Wagnerian medievalism and prose.

Maeterlinck wanted to write poetic drama, and he made an inordinate use of various devices which can, on the whole, be described as the components of poetry, but which are not poetry. We find in his work all the well-known devices repeated *ad libidum*—the same old castle, the gloom and cold which go with it, the subterranean vaults, the vast forests, comets, white sails, towers, rings and crowns lost in magic waters, the usual fountains—nothing is forgotten, nothing is new. And together with these same old poetic properties, we have the same poetic themes based on old fables and legends, and the same myths and fairy tales used in order to create that atmosphere of unreality which some people seem to think a fundamental prerequisite of poetry. Poetry in poetic drama is not only what should strike an audience as being the most complete way of expressing character, but also a form which should impose itself on characters and author, and by so doing acquire a kind of mysterious life which goes beyond both and which becomes an endless source of interpretation for successive generations of readers or listeners.

Maeterlinck has taken the trouble of explaining in the Preface to his *Théâtre complet*, published in 1908, what his conception of Poetry was:

> La haute poésie, à la regarder de près, se compose de trois éléments principaux; d'abord la beauté verbale, ensuite la contemplation, et la peinture passionnée de ce qui existe réellement autour de nous et en nous-mêmes, c'est-à-dire la nature et nos sentiments, et enfin, enveloppant l'œuvre entière et créant son atmosphère propre, l'idée que le poète se fait de l'inconnu dans lequel flottent les êtres et les choses qu'il évoque, du mystère qui les domine et les juge et qui préside à leurs destinées.
>
> (Preface, pp. x-xi)

Verbal beauty, passionate language and sense of mystery are indeed important elements of great poetry. Everybody will agree; but there is something more important. Maeterlinck has left out the one quality which welds all these elements together into the oneness of poetry—it is the quality of imaginative yet precise sensitiveness which compels its form and produces a kind of organic wholeness. His writings do show, scattered through them, as a veil which floats over them, the qualities which he mentions. They have at times verbal beauty; they show samples of passionate attachment to reality, and they also have sometimes a vague sense of mystery. But all these things are only the *disjecta membra* of the great body which never lives; they are not woven into the pattern of the work, and they add little to the knowledge of the characters, which are rather static. They are mostly descriptive passages of scenery, or of *états d'âme*, but they are not dramatic.

Maeterlinck, when he talks of "the passionate painting of what exists round us", seems to be well aware of the fact that realism is not the antithesis of poetry. What leaves one rather unconvinced is the distinction which he makes between lyrical and dramatic poetry. It seems rather difficult to accept his notion that the lyric poet can confine himself to generalities while the dramatic poet must give concrete, real forms to the obscure forces which surround man and are the texture of his tragic fate.

A la rigueur il est permis au poète lyrique de se tenir aux idées générales les plus vastes et les plus imprécises. Il n'a point à se préoccuper de leurs conséquences pratiques. . . . Mais le poète dramatique ne peut se borner à ces généralities. Il est obligé de faire descendre dans la vie réelle, dans la vie de tous les jours, l'idée qu'il se fait de l'inconnu.

(Preface, pp. xi and xii)

In fact, in dramatic poetry the mystery is no nearer a solution than in lyrical poetry. The mystery of *Hamlet* remains, and indeed it is partly because that mystery is unfathomable that it is a great play. Can we say that we are anywhere nearer the solution of the mystery because we can say that it is ambition which leads Macbeth to murder, or ill-conceived passion which leads Phèdre to crime and suicide? Have we solved the problem because we have found a name? Why ambition should have affected Macbeth rather than Marlborough, or why Phèdre and not Ariadne should be the chosen victim of the gods, we do not know and we cannot know. The more one tries to envisage those various categories of poetry, the more one realizes that one should not stress too sharply the demarcation line. The lyricism of dramatic poetry may only be, at least ought to appear as being, the lyricism of the characters of the play, yet in fact it is and can only be the lyricism of the creative mind, which must have lived imaginatively the drama of its characters. As for what we generally

describe as lyrical poetry, we know that it is indeed the spontaneous flow of the poet's heart, but of a heart which is ever the place
where conflicts rage, where contrasts live in a vivid form, and
where the dialogue between present and absent, between what is
and what is not, surges forth in the beauty of the song. The purest
lyrics of Burns, of Donne, of Herrick or of St. John of the Cross
are the expression of that "dialogue of one", between the
"I" and "Thou", on the human or on the supernatural plane.
The lyrical outbursts are certainly born from conflicts and contrasts and from the moving awareness of what is and what is not,
and even when love flows in its full plenitude and rings joyfully,
as in "O my love is like a red, red rose", we have that duality
between the temporality of nature and things and the transcend-
ance of love. The only oneness of lyrical poetry, or more pre-
cisely, of the short lyric, is the oneness of the single emotion
which underlies it with its congruent and divergent associations.
In dramatic poetry we have a poetic resolution of emotional
conflicts, through the *self-conscious* creative mind.

The main weaknesses of Maeterlinck's drama lie probably
in his conception of it. He thought that he could compromise
between the realistic tendencies of his time and his poetic aspirations by treating poetic subjects and situations in prose. Perhaps
that was not a willed attitude but the expression of his very nature,
which does not seem to be that of a true poet. Whatever explanation one may accept, the result is that his attempts to write poetic
drama in that way led him to making use of all the most outworn
conventions of poetry, in diction, subject-matter and situations.
He gave away, if ever he had it, the substance for the shadow.
His characters, on the whole, have no life; they are puppets which
he manipulates as he pleases. They confront us not with dramatic
developments but with a succession of events; they have beautiful
names, they surge from strange places and go nowhere, and they
perform with mechanistic exactitude those same gestures which
have been performed before them by various heroes of legend,
from Tristram and Iseult to Lancelot and Guinevere. With

Maeterlinck we are right in the middle of the neo-romantic revival of the end of the nineteenth century; his characters partake of all the foibles of the conventional romantic hero from Werther to René, the hero who is doomed and who knows it, the hero whose love only exists on the basis of its impossibility and its associations with the death-wish, because death is the only solution. Love is for these heroes the unattainable, the thing that ceases to be love if it reaches fulfilment; therefore they must all fall prey to an impossible yet an unavoidable love. Tristram and Iseult, Pelléas and Mélisande could not possibly be happy lovers getting married and living happily ever after. They express that aspect of love impossible to satisfy, the love which is above all the longing, the anticipation or the regrets for the thing lost, but never the actual, the present. It is a conception of love which shows the supremacy of imagination over reality and the trans-cendence of memory and the essence over existence—existence being the means of apprehending glimpses of the world of essences—but never being able to achieve, in the act of living, the plenitude of the imagined world.

We are back to the world of ideas of Plato and to meta-physical determinism. The romantics believed in the ideal world, and the importance which they granted to subjective experience led them to the grandiloquent poses of Victor Hugo or the Nietzschean assertion of the individual will. In Maeterlinck we do not have the Nietzschean will, but we have the self-indulgent poses and the complete disregard of reality which are the main weaknesses of late romanticism and we have, above all, the Mallarméan conception of silence as a source of poetry, derived from Plato:

Heard melodies are sweet, but those unheard are sweeter.

Keats had already sung the beauty of silence and music unheard, the superiority of the ideal over the world of the senses, the superiority of the essence of song or beauty over any existing song or beauty. The "ideal beauty" of Baudelaire and above all of Mallarmé was the abstract beauty of Poe completely detached from the phenomenal world. That beauty could only be reached through an elevation of the soul. For the great romantics, imagination operated through the phenomenal world; Poe, on the contrary, operated in the world of fantasy. Maeterlinck followed him, and vagueness, which had been one of the failings of the early romantics, became with him what it had been for Continental romantics, part of poetic technique.

We can see how far we are from the idea of beauty of the great romantics—Blake, Wordsworth, Coleridge or Keats—who did not believe that the abstracting power of the intellect could produce knowledge more complete than that of the senses; on the contrary, they believed that knowledge was particular and imaginatively apprehended through the senses. As poets they believed that the words, mysterious symbols of a reality beyond the senses, could not express all and could only hint and suggest; but they knew that it was the way in which these words were arrayed which made suggestions possible, and the more suggestive they were, the greater the poetry. Indeed, this is a point most relevant to Maeterlinck's drama; we must remember that the quality of silence and its creativeness depend entirely on the words which lead to it and frame it. People talk about the poetry of silence, forgetting that silence is by definition neuter; it can only yield what one puts into it, or extracts from it. The dead silent night might be heaven or hell according to the thoughts which beset the mind and the emotions which stir the heart. One must not construe vague pronouncements about the poetry of silence into the wide generalization that silence is poetry. If it were so, there would be no need for words, or for poets; all the silent, sullen, dumb of the earth would be poets, and perhaps they are, at least potentially, but only the words can tell us what is the truth —the quality of their silence.

One talks about what is beyond the word as being the true source of poetry, but one must not forget that it is the word which must lead to that source. Indeed, that kind of silence is really the prolongation of the word, and we can understand why its quality is determined by the word; in fact, that quality seems to me to be nothing more, nothing less than the creativeness of the word, and that is truly what poetry is. People talk of the silences of Maeterlinck's dramas, silences where souls speak to souls in matchless poetry. That is, it seems to me, a gratuitous assertion; if poetry there is, it will depend entirely on the words which have caused these silences and which surround them. Some people believe that emotions gain in intensity through being inarticulate. I think, with T. S. Eliot, that "those emotions are perhaps not significant enough to endure full daylight". I would also add that perhaps the poet has not enough power to express them, and that means that they do not truly exist, they are only virtual. There is here a confusion, and it lies in equating the very nature of poetry, which is to be a source of creativeness for every reader or listener, with what one calls the poetry of silence. The poetry of silence rests entirely on the words, which must be harmonized in such a way as to produce or to induce, in the reader or listener, silences filled with poetry. Something similar can be said about Maeterlinck's use of repetition, whose value has been greatly overrated. The poetic value of repetition lies in the context and not in itself. A simple phrase uttered in the middle of a dramatic situation is far more potent than any kind of concentrated language or imagery, but that phrase must startle and produce poetry by its power of tense meaning; the best examples are of course in Shakespeare: "Never, never . . .", or "Tomorrow and to-morrow . . ." Some of Maeterlinck's repetitions are utterly conventional and unbearable.

Maeterlinck was a typical example of "the divided sensibility" of the age in which he lived, an age in which every work of imagination had to have a philosophy. He wanted to be accurately realistic in his speech and poetic in his settings and themes, and he felt that one ought to speak not in verse, because verse would have been too remote from the customary speech of the theatre of his day, but in a kind of poetic prose which, with the necessary stereotyped scaffoldings, should rise to poetry. He was not aware of the truth—in fact he could not be, since he lived in that climate and was part of it—that the obverse of rationalism and materialism is sentimentality. His was the age which could once again divide man, the age which, believing in the supremacy of reason and in materialism, plunged into sentimentalism as the only means of escape, as the only way to give scope to the affective life which was there, part of man, and could not, whatever the attempt, be reduced to nothingness. In days when imagination had been once more superseded by a revival of pseudo-rationalism and scientism, the faith in reason was too great to have it contaminated by any admixture of sentiments; therefore sentiments had to be accepted by themselves, in isolation, without having been tested by mind; and that is why men accept living on two distinctly separated planes—on the plane of hard rational behaviour and high expectations, and on the plane of dreamland, escapism and sentimentalism.

They were inclined to think that since poetry as poetry is a creation of the imagination, anything which is not realistic, any kind of airy-fairy concoction which takes place in dreamland, any kind of debauch of colours or cacophony of sounds which smacks of the unreal, is poetry. True enough, *The Tempest* and *Kubla Khan* have only existed in the ideal or supernatural world, but they partake at the same time of the real and of the unreal world, and they bear the mark of the synthesizing power of the imagination which, operating on the two planes at once, left upon these imaginary flights the imprint of deeply lived experiences. *Kubla Khan* may be a dream, or the memory of a dream, but it is the dream of a man of our world who, for a timeless moment, had perhaps his "beatific vision". The fairy tales, whether we examine those of Lewis Carroll or those of Maeterlinck, cannot be situated on any one of these planes, for they are above all flights into unreason and they do not exist on any plane, neither on the supernatural nor on the natural. Fantasy is an attempt to get free both from the real and the unreal, the eternal and the temporal, heaven and hell. As an antithesis to realism, it fails, for it flies away from the world and has no contact with it. The result is not artistic creation, but fantastic visions of a completely unreal world, a world which has nothing to do with experience.

Maeterlinck's theatre, on the whole, fails as poetry, as philosophy and most of the time as drama, and the failure is generally due to complete confusion of the genres. The so-called poetry is frequently reduced to a matter of devices, conventions and worn-out themes; the philosophy is vague, undigested and above all untransmuted into the dramatic characters, who are generally the prey of mechanistic forces which leave our sympathy unmoved. A great many of these characters have obviously spent weary hours in the shadow of the *House of Usher*: through Maeterlinck's theatre the ghost- and ghoul-haunted world of Poe reaches the stage; the strange atmosphere of omnipresent death and all the tricks of Poe are here extensively used.

Had Maeterlinck's poetic gifts been greater and more genuine, he might have given us, not vague philosophical generalization, simple allegories and conceptionalized-emotions, but imaginative creations which would have conveyed the experience of a philosophy detached from the life and thoughts of their character. Yet one must not forget that Maeterlinck began to write at a time when the divorce between what was then esoteric art—symbolism and impressionism—and the masses, engrossed in the prestige of scientific achievements and materialism, was growing. If his attempt was a partial failure, the final results are not negligible, for he broke the ice which barred the access to certain esoteric lands, and he can claim the lasting honour of having inaugurated the symbolist theatre.

CHAPTER 2

Edmond Rostand

EDMOND ROSTAND is not a major writer, yet somehow he is an important one. His importance lies in the fact that he is not only a kind of reaction to symbolist poetry, but a combination of the two strains—idealism and realism—which at the end of the nineteenth century were contending for pre-eminence, and also the representative of a great tradition in French poetry, the tradition of rhetorical poetry. Rostand's romanticism is counteracted by his rationalism and trust in reality, and these two contending tendencies assume, in turn, the mastery of his creative mind, or blend harmoniously in order to produce his best writings.

Rhetoric, which is found in the best poets, from Shakespeare to Racine, has now become a term of disparagement, yet there is good and bad rhetoric. The aim of rhetoric being to persuade, it may take the form of a conscious effort combining words and gestures in order to create an emotive state which will win over the reader or listener, or it may be a logical, cogent display of reasoning which cannot fail to carry conviction. It is an attempt to convey to the listener or reader a definite experience by means of overwhelming or triumphing over his judgment. Therefore the experience of the listener or reader will not be creative, but will be imposed upon him by the poet; that experience will gain only a temporary acceptance, for as it has not been truly lived and re-created by the listener or reader, it will not become part of his experience; it will not be true knowledge—which is what real poetry should be—it will remain an inferior kind of poetry. The poetry will not rise from the event or the thing described in its simplicity, or complexity, but will be given life with an aim in view, and both its morality and beauty will tend to be explicit and not implicit, as they should be. Poetry in tragedy arises from profound emotions probed to their depths in attempts to lay bare the very sources of being. Poetry in comedy arises from intellectual dispersions or unsuspected associations; the mind, instead of being governed by an overwhelming passion, bubbles freely in irrepressible exuberance according to the theme and subject chosen. That kind of poetry does not imply any revelatory quality of the words, but it does imply the existence of a rhythmical pattern, a musicality of the lines, and also the use of figures of speech which appeal as much to the senses as to the intellect, the whole thing being not a compulsory surge from the whole being of the poet, but rather an "intellectual" creation resulting from the intellect working on emotions as well as on strictly intellectual materials.

It seems to me that the test of whether rhetoric is good or bad lies in its power of conviction. If the author forgets himself, and uses his characters, or one of his characters, in order to expound his own ideas, or if he allows the characters to speak beyond the stage to the audience, then we have bad rhetoric. If a character dramatizes himself unconsciously, or if his words and gestures do not match the emotions or feelings which he is seeking to convey, then we also have bad rhetoric, for the words are no longer there in order to express a given situation, but because the author, carried away by his verbal skill, cannot resist a display of his virtuosity. But if the intellectual excitement, the passionate vehemence or persuasive strength of speech is perfectly in character and situation, whether it be Henry V on the eve of Agincourt or Horace's and Curiace's passionate debate before they engage in single combat, we have excellent rhetoric, or, to be precise, excellent dramatic speech. Good rhetoric is essentially reason at white heat, set upon a goal and wilfully using all the means of impassioned speech and power of emotive suggestion in order to reach it. The words, like waves, roll, pervade and overwhelm the listener until he lies temporarily exhausted or dazed under the

33

impact of this mighty, dissolving stream. Rostand's rhetoric is above all the rhetoric of a burlesque poet, a poet who is making fun of others, as well as of himself. Although he is much less brilliant than either of them, his is the rhetoric of Pope or of Byron, the Byron of *Don Juan*, for instance, who laughs at himself first so that others may not do it. Rostand's Percynet, for instance, sees himself as Romeo, Tristram and all the great lovers of legend and history, but he says that with a smile, and therefore his utterances have a truly dramatic value for they fulfil their purpose. Only when he talks for one moment seriously, too seriously, of his love without any self-consciousness (as in the "stances") does he fall into sentimentality.

Rostand's passions are thoroughly intellectual. They come not from the heart but from the head; they are not forces which can wrench the human soul as storms can wrench minds or trees, they are thought out, although at times mentally felt and expounded with great skill. We have here a kind of rhetoric of passions reminiscent of that of Corneille and sometimes very successful, for like Corneille—though not to the same degree—Rostand was a master of words. But he did not write, he never wrote with his whole being; he wrote from a divided or rather complex, non-integrated personality. If he shared in the romanticism of his time, his Attic salt, his Mediterranean scepticism prevented him from taking himself too seriously and from striking humourless poses. He has his limitations, and they are very great, for he did not have the supreme quality of the poet, imagination, which can make great poetry; but he had equilibrium, and a sound grasp of realities. When that equilibrium is broken, when the balance leans towards the tragic, as in *La Princesse lointaine* or in *La Samaritaine*, Rostand is at his worst, for he is not a tragic poet; but when, as in *Cyrano*, he can temper the most serious situation with self-criticism and laughter—which forestalls laughter at himself—he is at his best, and he achieves a kind of elevation quasi-unique in his genre in France and very reminiscent of Byron.

La Samaritaine, for instance, illustrates the weak aspects of

Rostand's romanticism unmitigated by the realism and the sense of humour which generally redeem it. The theme is the triumph of ideal love over physical love. The more one advances through the play, the more one wonders with anguish and increasing disquiet what Jesus had to do in the apotheosis of this new Magdalen—Sarah Bernhardt. The part is all to obviously written for the great actress, who is given as many opportunities as Rostand could provide to display the irresistible charms of her feminine personality, and they are such that even Jesus who is far more man than God, is very nearly carried away by "la forme divine de son bras nu". Indeed, who could resist her, when with her fair locks rippling down her white shoulders she seeks to rouse the mob in the public square or to lead them out of the town, along the dusty roads towards Jacob's Well where Jesus sits? What a tableau, as Rostand calls it! Jesus speaks like Rostand himself; Rostand the inflated, self-conscious poet who could not only always produce a rhyme when needed, but also a triple and quadruple rhyme when those who required them were the ghosts of great prophets who had behind them centuries of vaticination.

Rostand certainly did not seem to understand anything about religion, or he would not have produced that cardboard mock pageantry which might perhaps grace a village fête in Provence and bring sentimental tears to the eyes of old matrons watching the scene, but which has no deep echoes. Jesus cannot be a dramatic character, even in order to partner Sarah Bernhardt. How can he choose, act, hesitate, suffer, since he knows all, suffers all and transcends time and space? To make of him the protagonist of a drama is to reduce him to the husk of what he is, and to show the shallowness of one's sensitiveness. The only drama the greatest drama of all, is the Passion of Christ. We cannot alter the story or the fable, as we may choose to call it, without shattering the whole framework of human sensitiveness. If Jesus moves on earth and utters human words, they must be move-ments and words which everybody knows, and which have by now become the very texture of the Christian soul. He may be made to behave and to speak in the manner and with the words of Rostand, D. H. Lawrence[1] or any other poet, but then it is no longer Jesus; he becomes a being whom pagans or Martians could perhaps understand, but Christians certainly cannot do so. This is not a point of historical truth; poets can, to a certain extent, alter history and give us poetic truth, but Christ is not *history* but *reality*, permanent and eternal reality, beyond the historical. The greatest poets, Dante or Milton, who have sought to convey to man the idea of the Divine, have understood that; for although Milton makes God and Christ speak, they do so at least in an epic, and not in a drama. A drama, if it deals with the life of Christ, can only take the form of mystery plays which give us as faithful a vision as possible of the life of our Lord as we know it from the Bible.

Pace to *La Samaritaine* and let us pass, with *Cyrano de Bergerac*, to a genre in which Rostand can truly be himself, and in which he has reached his plenitude as a poet-dramatist.

Rostand combines some of the technical skill of Scribe with some of the exuberance of language of Victor Hugo. Besides that, he is both a realist and an idealist. His idealism is akin to that of Victor Hugo; like him, he believes in violent contrasts and in the supremacy of the spiritual over the physical. Cyrano has echoes, sometimes conscious echoes, of Marion Delorme and Ruy Blas—the earthworm in love with a star. Like Victor Hugo, Rostand can unfold brilliant metaphors and coin striking antitheses, and even his most lyrical outbursts, such as Cyrano's words to Roxane in Act III, have that kind of rhetorical brilliance and verbal lusciousness which we find in Victor Hugo. There is no doubt that with regard to rhetoric and themes, Rostand is the most Hugoesque of contemporary French poets. One cannot talk of his imagination; as I have already suggested, I do not think he had much, and whatever he had (and this is where he parts

[1] Jesus, in D. H. Lawrence's story, *The Man Who Died*, suffers the same entirely subjective interpretation.

company from Victor Hugo), he certainly did not place a great deal of trust in it. He was too sceptical, too reality-bound, and, in contrast with Victor Hugo, he did not picture himself as the visionary, inspired seer who can descry unknown lands and point the road to his fellow-beings.

Rostand has a definite gift of visual imagery, of which we find many good examples in *Cyrano*, but as soon as he leaves reality he throws himself into a fantastic world in which he obviously does not believe. He has fancy, the kind of power which drags him in any direction but which is incapable of unifying various aspects of things and emotions into a living whole, and he has at times a power of dramatic expression which in its simplicity produces emotional tension and can rise to poetry. The end of the scene between Roxane and Cyrano is an example in which great tension between two characters can lift simple words to poetry. That scene is dramatic and very moving too, for here we see how Cyrano's hopes are drowned in the distractions of Roxane, who is completely carried away by her love for another. Rostand, or Cyrano, could dream beautiful dreams, but these dreams were countered by the wit of a man who knew their defects, and who knew that life could not always be a dream. The whole of Rostand's dramatic creation tends to prove that he believed in the supremacy of the ideal over the spiritual; indeed, in the end Rudel and Cyrano, the poets, the idealists, are those whose love triumphs; but that triumph never takes place in the world here and now, in the world of realities. When these heroes fall in the arms of their beloved, it is always too late, death is already upon them.

Protected by night Cyrano could, through the magic of his words, win Roxane's love, but he knew all too well that the whole thing would not stand the test of light and reason; he knew that Ideal is one thing and Reality another. Rostand did not believe, as Hugo did, in imagination, and his wit springs from that loss of belief. Hugo believed in his visions, in his apocalyptic dreams; Rostand also could dream, but he knew that dreams could not be realized, and he resolved the contrasts between dreams and reality into mockery, as when Cyrano, in Act I scene v, confesses his love for Roxane to his friend Le Bret:

CYRANO: ... Avec mon pauvre grand diable de nez je hume
L'avril,—je suis des yeux, sous un rayon d'argent,
Au bras d'un cavalier, quelque femme, en songeant
Que pour marcher, à petits pas, dans de la lune,
Aussi moi j'aimerais au bras en avoir une,
Je m'exalte, j'oublie ... et j'aperçois soudain
L'ombre de mon profil sur le mur du jardin.

LE BRET (*ému*): Mon ami! ...

CYRANO: Mon ami, j'ai de mauvaises heures!
De me sentir si laid, parfois, tout seul ...

LE BRET (*vivement, lui prenant la main*):   Tu pleures?

CYRANO: Ah! non, cela, jamais! Non, ce serait trop laid,
Si le long de ce nez une larme coulait!
Je ne laisserai pas, tant que j'en serai maître,
La divine beauté des larmes se commettre
Avec tant de laideur grossière!

(pp. 46-7)

This is extremely moving, it is dramatic and it is poetry. The whole scene, which oscillates between the sentimental dream and the dramatic self-mockery of the main character, is wholly integrated and shows the progressive creation of Cyrano's character.

That power to see himself as he really is, and to laugh instead of crying over what is unchangeable, gives the character a new dimension and increases his dramatic range; it is, if one wishes to call it so, a kind of sense of humour, a quality which is wholly absent from the great romantics like Wordsworth, Shelley or Victor Hugo, who generally wrote on one single plane, but which in this country appears very often in the poetry of the Scots, Burns, Byron and in our time MacDiarmid. The quality of self-critical humour and of laughing at the Devil and even at death

38

itself, is one of the main traits of Scottish poetry. The poetry of
the great romantics, with their faith in imagination, their kind of
mystical attitude towards the creative act, or the high seriousness
of Arnold who could see in poetry a substitute for religion—or,
for that matter, German subjectivity from Goethe to Wagner—
has no parallel whatever in Scottish poetry. The Scots seem to
share with the French a great reverence for the intellect. Rostand,
in that respect, is very French indeed; he refuses to confuse reality
and visions, he rarely takes himself too seriously, and when he
does it is fatal to his art. Strangely enough, another mediterranean, a greater poet than Rostand, yet a man who, like him,
believed both in poetry and in reason—Valéry—concluded his
artistic life with *Mon Faust*, a dramatic poem in which even
Mephistopheles is derided and made a victim of the author's
irrepressible scepticism. Cyrano believes in love but, man of the
world as he is, distrusts feelings and fears that other men may
laugh at him, so he forestalls them by laughing first. The important thing is that, however shallow Rostand's philosophy may be,
he looks at experience not from one single vantage-point, as the
great romantics generally did, but from various directions. He
may lack depth, but he has complexity and range; he does not
attempt to reach for a transcendental order, he deals with reality
as he sees it, and Nature, when he describes it, has none of the
immanence conferred upon it by Wordsworth or Victor Hugo.

As a play, *Cyrano* has many flaws. When at the end of the
balcony scene, for instance, Christian reaps the fruit of Cyrano's
rhetoric of love, we cannot help having a certain feeling of
revulsion, and we are made aware of the fact that Rostand's great
dramatic skill can at times fail him. The death of Christian, which
is not quite convincing, nevertheless increases the sympathy of the
audience towards him. The last scene of Act I is sheer fantasy, but
it does fit with the character of that strange man who is Cyrano.
On the contrary, the arrival of Roxane on the battlefield in Act IV,
scene iv, and above all the repast which follows, transform the
atmosphere of tension into one of tragi-comedy and burlesque.

It is a flight into absolute fancy, the characters become unreal and the interest flags. We find ourselves right in the thick of melodrama; the battle is completely artificial, and Rostand can display such a lack of sensitiveness as to make *en joue* rhyme with *je sens sa joue*. In spite of the fact that Cyrano's character is well drawn, the other characters are rather shallow. They are strongly reminiscent of Corneille's heroes in the fact that they are all, in various degrees, good; none of them is evil. The play has no metaphysical depth; life is shallow, language is without profound roots, yet it is nevertheless the language of a poet. Even De Guiche, who at the beginning of the play seems to be the bad one, in the end becomes the good Duc de Gramont who has seen the light and can express himself in poetry:

> Voyez-vous, lorsqu'on a trop réussi sa vie,
> On sent,—n'ayant rien fait, mon Dieu, de vraiment mal!
> Mille petits dégoûts de soi, dont le total
> Ne fait pas un remords, mais une gêne obscure;
> Et les manteaux de duc trainent dans leur fourrure,
> Pendant que des grandeurs on monte les degrés,
> Un bruit d'illusions sèches et de regrets,
> Comme, quand vous montez lentement vers ces portes,
> Votre robe de deuil traine des feuilles mortes.

(p. 197)

In spite of certain weaknesses, *Cyrano* is Rostand's major dramatic and poetic achievement. Rostand has often enough been dismissed as a mere writer of verse, or a kind of rhetorical poet who was not in fact a poet. Such opinions seem to me to imply a very narrow view of poetry. Granted, Rostand's poetry is different in quality and in degree from that of Shakespeare or Coleridge, or from that of Racine or Baudelaire; still, there are surely various kinds of poetry which can range from that of Shakespeare to that of Rostand.

Cyrano is a heroic comedy in verse, and therefore we cannot expect to find in it the kind of revelatory poetry which we find in

Othello, *King Lear* or *Phèdre*. The aims of the poet are here very
limited, but they are clear; he does not attempt to confront us
with unsolved mysteries, but with the everyday dualism of human
nature within definitely human situations.

The dramatic action of *Cyrano* is on the whole sustained, and
there are scenes of true dramatic and poetic beauty—the marvellous tirade of Cyrano on noses, for instance, and the reply to
the Vicomte which is a brilliantly developed metaphor, are
dramatic and produce, through the self-irony of the main character, a heightening of sensibility to which one could hardly refuse
the name of poetry. In the same way, the other beautiful speech
of Cyrano in the eighth scene of the second act is good wit-poetry;
there are plenty of apt images, there is movement, there is
rhythm, and it is dramatic; it gives us a full description of Cyrano's character—Cyrano who, once more, abruptly shatters his
apparent boastfulness with the confession of his utter dejection.
Only a poet, however minor he may be, could fuse such contrasting emotions into the unity which we find in many scenes of
Cyrano. The scene which follows is not poetry, but it is a good
drama, and it adds to the mounting tension. True, the balcony
scene, which is Rostand's lyrical flight, does not rise to the heart-
rending lyricism of *Romeo and Juliet*, or the poignancy of some of
Shakespeare's sonnets, but it is a very dramatic scene, which
trembles on the verge of sentimentalism but which nevertheless
avoids it and conveys in a poetic way the pathos of Cyrano's
situation; the audience is bound to share in that pathos, for it
knows that what he says comes from the depths of his heart, and
it cannot but feel sympathy for a man who makes use of the
sincerity of his passion in order to win a heart which he knows
will not belong to him. It is indeed a very "poetical" situation,
extremely delicate to handle without raising unwanted smiles or
laughter, but it seems to me that by now the complex nature of
Cyrano's character is so well accepted and his sincerity, which
makes him forget that he is playing a part, seems so genuine, as
to make the scene dramatic.

Rostand shows us that the greatest dangers which beset the poet are perhaps the discrepancies which might arise between his aims and the means which he uses to reach them. If, like Maeterlinck, he thinks he can reach poetry by using poetic themes and conventions, he will soon realize that the result will be neither dramatic nor poetic, for the two in that case should go together; but if, on the contrary, like Rostand, he attunes his poetic lyre to the situations he has chosen to describe, to the characters he has chosen to present, then he may, without flights to the summits which the former tried to reach, avoid the marshy ground where Maeterlinck got lost, and walk along a moderately high ground to the accompaniment of a music which, if it does not ravish us, never completely bores us, and which will save his name from oblivion. In his way, Rostand is a poet. He succeeds where Maeterlinck failed, and *Cyrano* is a work which has both an intrinsic and an historical importance. Aesthetically it is successful drama, historically, it is the meeting-point of a long tradition in French literature and the reconciliation of many contrasting traits, amongst the most important, the ideal and the rational; it has echoes of Victor Hugo, Banville, Scarron and others also, and it points the way to Valéry's more elaborate scepticism.

Cyrano marks the apex of Rostand's dramatic career. With *L'Aiglon* and *Chantecler* we have again a break in the equilibrium which produced Rostand's best drama, and consequently we have partial failures. The critics who try to gloss over these dramatic failures by describing them as poems are, to my mind, mistaken. There are true poets like Swinburne, for instance, or W. B. Yeats, who could fail in their attempts to produce good drama because they were first and foremost poets and perhaps not primarily dramatists. *Atalanta in Calydon* may not be a good play, but it certainly contains good poetry. But Rostand was not a poet of Swinburne's or of Yeats' magnitude; he was a versatile, masterly versifier, he had the gift of words, he could juggle with them to the point of inebriation, and also to lapses of appalling bad taste, and he only was a poet when he was a successful dramatist. He could sometimes write good descriptive poetry, and his images often have a Hugoesque splendour, but they are generally clear, visual images, free from psychological complexities or metaphysical symbolism tending towards apocalyptism as is the case with Claudel, for instance, who, like Rostand, resembles Victor Hugo but in a different way. Rostand obviously is, and could only be, a minor poet; in him there is no depth, no power of vision, no confrontation between being and non-being, between time and eternity, none of that awareness which can illumine a man's soul when confronting his finitude and his fate with the infinity of the universe, and which can give rise to moving, heart-rending songs which enable him to transcend time and his earthly plight. Rostand is the kind of poet who, deprived of the lyrical gift to sing himself out of time, can only make poetry out of the characters which compose his drama; and when he fails to be dramatic, he also fails to be a poet. His limited realistic vision, his intellect, which in order to avoid any possible suggestion of presenting Rostand as a thinker should really be described as good common sense, confine him to a kind of poetry which is more often verse than poetry, and which never goes beyond drama.

The critics who try to console themselves by saying that in *L'Aiglon* and in *Chantecler* Rostand's lyrical poetry redeems the lack of dramatic tension, the practical failure in drama, confuse the shadow for the substance. The so-called symbolism of *Chantecler* is so obvious that it does not deserve that name, and it does not require any explanation. Any normal twelve-year-old child would grasp it at once without having to ask his father any awkward questions; in fact, its obviousness rejoins in its results the very transparent camouflages put on by Maeterlinck's characters. At any moment we expect Chantecler to say: "Well, of course you know who I am, don't you?"—just as we are surprised not to hear at certain moments the famous Blue Birds saying these same words. These animals have nothing animal about them; they talk and behave as Rostand and his friends probably did, and we feel that somewhere, some time in Rostand's life, there must

43

have been some hen-pheasant who tried to lure him away from the Dawn, some denigrating blackbird-like colleague, and some highfalutin' lady whose "at homes" were the meeting-place of all the blue-stockings and the wigged hollow-heads of Paris. If, because Rostand obviously speaks through those various characters and borrows more often than not Chantecler's voice, we call that lyricism, we are singularly mistaken. Some speeches certainly sound personal, at times to the point of incongruity, as when Chantecler-Rostand talks of Chénier's death; but lyricism is something more than personal expression of feelings, as Lamartine and Rostand ought to have known. It all depends on the feelings; those expressed here are pretty common alloys, and would require a great deal more refining before they could reach the state of the pure metal. There is in the play a certain amount of wit verse, the kind of wit which brings together things far apart, or suddenly reduces the distances which separate things similar; part of scene iv in the first act is a case in point. There is also some kind of poetry, mostly verbal—the hymn of Chantecler to the sun, and his confidences to the hen-pheasant—interspersed with very bad lapses; and there are throughout the play unbearable puns, unbelievable samples of lack of taste, and a kind of verbal headiness which sprawls endlessly across numerous scenes. It is, all told, a very elaborate, over-elaborate fantasy, which is ingenious, and in parts entertaining as a review, but which will grow older and older, and will not improve with age.

L'Aiglon is on a higher level than *Chantecler*. It is, after *Cyrano*, the most accomplished drama of Rostand. Here he has once more moved away from that mixture of realism and idealism, sentiment and irony, bravado and heroism, which characterizes *Cyrano*, and we are once more faced with a very romantic theme, that of the hero condemned to failure. The action is therefore static; the main character, although he has impulses and velleities of movement, remains motionless. The words are like the sails of a windmill gyrating without anything to grind; they strike the air, and nothing but the air, producing a powerful impression of fruitless effort. The result is bombastic, swollen language, gongorism, and long scenes placed where they are for no other purpose than to enable the poet to indulge in a certain form of rhetoric.

The hero is a cardboard hero, an opera prince without any life of his own. He seems to be a combination of certain very feminine aspects of Rostand's character, crystallized in a form which would suit Sarah Bernhardt's acting. The truth is that, although Rostand may be able to conceive a verbal exteriorization of tragedy, and may have the gift of passionate rhetoric which can produce at times epic poetry, he cannot be a tragic poet. He can obviously write mock-heroic verse, as in *Cyrano*, and also heroic verse, as in *L'Aiglon*. The entrance of Flambeau in the ninth scene of the second Act is a good sample of heroic poetry containing striking images:

> Nous qui pour arracher ainsi que des carottes
> Nos jambes à la boue énorme des chemins,
> Devions les empoigner quelquefois à deux mains.
>
> (p. 92)

Flambeau is the best-drawn character of the play, and it is in him that we find that mixture of heroic grandeur and irony which was greatly responsible for Cyrano's attractiveness. He has bad lapses—at the end, for instance, when he dies saying "Je me suis fait une légion d'honneur"—but on the whole he is moving, convincing, and his language sometimes bears the imprint of epic poetry. There are other samples of epic poetry: the beginning of the tenth scene in Act I, for instance, contains good epic poetry. Indeed, the thing to remember about *L'Aiglon* is that it is only a partial failure, for in spite of lengthy, lifeless scenes, in spite of appalling samples of bad taste and most common puns, such as: "vous ragusassiez!", *L'Aiglon* is at times dramatic and contains a certain kind of poetry. The duke is weak, sentimental, as when he offers to decorate Flambeau, pompous, petulant and childish, as when he wilfully alienates himself from his grandfather's goodwill, or merely shilly-shallying, as when he should be strong and escape in order to reach the throne; all these traits show that this sickly and nervous young man was not fit to reign. Like Hamlet[1] whose presence seems to have been haunting Rostand at that time, the young duke is incapable of action. He is ever hampered by what looks like very futile reasons. He nurses Hamletian feelings about his mother's unfaithfulness to the great man, his father. Just as the ghost plays an important part in *Hamlet*, in *L'Aiglon*, Napoleon's great shade dominates the play and overwhelms the weak, golden-haired young man who is torn between his urge to fulfil his father's wish and the anxiety of feeling unequal to this great task. Yet he could at times redeem himself, with the self-irony of "les soldats de plomb de Napoléon II", and Rostand could every now and then knit his speech with splendid Hugo-esque images, as when, in Act I, scene viii, the doctor, talking about butterflies in an album, asks the young duke what he is looking at, and the duke replies with the very apt and dramatic words: "L'épingle qui le tue"; or later, in scene xiii, in spite of the weak rhymes:

> Mais haussez au soleil la page diaphane;
> Le mot 'Napoléon' est dans le filigrane!

Or in the middle of the rather sentimental speech of the duke to Flambeau, in the otherwise good scene ix of Act II, when he says:
> Je dois, malgré tant d'ombre et tant de lendemains,
> Avoir au bout des doigts un peu d'étoile encore . . .

There are many examples of such verbal felicity, which, when they fit with the character, are good rhetoric. Even more, the end of scene iv in Act II contains good descriptive, direct poetry; the tension caused by the feelings involved is strong, the images used extremely apt, and the result is quite moving poetry.

[1] Hamlet is not incapable of action because he is a weak character or lacks physical courage, it is only because he has too much purity of mind and wants first to discover the truth which underlies his "world out of joint".

CHAPTER 3

Henri Ghéon and Jules Supervielle

HENRI GHÉON has written some poetry, but he is not primarily a poet; he has written poetry in the normal way in which many novelists and other men of letters write poetry during certain phases of their lives, but not as their primary artistic expression. Henri Ghéon is first and foremost a prose dramatist, and although he has not conquered the commercial stage, he is quite an important dramatist. This is not the place to attempt to assess him as such, and even if it were, the task could only be a tentative one, for the fact is that for the moment a good number of his plays are still unobtainable, some of them never having been printed. There are more than 100 of them, and although not a few are merely one-act plays, we are faced with a prolificity and, above all, with a widespread success in a certain field, which can neither be neglected nor explained away as a passing craze or as merely the result of propaganda. Henri Ghéon wilfully set himself an uphill task. He deliberately refused to court popularity and to indulge in the tastes of the day. To know what those tastes were and to have an idea of the state of the theatre at that time, one has only to remember the masterly analysis by Copeau published in *L'Ermitage* in February 1905. It is an analysis which gives the measure of Copeau's extraordinary clear-sightedness and vision. Few are those who could claim to have known more than Copeau about the theatre, and his writings should be pondered now, for a great deal of what he said is unfortunately truer than ever.

Henri Ghéon was a friend and an admirer of Copeau, and he began writing for the theatre under his inspiration. His ideals

47

were those of Copeau, and like him he wanted to restore intellectual integrity and poetry to the stage. He did not write to
please the snobs, the managers of commercial theatres or the star
comedians. He wrote to carry out his vocation, which was
to restore Christianity in the theatre. Although Copeau was
not animated with the same Christian zeal, his priest-like attitude
towards art could not fail to range him by the side of Ghéon,
and he supported him whenever and wherever he could. There
is no doubt that the support of men like Copeau, Maritain, the
Pitoëffs and Dullin was of great importance to Henri Ghéon, who
had refused to try to please worldly society and the pundits of the
day. His aims were different; he wanted to reach the broad public,
and he felt that if all the gods of Olympus could participate in the
life of the theatre, there was no reason why God, the true God,
and His saints and angels could not occupy an even greater place
in that theatre. He felt strongly, and argued, that if the origins of
drama were religious, there was no reason why our religion,
Christianity, should not play in our theatre the part played
by the gods in the creation of the great Greek tragedies. He
was in no way convinced by Gide's specious arguments about
Christianity being a leveller of character.

Henri Ghéon wanted to create a popular Christian theatre;
for him art was prayer, and he wanted to regain for religion the
ground which it had lost since the Middle Ages; he wanted to
return to the atmosphere of that era when miracle and mystery
plays were part of the ritual of the Church and could hold the
attention of all the faithful. He knew that in order to regain that
lost territory he had to begin with the masses and with the young
people; and he knew that he had to forgo the advantages of having his plays accepted by well-established commercial theatres.
Up till now, most of his plays have been performed by amateur
companies, and, except in this country, outside the big cities.
His aim has been to prepare public and actors to accept a truly
Christian theatre, so that once the new ground has been broken,
a poet of the magnitude of Claudel or some other yet unborn

might have his great Christian symphonies accepted by all. Many of his plays, such as *Le Pain, Le Comédien, La vie de Saint-François, La Farce du Pendu dépendu*, have been produced with success and there is, above all, his best play, *Le Pauvre sous l'Escalier*,[1] which is one of the finest examples of religious drama.

Although he has scattered some verse across his plays, Henri Ghéon has only written one play wholly in verse; it is *Les Trois Miracles de Sainte Cécile*. Miracle plays and mystery plays are not *per se* poetic drama, even although they may contain a great deal of poetry. Indeed, there is between the two genres an unbridgeable gap. "Poetic drama" is art, an imaginative creation which implies "a suspension of disbelief" in order that such a creation may be accepted on its own terms, as a living thing. The miracle and mystery plays based on the Bible and on the lives of the saints have a foundation of historical and revealed truth which cannot be deeply altered in order to fit into imaginative creations. Above all, they are not primarily works of art or spectacles for entertainment, they are acts of faith; they are not imitations of actions, they are the real thing re-enacted with the full affective and intellectual participation of the audience. The actors are not "acting" a drama, they are living through episodes which are part of their faith and of that of the audience; there is no "suspension of disbelief". The actors who represent the passion of Christ do so as an act of faith, their prayers are genuine, heartfelt, and the Christ whom they impersonate is something as real as is humanly possible; they want His presence to be truly felt. The members of the audience, each one in his heart, live the great drama and feel in themselves Christ's living presence. Poetry does not add to the core of faith of the mysteries and miracles—though it could, if we mean here by poetry the direct expression of the essence of things. But in general the tension rising from the events in miracles and mysteries is such that words are hardly necessary, and if they are used, the simpler—I mean the more direct, the more closely linked with the thing itself—they are,

[1] See synopsis at end of chapter.

49

the better. The best words are those which have kept their primitive force of "imaging", or, if the emotion cannot be imaged, words arrayed in order to produce rhythms effective enough to arouse an emotional state conducive to the birth of that emotion. The poetry of the ballad, the poetry which still retains its elemental force, is the only one which would suit mystery and miracle plays.

Although one must not set too great a store on the theories of poets about poetry, these theories are always, if nothing else, an indication of the kind of poetry their author would like to write, or would not like to write. Henri Ghéon's brief comments on poetry are quite interesting, for they foretell his failings: Ghéon constantly endeavoured to escape from what he described as the tyranny of the "image". "That pest", he said, "dates from Rimbaud."

> Since the day when Rimbaud saw a mosque in place of a factory, and coaches driving along the roads of the sky, every kind of means has been used. We have fallen below the level of the *précieuses*. Poetry is first and foremost rhythm and music, it is time we returned to this vital concept whence should have sprung, full of life, the poetry of the twentieth century, music and reason. That is why our greatest poet is still La Fontaine.

Pace to his choice of the greatest poet; what counts is his obsession about the tyranny of the images. Ghéon may have succeeded as much as he wished in avoiding images; on the other hand, he may have been incapable of "seeing images". The fact is that there are hardly any images in his poetry, and an examination of his only verse play (*Les Trois Miracles de Sainte Cécile*) shows that lack of images as well as the shortcomings of the theme as matter for poetry; it also betrays a fundamental lack of imagination in the author, but that is not the point for the moment.

The first tableau, with the Claudelian theme of God claiming all, is doggerel verse which, deprived of substance, relies too much on the mere jingle of sounds repeated at certain intervals in order to create rhythm. The trouble is that there is no force, no tension which could make its mark on the mind and establish a living rhythm to act as the skeleton of the poem—which, without that rhythm, remains a mere sequence of light verse to be spoken by young sixth-form girls. The main cause of the failure of the poetry lies probably in the theme itself. Cécile carries everything before her; Valérien does not exist at all—in a few words Cécile transforms him. Perhaps it should be so, for miracles cannot be understood, yet the whole thing, which is meant to be a paean of joy, is too tenuous and too exclusively *ad usum puellarum*. The second miracle—"l'épreuve de la vie et la mort"—follows a different pattern. Here the words underlie a reality impossible to escape, a reality which involves the existence and the true being of the main protagonists of the drama. Cécile, Valérien, Tiburce are brought down from the heights of space where their joy could expand boundlessly, into a society which contains them and can decide their human fate, and, when face to face with the supreme hour, they reveal themselves as human beings in all their moving aspects. The words carry as much poetry as the author can give them. Ghéon has neither the lyrical sweep which, from a central core, can make words ripple into circles ranging as wide as the inner eye can see, nor can he create that ethereal music, that feeling of mystery, which keeps the reader anxiously waiting for the dawn of new worlds. He has none of these qualities, and he remains on a minor key, bound by the limitations of his imagination. The poetry rises from the situation of the characters, a situation which is extremely moving and which resolves itself at times into good poetry. The metre is the alexandrine, which has nothing of the incomparable vowel-music of Racine, but which nevertheless conveys directly and aptly the feelings of the characters:

Ami, si vous m'aimez, quittez-moi sans regret!
Donnez tout votre coeur à l'aube qui va poindre;

> C'est là, c'est là que j'irai bientôt vous rejoindre,
> C'est là que, pour toujours, Dieu veut nous marier:
> ... Si vous manquez le pas, comment vous retrouver?
>
> (p. 107)

This brings back faint recollections of the words of Prouhèze to Rodrigue in *Le Soulier de Satin*. The thought-content is the same, and scene iii is very moving and contains good poetry. Cécile has a passionate eloquence, which carries conviction, Valérien is more human, and perhaps more moving in his solicitude for his wife and for his brother. Cécile is possessed, fixed on one single idea, and nothing can shake her; she is, of course, too much of a piece to be the central character of a play, for she is the same from beginning to end, but there is no doubt that her qualities—youth, courage, unshakeable belief—and her human situation do give rise to pathos strong enough to produce poetic drama. The scene with Tiburce which follows is moving, contains good poetry and is psychologically sound:

> Du courage, ma sœur! Dieu vous laisse et nous prend:
> Il est moins sûr de nous que de vous; votre rôle
> Est de rester derrière, en poussant par l'épaule
> Celui de nous qui refuserait d'avancer ...
> Quand nous serons au port, il viendra vous chercher.
> Mais tout est doux en lui, même l'attente:
> Il vous parlait, on croit qu'il s'est tu et ... il chante.
>
> (p. 113)

The end of the miracle, the second tableau, sees the hardening of Cécile's character, her stabilization at the suprahuman level, the faintest trace of human emotion is wiped out, everything gives way to the feeling of exultation at the thought of the coming sacrifice and earthly liberation. Cécile's monologue is too long and certainly unactable; the supreme mastery of all concerned, Cécile and the soldiers who have tortured Valérien and Tiburce, is perhaps too remote from the human.

The third miracle—the end of Cécile—is harrowing and well-nigh unbearable. Here is poetry, simple, direct, describing the extraordinary event which took place, the miracle of Cécile's death—something completely different from poetic drama. The last episode of the life and death of St. Cecilia—*Le martyre de Saint Valérien*—is also a miracle play and not poetic drama or tragedy, and again it contains good poetry. Tiburce's speech and that of Valérien bear traces of the inspiration which lifts them, and are poetry. But Tiburce, Valérien and the others are not characters of drama—for there is here no crisis, no internal fluctuations, but only the participants of an action which is the whole thing, and which is never an imitation of an action in order to create aesthetic emotion, but always a reincarnation of that original action with all that it entails of complete faith and complete adhesion of performers and spectators to that faith. The fault may be mine, but I found the scene of the torture and flagellation on the stage far too long and exhibiting too strong a masochistic flavour of bliss through suffering. We all know that the paths to sainthood and supreme virtue are not easy; we cannot fail to feel the greatness of men animated by high ideals and capable of giving their lives for their faith; but death, when it comes, should be brief and not endlessly prolonged and made to advance step by step, slowly counter-pointing its horrors with hosannahs of joy. The emotional pitch lies too much beyond the human and risks provoking revulsion or a temporary escape into pathology.

The fact that Ghéon's contribution to poetic drama is small should not make us forget that he is definitely one of the remarkable dramatists of our time. His strong Christian or rather Catholic bias, his avowed didactic intentions may limit the appeal of his drama to those who share his beliefs. On the other hand, he has written plays like *Le Comédien et la Grâce* and *Le Pauvre sous l'Escalier*, which are capable of being appreciated by all lovers of the theatre. Although they are in prose, it is at times a very poetic prose, and the depth of feelings, the thought which underlies the characters, and the imaginative reality of those characters, show that Henri Ghéon's gifts were great, perhaps greater than those of playwrights whose versatility and art of courting the public favour have won them fame greater than his; still the time may come when people will realize yet more fully that theatricality is not drama. When the dust which partly fills our eyes has settled down, when tinselly glitters have faded away into their normal dullness, then the importance of Ghéon's contribution to drama may be fully recognized.

Supervielle is one of the most important poets of our time. He testifies to the existence of a poetic vein which has been rather intermittent in the normal flow of French literature. It is the vein of spontaneity and naturalness, and a rare vein indeed, which stands out in contradistinction from the extreme consciousness which is one of the main characteristics of French art; it is the vein of Villon and Verlaine, of poets who naturally transmute every element of life into poetry. If the poetry of Verlaine can more easily be covered by the term "lyrical" in the current meaning of the word, the lyricism of Villon is that of a greater mind and of a greater imagination; it is a lyricism full of a dramatic force rising beyond the "song", into realms where man faces the nakedness of his destiny and sings the sorrows of his tormented heart. The lyricism of Supervielle is nearer that of Villon than that of Verlaine; if he does not have the vivid imagination which gives Villon's poetry its poignancy, its unforgettable rhythms, he has the exquisite sensitiveness of the poet who can detect life in the frailest things, a sensitiveness which enables him to share his cosmic love with the living world. If his poetry does not bear traces of the unbearable tensions and drama which assailed and haunted the heart and the imagination of Villon, it does not lack drama either; and the traces of the duologue between soul and self, between what was, and what is and will be, are never absent from it. A poem like *Un Portrait* is a dramatic poem. Supervielle's poetry does not lack dramatic quality, but the question, the only question for us now is: has he written any poetic drama?

Bolivar is a pageant based on the historical life of a hero, Bolivar, who was the liberator of a good part of the South American continent. In a pageant which extends over thirty years and involves many well-known historical events, the characters are part of a great pattern. They therefore tend to be all of a piece, for their primary importance does not lie in the depth of their psychological complexities, but rather in the relations of their feelings and actions to the woof of history which with their lives they form. That does not mean that the *dramatis personae* of a pageant have no individual human reality. Far from it; they have a reality, however sketchy it may be, their personalities being woven into an historical pattern; they are given some moments to pause for lyrical complaints or epic surveys, but those moments are generally too brief. In a genre which is above all movement, there is not much time left for those pathetic contemplations of the self in its own ruin which are the source of some of the most moving poetry. In Shakespeare's epic on the lives of the Henrys, for instance, there are splendid moments, there is beautiful poetry of all kinds, from epic to lyrical. But where is the moving pathos, where is the poignant, piercing note which we find in the tragedy of Richard II, in the undoing of a man who could not avert catastrophe, who seems to have been born to endure it, and who could only say:

> Let's talk of graves, of worms, and epitaphs
> Make dust our paper, and with rainy eyes
> Write sorrow on the bosom of the earth?

This brief allusion to the Master is merely in order to try to point out that, although Supervielle is a remarkable poet, the pattern he chooses with Bolivar does not afford him much opportunity for poetry. He has wisely decided to treat Bolivar's life solely as a dramatic theme which obviously could inspire him with very genuine feelings, since he not only shares the humanitarian, brotherly feelings of his hero, but also his love for a land which is as important to him as is his mother country. The author of

Bolivar, who knows as well as any man living what poetry is, has given us here as many samples as possible of his poetic vision and language, but has treated his subject not as poetic drama but as a pageant which can stand the adornment of music and good staging, and is good theatre.

In *La Belle au Bois* the author has telescoped into one three well-known fairy tales—*Puss-in-Boots*, *Blue Beard* and *The Sleeping Beauty*. The Prince Charming is a man of our time who, at the end, records the fact that these ethereal figures, which have for a moment intermingled with, and partaken of, the ups and downs of life, return to the separateness of the pages of the volume which contains them, to the realm of fantasy and memory where a fictitious lasting bliss outweighs any sort of happiness of the flesh. Here we find once more the freshness of approach to things, and the unmistakeable art of telling a story which characterize Supervielle. We find beauty of language, we find fantasy, but the play does not come within the category of poetic drama; the author did not intend it to be so. It is a fairy tale, very poetical in its atmosphere and the brittle grace of the characters, it has an organic life mostly lived at the fantastic level, yet bringing to us the wisdom born from the confrontation of two remote aspects of civilization; it is obviously the work of a poet, but it is not poetic drama.

Schéhérazade is also a fairy tale, a delightful fantasy rich in poetic beauty. *Robinson* is a pantomime, an enchanting comedy which contains genuine emotion and genuine poetry; yet neither of them could be described as poetic drama. The plays mentioned are in prose—the prose of a poet, a prose intermingled with verse, but nevertheless prose. Another problem, perhaps even more important than the latter, because it determines it, is the problem of the theme. Themes of pageantry, fairy tales and pantomimes are definitely not themes for poetic drama. These themes are most suited to Supervielle's genius, and his treatment shows his inimitable gift as a raconteur. He is the story-teller who seems to have discovered the art of telling a story in which all things live and talk, and that not in a humanized way, but each according to the law of its own species. He has the supreme gift of keeping his reader in suspense, and although the suspense of the novel is not quite the suspense of the drama, and although in these two genres characterization and action proceed in different ways, sometimes even in opposite ways, he is, together with Giraudoux, amongst those who, have shown that a good story-teller can also be a good dramatist.

Supervielle's best play, and his nearest approach to poetic drama, is *Le Voleur d'Enfants*. Here we have fantasy, but fantasy not divorced from reality. The character of Bigua, the colonel "who goes through life surrounded with a mist of innocence", is very real indeed and capable of profound pathos. The fantasy of the beginning of the play does not remain for long suspended in mid-air between real and unreal, it leads us down to earth into a situation which, however strange, is humanly possible, and to feelings which, although not ordinary, are extremely moving and bear the mark of truly lived experiences. In fact, at the end of the play we realize that the butterfly flights and fairy lights of the fanciful mind of the beginning have been fused into an imaginative creation which bears the imprint of poetic experience. The dialogue is brilliant, the wit displayed is dazzling, the pathos of feelings extremely moving, the ideas and the themes outlined are those of Supervielle's poetry. The treatment of the subject is essentially poetic, and that in the best Supervielle manner. That is to say, without poses or clownish performances catering for applause, but in that carefree natural, unpretentious way of treading the most difficult ground which characterizes the true poet. Supervielle is, since the death of Claudel, the most outstanding living French poet, and my feeling is that with his great technical skill, his remarkable imagination and his dramatic apprehension of the plight of man, Supervielle could yet produce poetic drama worthy of his high stature.

SYNOPSIS OF "LE PAUVRE SOUS L'ESCALIER"

The action takes place in the fourth century A.D., in the house of the wealthy Roman senator, Euphemius. The play opens with the janitor explaining to a pedlar that fifteen years before, on his wedding night, the only son of the house, Alexis, had run away from his home and had never been heard of since. His father, his mother and his wife, Emilie, are still hoping that he may come back, and they have sent emissaries to try and discover him. Emilie's mother, Sophie, is impatient with all this and she urges her daughter to marry again. The three emissaries return and report the inanity of their search; then Alexis, disguised as a beggar, arrives and asks to be allowed to live in a little recess under the stairs. Senator Euphemius, who is a very religious and kind man, accepts; Emilie has suddenly guessed that it is Alexis, and she tries to draw him out, but Alexis keeps his secret. Two years later in a very touching scene, Emilie tells the beggar that when he arrived she thought he was Alexis and she asks for his advice about marriage. Emilie is about to choose one of the three pretenders who have been pursuing her, but at the last moment she cannot, and she asks the beggar to communicate to them her decision. He does so in a convincing manner. Fifteen years later, Alexis, exhausted by illness, is dying and the Barbarians are threatening Rome, swept by fear and hoping for a miracle. Both the Pope and the Emperor are praying for this miracle and for the discovery of the man who can save Rome. After a last, very moving conversation, in the course of which he tests Emilie once more and nearly reveals his identity to her, Alexis dies in her arms, and just then she discovers the truth. The Emperor arrives, sent by the Pope, who has decreed that the beggar is a holy man. He takes a paper which is in Alexis's hand and which is a revelation of his identity, a confession of his doubts and worries about the sorrows he may have caused to his wife and to his parents, and a token of humility and generosity such that it clearly marks him for sainthood.

CHAPTER 4

Paul Claudel

THE standard modern approach to a play seems to be the Ibsenian form of character and plot with an ascending graph of dramatic tension. A play must have an obviously exciting action and a single focus. Delacroix's *Barricade* with its single, strongly outlined action conforms to these standards, while Rembrandt's *The Night Watch*, with its complexity and wide range of emotions involved, does not. By such criteria, *Hamlet* is a badly constructed play and Claudel's theatre is a complete failure.

A great innovator in verse, and above all the most powerful imagination which has been at work in French literature since Victor Hugo, Claudel is a poet whose works must first and foremost be considered as an imaginative synthesis. If we neglect the pre-eminence of the imagination, if we attach too much importance to the psychology of the characters and to the logic of the action, if we isolate those aspects of drama from the poetic pattern which contains both and is more important than they are, we shall be over-emphasizing certain aspects of the plays to the detriment of others, and we shall severely curtail our appreciation of the whole. If, on the contrary, we do what one ought always to do with poet-dramatists, if we give our greatest attention to poetic wholeness and think more in terms of symbolism and imaginative truths, than in terms of character and logical development of actions and situations, we shall preserve unbroken the subtle, imaginative texture of each play and shall see it as an harmonious whole.

It is true, of course, that Claudel wrote in terms of drama, but the dramatic nature of his work could not by any means be used, when dealing with poetic drama, as the only basis of an inter-pretation or a critical appreciation of that work. In the end it is nothing more than a convention in order to express certain truths which were in the poet. That "convention" has its import-ance, and when a poet writes for the stage, one has the right to ask oneself whether or not he has achieved drama; yet when deal-ing with poetic drama, what finally counts is not drama, but the dramatic poem. The purely dramatic aspect of a poetic drama can be used and should be used as a means to throw light on certain aspects of the work, yet in order to have an all-embracing and complex grasp of that work one must try to reach the imaginative core which determines its nature and gives it its reality. What surely counts in a work of art is its imaginative truth, a truth which is the highest form of beauty, and a truth in which ethics are in the end a matter of aesthetic achievement. One must be wary of confusing the morality of human life and the morality of dramatic characters; if we did so, we might apply purely social criteria of morality to actions and to human beings which should only be judged in relation to the wholeness of the work of art and there-fore in relation to life on the metaphysical plane.

To begin with, Claudel is not a psychologist; he may be unable to descry the intricate workings of the human heart, or he may not be interested in those workings, except in as much as they correspond to certain aspects of his imaginative vision of the cosmos, which, so far as results are concerned, comes to the same thing. He is not concerned, like Shaw or Sartre, with the propa-gation of certain philosophical and moral beliefs and ideas in terms of human psychology and human behaviour. He is, it seems to me, concerned with expressing and conveying to men the truth which lies at the centre of his whole being, in terms of symbols, metaphors, analogies and images, as befits a poet. The truth which Claudel feels is God's truth. The structure of life and of the cosmos which he describes is not the one seen by the human eye but the one seen by the inner eye of the imagination. The way he attempts to express his vision is by means which make of his characters, actions and situations the second terms of analogies, or the words or objects standing for vast images, metaphors and forces which lie beyond the seeing eye and are part of a pattern in which eternity only touches time at certain points and through the medium of the creative mind. Therefore if we wish to recapture glimmers of the vision which filled the poet's eye, we must not attempt to give those terms, characters or situations an intrinsic, self-contained, logical meaning, but consider them as the apprehensible signs of vast constructions which might be glimpsed at, but which can only be apprehended, as far as they can be apprehended, in a referential way. If we examine the plays from the vantage point of poetic oneness, we may even feel that certain flat passages, halts in the progress of the action and flaws in the growth of characters could be considered, even in their negative values, as parts of the symphonic structure of the plays. They may be necessary to throw into relief certain other aspects which perhaps can only fit into the whole when set into that kind of dull or negative context. I do not wish to say that all weaknesses of style, construction or characterization are willed or could be explained away in that fashion. I merely mean to suggest that those weaknesses would lose a great deal of their sharpness of relief if viewed as the possibly necessary dull colours of a landscape which may be closely scrutinized in its details, but which should be finally contemplated from a distance and as a fully integrated whole.

Claudel's first plays, *Tête d'or* and *La Ville*, are not good plays, but they already contain good poetry and they are the work of a man who already shows the portents of a major poet.

Le Repos du Septième Jour, which in some ways continues and concludes *Tête d'or* and *La Ville*, is much less of a drama than either of them. There is a certain amount of pathos in the Emperor's plight, and in his meeting with his mother; there is sometimes a kind of atmosphere of tragedy, but on the whole, human passions only appear as extremely faint reflections of the fundamental problem of good and evil. The *dramatis personae* are really the Emperor of China and God, or rather, in the end,

Claudel himself, in the exultation of his newly found religious plenitude. Therefore there is no drama, although we have good dramatic poetry forming part of a poem which is, on the whole, on a high level. Somehow here one cannot help being reminded of Dante. The Emperor has not lost his way in a dark wood, but something similar has happened to him. The harmony of his empire, of which he is the kind of supra-human centre, has been broken. The dead cannot rest because of the sinful behaviour of the living and they therefore render life almost impossible. The Emperor decides to plunge into the underworld and to find out the roots of the trouble. We are back in the *Inferno* and in the atmosphere of Dante's theology—we have the circles, we have the various guides, and we have an explanation of sin and evil which compares with Dante's metaphysics. The first step into sin is that of Paolo and Francesca, "la douceur de faire le mal", a form of evil which can only be refined by the fire which is God's love. There is no need to press further the parallel between the two poets; sufficient to say that the Emperor, like Dante, finds his Beatrice, the angel of the empire, who leads him to the heights and imparts to him the divine wisdom to save his people. The Emperor returns to earth, Christ-like, his sceptre transformed into a cross, his face made unrecognizable by leprosy, and filled with the faith which has come from the west and will save his people. He lays down his life with the certitude that he has brought the Kingdom of God unto earth. This is a poem which contains passages of striking beauty. The scene between the Emperor and his mother is very moving poetry, with penetrating rhythms and subtle texture; the pathos of the scene is undeniable. The long scene with the Daemon, packed with metaphysical arguments, shows Claudel's visionary power and the depth of his thought; at the same time it shows clearly enough why he is not on the same level as Dante. He lacks that clearness of vision, crispness of diction and rhythmic harmony which carried Dante to the summits. Claudel's visions, however impressive, remain confused, apocalyptic, and they are at times expressed in abstract terms and with a tendency to repetition; he cannot control his wealth. In Dante we have simple words, but words which image, and concision and concreteness are amongst his main assets. Still, there are very few poets who call Dante to mind. The scene between the angel of the empire and the Emperor, and above all, at the end of the poem, the alternate song of the new Emperor and the Recitant, are beautiful poetry. It is probably Claudel's most profoundly religious poem, a poem pervaded with feelings of holiness and joy which show the timelessness of Christ.

L'Échange is a drama. Louis Laine and Léchy Elbernon have in them the violence of people who have not been tamed by centuries of organized social life and accepted moral principles. Their passions, their uncontrollable desires, urge them to ruin. Thomas Pollock Nageoire is a mixture of the old and the new world; under the thin film of ruthless business competition still lurks the old moral man of the ancient world, and in the end, thanks to Marthe, he rediscovers his soul. Marthe represents what is best in women, firm faith in her principles, boundless human love, and trust in God's way. Her character rises to tragic pathos, her innocence is burdened with a fate which she does not deserve, she is acted upon by the violent passions of the other protagonists of the drama. She has upon her the marks of tragic grandeur, her suffering sounds real, and she can express her loneliness and plight in beautiful poetry, as in the very moving scene when Laine comes to tell her that he is leaving her, or when, at the beginning of the third act, she is alone on the seashore, away from her ancestral roots, without a friend near her. That monologue is certainly good poetry, although it is perhaps rather long. Marthe, the chosen instrument of God's will, belongs to the same family as Violaine and Dona Musique, the women born to heal wounds and to bring salvation to men, and her part contains the best poetry. There is also good poetry in the part of Léchy Elbernon, chiefly when, at the end of the second act, in front of Marthe, she asks Laine to follow her:

Aime-moi, car je suis belle! Aime-moi, car je suis l'amour,
et je suis sans règle et sans loi!

Et je m'en vais de lieu en lieu, et je ne suis pas une seule
femme, mais plusieurs, prestige, vivante dans une histoire
inventée!

Vis! sens en toi
La puissante jeunesse qu'il ne sera pas aisé de contraindre.
Sois libre! le désir hardi
Vit en toi au-dessus de la loi comme un lion!

Aime-moi, car je suis belle! et où s'ouvre la bouche,
c'est là que j'appliquerai la mienne.

The theme of *L'Échange* is very much that of *Partage de Midi*.
God's will cannot be transgressed with impunity, and evil and
all the suffering that it implies must be accepted with the belief
that the ways of Providence, although inscrutable, lead men to
the supreme good, and to happiness. We shall see with *Partage de
Midi* the dramatic and theological implications of such beliefs.
At this juncture one should note once more that the time has
not yet come in Claudel's work when poetry and drama are
absolutely one.

L'Échange clearly illustrates the contention that what counts
most in Claudel is the theme expounded by the story and the
actions and the symbolical value of the characters and their
speeches. As Claudel himself has made it clear, the characters
are purely representations of conflicting aspects of his personality,
and he evolves them into actions and situations which will reveal
to us and to himself what happens when certain forces of life are
in conflict. The theme is the one which forms the crux of his
experience, which is that God's ways are inscrutable, and that not
until he understands them or accepts them can a man reach
happiness ranging in intensity from earthly satisfaction to heavenly
bliss within God's will. The forces involved are two variations on
the theme of sex—the sex-destruction impulse of Léchy, and sex-
restlessness in Laine, counter-balanced by the saintliness and faith

in the spiritual of Marthe, with Thomas Pollock Nageoire as a necessary object upon which divine grace will operate through Marthe. The characters are symbols of those forces, and, as is most of the time the case with Claudel, they tend towards the straight line, or the single colour, black, white or red. They are not depicted in their subtle psychological complexities, with their hesitations, impulses and changes, like the masterly creations of Racine. They are all of a piece, actuated by one single motive, which urges them on unswervingly. They are not, therefore, true to life, they are beyond life, and they are expressions of life, they are life seen from a huge distance, from a point whence men's ways and passions merge into the few main streams which could be said to form the flow of mankind; or they are seen as the representations of the mysterious essences which underlie the actions of men. Therefore they are never fully explained, for they do not know themselves, they always stand in a kind of half-light, termini of forces whose roots we cannot reach, and they move and act in inevitable ways as instruments of a purpose which is beyond man. Tête d'or goes to his end devoured by his self-centred ambition, the ambition which, when it is God-centred, as in the case of Rodrigue, can lead to heaven. Mara and Léchy hate and kill with the same steadfastness, the same singleness of purpose and faith in their actions which guide Marthe to forgiveness, and Violaine and Prouhèze to heaven. Ysé and Mésa accept their adulterous love with the full knowledge of their guilt, and yet with the hope that their love, part of God's will, will be forgiven and admitted to heaven. Claudel's characters live a kind of elemental life; they are forces, black or white, which terrify us or fill us with admiration or pity, they are forces which we dimly recognize, with which we feel vague affinities, but which we could not analyse or imitate, for they are beyond life. In fact, they are poetic representations of the conflicting aspects of man's nature, and as such partake of its mystery. Their life, although it takes place on the plane of reality, is based on a transcendentalism sometimes recognizable, acceptable and part of the human experience and sometimes unreal, which makes their complete grasp impossible.

In *Partage de Midi* Claudel, though touched by the light of God's grace, still retains some of the violence and pride of the pagan. The play, which is very moving, and one of the most lyrical plays ever written, owes a great deal of its pathos to the conflict between the beliefs and the uncertainties of the main protagonists, between the awareness of sin and the overwhelming desire to plunge into it, between the knowledge of God's love and God's will, and the deadly urge to transgress them, carried away by the feeling that absolute possession of the being which belongs to God can only be achieved by death. Ysé knows her incompleteness and she knows that, in spite of her passion or perhaps because of her passion, there exists an ineffable state, which human love, physical or spiritual, cannot create. Only in death can she reach that absolute, and so she consciously wills her death and that of her lover, in an attempt to fulfil themselves in the face of God, and they die in an apotheosis of pagan grandeur, yet still trusting in the mercy of God, who will, they hope, sanction their love in eternity.

The lyrical sweep of the verse matches the tense pathos of the emotions and makes the play one of the remarkable achievements of the theatre. In this play the characters have lives of their own. We do not have the feeling of constant supernatural intervention. In spite of what Claudel says, "that in order to take man away from himself, to enable him to have the knowledge of the other, there is only one appropriate instrument, the woman", in spite of that aspect of Claudelian dogmatism that God makes use of certain human beings as vessels of His will, the dogmatism is not too apparent here. It is true indeed that Mésa is a man who has had his revelation, without having become fit to be admitted into God's bosom, because he has retained his human pride and the arrogance of his purity without the awareness of sin, and thus without God's grace; therefore the woman is the instrument with which God will break him, will bring him to Him through sin and humility. One can feel that, and one can feel also that if the central character of the play, Ysé, had been all of a piece, a single-minded instrument of divine providence, like Violaine for instance, the play would have been mechanical. But on the contrary, Ysé is, up to the end, a real human being, unpredictable, uncontrollable, a force of nature, and a force which can only manifest itself through and by other beings, a force which becomes part of the pattern of life, which in the end she drags down with her into catastrophe.

But just as Claudel transformed *La jeune fille Violaine*—a great drama—into the mystery play called *L'Annonce faite à Marie*, in the same way we can see in *Partage de Midi* differences between the original and the final form which are not to the advantage of the play. The new preface to the play, published in 1948, completely different from the original introduction, shows Claudel's dogmatic preoccupations which seem to be posterior to the play and therefore should not be taken too literally. Whether the third act has been slightly modified or not in order to fit in with Claudel's theological view, I could not say, but the fact is that those preoccupations are too apparent there, and that the play would have been much greater without them. In fact the third act, which is beautiful poetry, is dramatically weak, for the solution that it offers is that of a morality play and not that of a true drama. The *cantique* of Mésa is beautiful, but no longer quite in character. Above all Ysé, the vital character of the play, emerges, perhaps too clearly, as the chosen instrument of God; she has been the "jack" employed to lift God's elect—Mésa—to Him. Such a view of the relationship between man and God perfectly fits pagan deities, but does not fit the God of the Christians. Whatever determinism one may believe in, whatever the force and the extent of God's will, we cannot accept the idea of a God deliberately choosing certain victims for sacrifice, even in order to see the accomplishment of His ways which lead to the supreme good. It is possible to believe in metaphysical determinism and to accept the view that whatever is or exists could not be or exist otherwise than as it does, but it seems to me impossible to believe in God choosing certain of His creatures to scourge them in order to carry out His purpose. That is the God of the Old Testament; the God of Claudel seems to me too intent on ruling the lives of His creatures, on punishing them or rewarding them. He never leaves them any respite. He is too anthropomorphic. He is not the God of Love, and certain aspects of His nature are rather repellent. Dramatic characters can only suffer from the obviously set purpose of their creator, they are too clearly there for a chosen end. Here it is not the Greek's *ananke*, which is greater than the gods and which makes one pity the human suffering; there we had the pathos of men and women overwhelmed by superior forces, here we have men and women deliberately used to carry out God's will, God's conception of man's salvation. How can we pity Mésa, Ysé, and the others, if all that happened was entirely due to God's will, for their own good and for their eternal salvation? Who, if he believes in God and eternity, will prefer his earthly joys to eternal bliss, whatever human pains he has to go through in order to reach it? In spite of his ardent Catholic apologists, one has the feeling that it is Claudel's theology which is somehow wrong, for one cannot accept with equanimity the conception of a God who uses His creatures like puppets, a conception which seems to me far too remote from the doctrine of love and forgiveness which brought the Redeemer to earth. The vindication of the idea: "Le mal est dans le monde comme un esclave qui fait monter l'eau" is difficult and well-nigh impossible to carry out, and the attempt is harmful to the harmony of the play, for the *dénouement* is slightly strained and does not quite become the hall-mark of unavoidable necessity. Ysé cannot be both Mésa's predestined lover and the instrument which through sin and suffering is going to bring him back to God; she cannot be both the jack-sin which through death is going to bring Mésa to heaven and the eternal reward which Mésa will enjoy in heaven—unless Claudel, by a kind of casuistry which few could accept, separates body and soul, presents the love of Ysé and Mésa as God's will, and its consummation on earth as Satan's design. And even that would only be another aspect of the dichotomy which in Claudel's theology impinges seriously on the drama. Nevertheless this flaw in Claudel's theology does not quite endanger *Partage de Midi* to the extent that it endangers *Le Soulier de Satin* or *L'Annonce faite à Marie*.

L'Annonce faite à Marie is considered by many as Claudel's masterpiece. It unquestionably is, with *Partage de Midi* and *Le Soulier de Satin*, one of the greatest plays of our time; yet I must confess that I prefer *La jeune fille Violaine*, second version, to the final version which is *L'Annonce faite à Marie*. I should of course feel much more confident if I had seen *La jeune fille Violaine* staged. It seems to me that as drama, as distinct from mystery play *La jeune fille Violaine* has the advantage. Here the symbolism, didacticism and theological views of the author are less prominent and the characters retain a greater degree of ambiguity and humanity, all combining to make it one of the most moving Christian tragedies. Both plays contain some of the most beautiful and moving poetry ever written.

Claudel says that *Le Soulier de Satin* is a "résumé" of his whole poetic and dramatic work. This is indeed true, and to my mind that truth embodies both the outstanding aspects and the weaknesses of the work. Here we find the main themes of Claudel's poetry and drama reappearing and being given a final form which bears the imprint of Claudel's personality. We have the theme of the superman thirsting for power, as outlined in *Tête d'or*, and we have spread across it and lifted to the heights where Claudel wants to see it the great theme of *Partage de Midi* summed up in the exergue to *Le Soulier de Satin* which is made up of the Portuguese proverb, "Deus escreve diretto por limbas tortas," and the words of St. Augustine, "Etiam peccata." We find once again the whole imagery and symbolism of Claudel, but we find something more—an attempt to produce a vast synthesis which, although it is situated at a certain moment in time, is an apotheosis of the Catholic religion and its achievements on earth and a glorification of the main tenets of its dogma. That attempt could partly be accounted for by the maturation of Claudel's personality, and by his desire to communicate to others in a concrete form the answers which he has at last found to questions which have certainly tormented his soul for a long time. He has by now reached certitudes, he is beyond the struggle between human love and the divine law which forms the texture of *Partage de Midi*; he knows now the ways of the saint. There is grandeur in such visions, in such a splendid faith in oneself and the ways of the Maker, but there is also an inherent artistic weakness. Instead of allowing the action to take its course according to the various characters of the *dramatis personae*, instead of allowing the poetry to rise from the events, from the genuine feelings of the characters, as the end is known in advance, both to us and to the mind which unfolds the drama, there is an unavoidable tendency to force the characters into channels which have been prepared for them and which they must follow. This results in a lowering of dramatic tension and a weakening of the poetic expression, which is no longer a spontaneous emanation of an organically living character, but bears definite marks of the passionate eloquence and convictions of the author.

Le Soulier de Satin is indeed in more than one way a summing up of Claudel's dramatic career. It is an exhilarating piece of writing, a vast Calderonian comedy, the scene of which embraces the world and attempts to sum up a whole aspect of the life of human society. The result is very impressive, yet one may doubt the possibility of creating drama by trying to bring together various abstractions and by attempting to synthesize historical movements, actions and creeds into dramatic characters.

One of Claudel's errors is to believe that because he involves the universe, because his heroes encompass the world and literally juggle with it as if it were a geographical globe in a study-room, he has widened the scope of the drama. In fact, he only widens the field of his eloquence, but does not increase by a single jot the tension which makes drama. Rodrigue is that enormous man who says:

Ce n'est pas pour devenir à mon tour silence et immobilité
que j'ai rompu un continent en deux et que j'ai passé deux
mers. C'est parce que je suis catholique, c'est pour que toutes
les parties de l'humanité soient réunies.

And after America he conquers Asia, and he would have won
over England had the King of Spain accepted his offer. The whole
of Europe is brought together by Don Juan of Austria, the son of
Dona Musique and of the Viceroy of Naples, and the dream of
Prouhèze to hold Africa for the faith is continued by the expedi-
tion of Juan of Austria and her daughter, Marie de Sept-épées
whom we see at the end of the play sailing towards Lepanto.
The symbolism is obvious: the whole world is united into a
Catholic synthesis. After the battle of the White Mountain we
find all the great saints of Christianity gathered in Prague. St.
Boniface from the Saxon lands, and St. Dennys from Greece; the
Black Monk Luther had to be held at bay. Practically every great
historical event has been forced into this drama in an attempt to
produce a vast panorama of Catholic achievement. Even Napoleon's name has to come in, although he lived two centuries after
the time when the action is supposed to take place. It may, of course,
have been another Napoleon—still, he is called great, and history
has known only one great Napoleon. Everything is there, the
Armada sailing to England, and the rest of the fleet sailing to
Lepanto; we have Queen Elizabeth and we have Mary Queen of
Scots who, impersonated by an actress, makes an appearance on the
stage. In fact, the desire to bring everything in is too pronounced,
the symbolism too obvious. Rodrigue is a symbolic hero who represents the Catholic aim to embrace the world, and he has tried to
conquer it materially and spiritually. He does not lack grandeur, and
we cannot but be carried away by his splendid vision of one world:

C'est pour qu'il n'y ait pas de trou que j'ai essayé d'élargir
la terre. Le mal se fait toujours dans un trou.
On fait le mal dans un trou, on ne le fait pas dans une
cathédrale.

One cannot fail to be moved by such ideals of world unity, and in days when that unity seems to be the only alternative to complete annihilation we can only subscribe to it; and yet we cannot recognize it as part and parcel of the play. Rodrigue is the superman, the hero, so great as to be the symbol of all heroes, including the saint. The King of Spain, who sits in Madrid and directs the conquest of the world by the Catholic faith knows it well when he says, in the course of a beautiful and impressive scene:

Tant pis! Lui-même l'a voulu, je ne vois aucun moyen de l'épargner.

Je veux lui fourrer d'un seul coup dans le cœur tant de combustible qu'il en ait pour toute la vie!

Au-dessus de ce monde là-bas qui est en proie à l'autre, d'un monde à l'état de bouillonnement et de chaos, au milieu de cet énorme tas de matière toute croulante et incertaine,

Il me faut une âme absolument incapable d'être étouffée, il me faut un tel feu qu'il consume en un instant toutes les tentations comme de la paille,

Nettoyé pour toujours de la cupidité et de la luxure.

Je me plais à ce cœur qui brûle et à cet esprit dévorant, à ce grief éternel qui ne laisse à l'esprit point de repos.

Oui, s'il n'y avait pas eu cet amour, il m'aurait fallu y suppléer moi-même par quelque grande injustice.

As a first test Rodrigue has to conquer and to mould the newly-born continent of America; yet we know all too well that such an historical personage never existed. It is not a matter of taking liberties with history; we know and we agree that a play is not history, and that what counts is the poetic reality of the characters, but there are limits even to the imaginative acceptance of certain concrete facts. We can invent or arrange incidents of Caesar's life, but we cannot go as far as inventing a world-conqueror who never existed, without placing ourselves on the plane of fantasy, and here the historical claims are so precise and yet so violently opposed to what everybody knows that they depersonalize the character of Rodrigue and make it an abstraction completely devoid of reality. In spite of what some of Claudel's fervent apologists say, there is no "total drama". Such an expression has no meaning. Drama implies conflict of certain forces at a given time, and if it expands in time and place and contains, as it does here, various aspects of social life, it becomes an epic, which may be dramatic but is not quite a drama. The Kingdom of Denmark looks like a pin-head when compared with the vast dominions over which Rodrigue rules; yet Hamlet lives in a way in which Rodrigue does not, because the latter lacks individuality and is merely a symbol. Neither can we accept as valid the analogy of the *Divina Commedia*. There the poet, through his supreme imagination, welds together the contingent and the transcendent in an attempt to lift himself to the level of the ideal, which links him with the eternal, and he is the poem. In *Le Soulier de Satin* Rodrigue and Prouhèze have high ideals which lead them both to sainthood, but they are only part of vast plans for the glorification of a great creed and are only means to that end. Prouhèze is the means to bring Rodrigue to the gates of Heaven, Rodrigue is worthy of her and endures everything in order to reach sainthood, for which he is predestined. They may come near enough to sin and evil, but we know that they will not yield, that God will prevail, and that certitude saps the dramatic spring of the action. In fact, the character of the saint is not made for drama but for mystery plays. We know that saints are made of a substance different in certain ways from that of common mortals, but we know also, and this is what counts from the dramatic point of view, that their suffering is part of a process which refines them for eternity. We tremble in awe, and pray that one day perhaps the same divine grace may lift us out of ourselves, but we realize that such characters have nothing to do with drama. It is not the determinism of the motives which hampers the drama, it is the triumphant certitude of the end.

Phèdre also is overwhelmed by ruthless determinism, but with her we witness the harrowing struggle of a human being against forces which are bound to crush it, we are not aware that what takes place is for her good, and we can only suffer and sympathize with her fate, which is that of a being who pays for crimes for which she is not responsible. With Claudel there is no absolute struggle between good and evil. Evil is only part of the good, a means to the good; it is analogous to the stoic grandeur of Corneille's heroes, who do not know evil and only experience conflicts of duties in a theatre which involves a morality without religion. In Claudel the immanence and omnipresence of God reduce evil to the Spinozan concept of a part of the great whole:

> Qu'importe le désordre et la douleur d'aujourd'hui puis-qu'elle est le commencement d'autre chose, puisque
> Demain existe, puisque la vie continue, cette démolition avec nous des immenses réserves de la création,
> Puisque la main de Dieu n'a pas cessé son mouvement qui écrit avec nous sur l'éternité en lignes courtes ou longues,
> Jusqu'aux virgules, jusqu'au point le plus imperceptible,
> Ce livre qui n'aura son sens que quand il sera fini.

Right from the very beginning of the play the prayers of the Jesuit Father state in unmistakable terms the theme of the play.

> Mais, Seigneur, il n'est pas si facile de Vous échapper, et s'il ne va pas à Vous par ce qu'il a de clair, qu'il y aille par ce qu'il a d'obscur; et par ce qu'il a de direct, qu'il y aille par ce qu'il a d'indirect et par ce qu'il a de simple,
> Qu'il y aille par ce qu'il a en lui de nombreux, et de laborieux et d'entremêlé,
> Et s'il désire le mal, que ce soit un tel mal qu'il ne soit compatible qu'avec le bien,
> Et s'il désire le désordre, un tel désordre qu'il implique l'ébranlement et la fissure de ces murailles autour de lui qui lui barraient le salut,
> Je dis à lui et à cette multitude avec lui qu'il implique obscurément.

The woman is going to be once more, as in *Partage de Midi* the instrument of salvation, God's bait, which will hook and drag the human heart to Him. Sin and utter despair are made to serve; the dark night is necessary to light. Evil is therefore part of life or part of the necessary individuation of creation, but not the part of the perfect unity of being. Faust's life, for instance, is not righteous in any of its parts, and yet in the end righteousness is accepted for the whole. The faults of Faust in time are blessings in disguise and in the end, grace redeems for eternity what was imperfect and insufficient in time. As Spinoza says, "A thing is seen within the form of eternity, when all its parts or stages are conceived in their time relations and thereby conceived together." The blots in Faust's life were necessary blots, yet Mephistopheles, the tempter and main agent of the plot, is not part of God's plan, he appears as something beyond God's will, a necessary evil of creation perhaps, a force which is outside God's original pattern, and yet sprung from it and therefore tolerated in the whole as a part of a system which tests man's sense of personal responsibility. God is love, and suffering, though part of life, is beyond His actual will, but within His original will, the will which created life, and which is a process which God Himself cannot reverse until it has reached the end which He has Himself fixed.

Claudel's theatre in general, and particularly this play, is, above all, a vast synthesis of Catholicism and its achievements; the very souls of the various European nations are explained in terms of Catholicism. The Third Journey begins with scenes of epic grandeur and of obvious symbolism. Juan of Austria has marched into Bohemia in order to stem the onslaught of the enemies of Christendom; the scene which follows, the vision of Spain, her traditions and her gigantic struggles as the defender of the faith, is reminiscent of the Victor Hugo of *Ruy Blas*, but definitely to the advantage of Claudel, who shows a superb sense of the colossal and cosmic, and at the same time a very profound sense of the human. We not only have broad historical frescoes, we also have a definite feeling of life; there we can see the count-less barbarian migrations swaying to and fro across Europe, we can see all the physical and spiritual foes marshalled against a chosen cause; and we realize that not only is Claudel's theology as such difficult to accept, but also that the application of some of its tenets to dramatic art makes drama impossible. The main protagonists of the drama, in as far as the love of Prouhèze and Rodrigue is part of the drama, have no freedom of action, and that lack of freedom is not due to an inner compulsion but to definite manifestations of divine power. One may say that divine power can only manifest itself through the consciousness of its existence based in the soul, but in the case which concerns us we find ourselves faced with the application of one of the most serious aspects of the Christian dogma, which differentiates be-tween intuitive revelation of the divine, and the definite manifes-tation of the divine will to the human creature. From the beginning Prouhèze pledges herself, in her beautiful prayers to the Virgin, that she will not fail, and asks that, should she forget her prayers, divine presence should intervene every time, when-ever it is required, and her prayer is heard and accepted; when Rodrigue goes to meet her, he is struck down seriously wounded in defence of St. Jacques's church, and when Prouhèze's will wavers, her guardian angel is always at hand to keep her right up to her normal level of Corneillian heroism or rather, of pre-destined sainthood. The scene where the moon speaks sets out once and for all the kind of relationship which we can expect between the two lovers. Their love, in order to transcend death, must remain an ideal love within the law. The double shadow is the pure being formed by the ideal union of Rodrigue and Prouhèze in eternity, and their love can only exist there and nowhere else:

Oui, je sais qu'il ne m'épousera que sur la croix et nos âmes l'une à l'autre dans la mort et dans la nuit hors de tout motif humain!

Si je ne puis être son paradis, du moins je puis être sa croix!

Pour que son âme avec son corps y soit écartelée je vaux
bien ces deux morceaux de bois qui se traversent !

Puisque je ne puis lui donner le ciel, du moins je puis
l'arracher à la terre. Moi seule puis lui fournir une insuffisance
à la mesure de son désir !

Moi seule étais capable de le priver de lui-même.

Il n'y a pas une région de son âme et pas une fibre de son
corps dont je ne sente qu'elle est faite pour être fixée à moi,
il n'y a rien dans son corps et dans cette âme qui a fait son
corps que je ne sois capable de tenir avec moi pour toujours
dans le sommeil de la douleur,

Comme Adam, quand il dormit, la première femme.

Here we have one of the key passages of the play, and above all
we have what is surely truly great poetry, the kind of poetry
whose moving beauty and cosmic range reach to the very
sources of being. I do not think that there is anywhere in *Le
Soulier de Satin* more beautiful poetry than this meditation of the
moon, and it is a meditation which derives a great deal of its
pathos from the fact that it is congruent to the play, and contributes to the knowledge of the main characters. It lifts the
lovers to a plane above the human and it shows them as part of a
vast design in which they retain some of their moving humanity.
The action continues with Rodrigue in front of Mogador and
when he wonders what to do, the hulk of the old boat *Santiago*
surges to the surface of the sea and reminds him of the great
benevolent presence of St. Jacques who watches over his destiny.
Had his will failed, Prouhèze's would not have failed, for the
guardian angel, who had visited her when asleep in her tent on
the shore, had screwed her courage up to the final pitch of self-
sacrifice and sainthood. That scene is the central scene, one of the
most moving of the play, and one high-water mark of poetry in
the play. There the guardian angel, with the image of the revolving globe casting its shadow on the tent, explains to the full the
implications of the words of the Jesuit Father at the beginning

of the play, and the meaning of Claudelian theology. Here we learn that the loved being exists not by himself, but only in the *loved one*, in order to make him what he is destined to be, and not what the other would like him to be, or what he himself would like to be. This is a point of view which undoubtedly implies predestination and grace. By accepting the law, the being reaches eternity, and in order to reach eternity also, the other being can only wish for death. But before death, and in order to be able to offer her soul to God, and therefore in order to be able to live in eternity with Rodrigue, Prouhèze must claim her soul back from him and renounce all in order to have all eternally. At this point Christian theology meets the longing for the unattainable and for death of the Romantics. Here we have a superb unfolding of the mysterious ways of God in beautiful poetry, but it is more a kind of ritual than a dramatic scene; we watch the image of Prouhèze's fate, we learn through her dialogue with her guardian angel about God's unfathomed ways, but we are, I think, rather more awed by the breath-taking contrast between the finite and the infinite, by those glimpses of the eternal and of the ways to reach it, than moved by the suffering of the human beings involved. We cannot pity them, we cannot suffer for them, for theirs is the state which every true believer should hope to reach, and the non-believer will, I am afraid, find the whole thing difficult to comprehend. The predestination is evident, the guardian angel already holds in his hands the stone which is to be the cause of the shipwreck of Rodrigue's boat, the revolving globe shows the lands and seas which Rodrigue is going to cross, the labours he is going to perform, and the scene ends with the immense image of the Immaculate Conception stretching across the sky. It is a beautiful scene, difficult to quote in extracts:

Je suis Agar dans le désert! Sans mains, sans yeux, il y a quelqu'un qui m'a rejoint amèrement dans le dèsert!
C'est le désir qui étreint le déséspoir! C'est l'Afrique pardessus la mer qui épouse les terres empoisonnées du Mexique!

DONA PROUHÈZE: Eh quoi! Ainsi c'était permis? cet amour des créatures l'une pour l'autre, il est donc vrai que Dieu n'en est pas jaloux? l'homme entre les bras de la femme. . . .

L'ANGE GARDIEN: Comment serait-Il jaloux de ce qu'il a fait? et comment aurait-Il rien fait qui ne lui serve?

DONA PROUHÈZE: L'homme entre les bras de la femme oublie Dieu.

L'ANGE GARDIEN: Est-ce L'oublier que d'être avec Lui? Est-ce ailleurs qu'avec Lui d'être associé au mystère de Sa création,

Franchissant de nouveau pour un instant l'Eden par la porte de l'humiliation et de la mort?

DONA PROUHÈZE: L'amour hors du sacrement n'est-il pas le péché?

L'ANGE GARDIEN: Même le péché! Le péché aussi sert.

DONA PROUHÈZE: Ainsi il était bon qu'il m'aime?

L'ANGE GARDIEN: Il était bon que tu lui apprennes le désir.

This beautiful symbolical scene is followed by the scene between Prouhèze and Camille which completes the exposition of Claudel's theology. Here we have once more confirmation of the idea that the good and the bad are all instruments of the greater power, and therefore we are entitled to think that the bad ones have perhaps as much right to be admired and accepted as the good ones. Camille is used to bring Prouhèze to the place where she must go, but it could have been the other way round; both are part of the same "necessity" and although we may for a brief moment, when Camille bullies Prouhèze, forget that necessity and sympathize with the sufferer, we are soon made aware of the fact that Camille performs, like everybody else in the play, his appointed task, and that Prouhèze will save him as well as Rodrigue. Camille recognizes in Prouhèze the presence of grace, and just as Mara asks Violaine, he asks her to be a saint and to save him, and in both cases charity triumphs. All the characters in *Le Soulier de Satin* know that they are in God's hands, and in spite of the fact that they know they are destined to each other according to eternity, as all the other extraordinary pairs of lovers were, Prouhèze and Rodrigue also know that they must accept their fate, which consists in not belonging to each other, and in making of that predestined love the means to reach sainthood. Prouhèze knows that if ever she transgressed the law like Francesca da Rimini and Paolo, she could only give Rodrigue the desire of the damned, and not the pure love of Beatrice which she knows is meant to be hers. We are driven back again to that Claudelian belief which implies the use of the woman and the awareness of sin as a means of salvation:

> Pour les uns l'intelligence suffit. C'est l'esprit qui parle purement à l'esprit.
> Mais pour les autres il faut que la chair aussi peu à peu soit évangelisée et convertie. Et quelle chair pour parler à l'homme plus puissante que celle de la femme?

We are back to the old insoluble problem—how can this desire be evil, if it is part of a pre-ordained order of things beyond man, and together with it the other problem which presents a similar intractability, the problem of the relationships between body and soul? We are faced here with the conception that, while the soul is the unique thing which may through some mysterious correspondence be linked with another soul, flesh is the common element without any character of uniqueness which must be transcended in order to reach the higher order. This is a difficult point, for it implies a separation between body and soul, a separation which has in fact been rejected by many Christian thinkers, and is contradicted by the dogma of resurrection and the Assumption of the Holy Virgin. Surely the body is as much God's work as the soul, and an individuation of the soul in eternity presupposes the existence of a certain substance which may well have existed or may exist again in time. From the point of view of drama, that dissociation between body and soul and the knowledge that what we see on earth is only the shadow of actions which take place beyond, together with the fact that from the very beginning we know that under divine guidance the characters can only reach their appointed ends, weaken considerably the dramatic tension. Prouhèze knows that she is God's instrument and that she alone can open for Rodrigue the gates of Heaven, so she never sees Rodrigue except when, after her life of suffering on earth, she is about to die, and she leaves him with her daughter who, strangely enough, in an immaculate way, is also his, and when she already sees herself in the sky as the star which will guide his way.

Le Soulier de Satin is a hybrid combination of the miracle and mystery play, an enormous creation worthy of Claudel, who is an enormous man, a man of genius, who can sing with an harmonious Orphic voice or shatter us with a Cyclopean roar. It is work which contains wonderful things—flights into realms of great poetry and patches which look like sack on silk. Take the so-called comic element in Claudel, for instance, which is probably meant to convey that kind of universality, of fullness of life which we find in Shakespeare's plays; the trouble is that these grotesque interludes which Claudel has introduced seem to have been brought in merely because they are part of the recipe, but they do not add a jot to the drama, which is better without them. The fool in *Lear*, the grave-diggers in *Hamlet* are not interludes in the action, on the contrary they heighten the dramatic tension by prolonging it and by giving it, so to speak, time to rebound to greater heights. One has to gather breath in order to continue those vertiginous ascents. In Claudel these comic scenes are not out of tone, but they are irrelevant, they are interesting writing, but they are not part of the drama. There are many other things which do not fit into the drama, and which seem to be there for Claudel's merriment—the dance of the black girl, naked in the moonlight, is a flight into fantasy which is out of the real experience of the drama; then there is the enormous machinery required to bring the world on to the stage; there is the weakness inherent to the part of the narrator who, being the link between the audience and the stage, introduces grotesque elements when they are least expected, and also a kind of magic carpet atmosphere (as when he brings Prouhèze's and Rodrigue's mothers together) which would be acceptable in a fairy tale or in a puppet show, but not in drama.

We have in *Le Soulier de Satin* a kind of expressionism which is not alien to Claudel, but which is probably more marked in this play than in others. Certain poses of the human figures are forced, like the El Greco pose of the man who holds the gilded statue of the Virgin at the entrance of Don Pelage's house, and we have the striking contrast of colours, black and white, and the dark green or red, which symbolize all the violence of Spain. But above all the *dramatis personae* are too symbolical, they are not characters but the representations of abstractions, perhaps types; their speech is very symbolical and often ends in sheer eloquence, and their actions are even more symbolical, and meant to bring to mind memories of some of the greatest events of Christian religion. In fact, it is only in that light that we can understand them, and it is only in that context that they acquire a moving greatness. Three times struggled Prouhèze against the bushes before she fell at the feet of her guardian angel. Then we have the symbolism of her whole struggle with the angel, and of course side by side with it the symbolism of the life of Rodrigue, who, like Christ, conquered the world and was brought to death amidst derision and suffering.

But these restrictive remarks are not meant to detract from the fact that *Le Soulier de Satin* is a major work which shows the full maturity of the poet who seems to me the most outstanding literary genius of our time, and without question, the most important French poet-dramatist since Racine.

PART II

The Prose Writers

CHAPTER 5

Jacques Copeau

AS a critic, a man of letters and above all as a producer and actor, Jacques Copeau has exercised a unique influence on the French stage in the last decades. In spite of the existence of writers like Maeterlinck, Rostand and many others, acting and producing during the last decades of the nineteenth and the beginning of the twentieth century were practically in bondage to realism and commercialism. The plays which were produced had to be, first and foremost, commercial successes, and in order to make them successful, for such seems to have been the mood of the time, those plays had to be true mirrors of life, in both their substance and their production. In those days realism and naturalism had secured a solid grip on all the arts, and to have an idea of it, we have only to think of the feats of ingenuity which were performed at the Théâtre Antoine. Instead of aiming at placing the spectator in a world of make-believe, in a world of poetic convention, with imaginative themes and heightened speech, authors, producers and actors were all thoroughly engrossed in the most slavish imitation of what is described as "reality". The stage had to be a mirror with a smooth, polished surface, reflecting in their most minute details the trivialities of everyday life; gestures had to conform to the same pattern, and stage diction sought to remain as close as possible to that of the plain man. Art tended more and more towards photography, indeed, the time was ripe for the development of photography, for the cinema, which was going to outpace all other attempts at being realistic and compel the other arts to revert to their essence. André Antoine, whose *théâtre libre* was founded in 1887, sought to combine realism with non-commercial plays. He reduced the scenery to the minimum, but that scenery was realistic to the point of having real butchers' meat on the stage. A few years later, in 1893, Paul Fort founded the *théâtre d'art* whose aim was to produce poets' plays, and whose ideals were certainly different from those of Antoine. He declared that "the theatre should be a pretext for dreams". He was echoed in this country by Gordon Craig who said: "Realistic scenery is ana-thema, the stage is an artificial place in which the natural looks as wrong as an artificial flower in a garden." Together with him, William Poel and Granville Barker sought to free the stage from the various contraptions which overburdened it and to return to the primacy of the text. France, the country of political revolu-tions, was as usual the most traditional in the arts, and was therefore the last to free her stage of the shackles of realism; and that was the work of Copeau.

Jacques Copeau was a man of great and varied gifts. He saw at once the ills from which the theatre was dying; indeed, few men have had his clear-sightedness, his sharp vision of the true state of the theatre and of the remedies to be applied, and cer-tainly fewer have had a loftier conception of their art. He was a kind of Flaubert of the stage, a monk in a new monastic order. For him the theatre was a kind of ritual, something mysterious, religious, as it had been at its beginnings. We have all seen pictures and read descriptions of the austere settings of the Vieux-Colombier with its blue-grey back-cloth, its scanty furni-ture, and of Copeau and his company performing with ritualistic, impressive dignity. His influence was tremendous, his presence blew away all naturalistic cobwebs and realistic trappings, and poetry returned to the stage with all the honour which it had enjoyed in great ages. The actor became the object of his unfail-ing attention, he knew that good acting is a whole-time job which requires the full growth and the continuous liveliness of gifts without which stage performances can never reach the level of memorable artistic experiences. The list of the actors and producers who won their first laurels with Copeau affords us a glimpse of his achievements; it is a list which comprises the names of some of the most remarkable actors and producers of our times—Jouvet, Pitoëff, Baty, Michel St. Denis, Dullin, and, as a pupil of Dullin, Jean-Louis Barrault; it is, I think, difficult to muster a more brilliant galaxy.

Copeau had been revolted by the state in which he found the theatre at the end of the nineteenth century, and his observations, made in an article entitled "Lieux Communs" and published in *L'Ermitage* on 15th February, 1905, give us an idea of his analytical powers, of his wisdom and of the magnitude of the task he set himself. Here are some of his remarks: "The theatre, even the theatre which describes itself as serious, has fallen into the lower realms of frivolous occupations. The most fatal kind of inspiration which might visit an artist is dramatic inspiration. He knows that and shuns it. If he accepts it, he will be reduced to surrender or to starvation. The indifference of the public and the apathy of dramatic criticism are the accomplices of this state of affairs. The theatre managers and their hirelings have one single pre-occupation—will my play make money? They have of course very heavy burdens to bear, but none is heavier than the actors' greed. Vain and arrogant, the latter are the true masters of the situation; their whims, their despotic ignorance rule the stage. A play is unrecognizable once it has passed through their hands. They modify the text, add, delete and transform it to suit themselves; they are supposed to be the collaborators of the authors, and they are their tormentors. The authors are only concerned in seeing their plays performed, their characters are made to suit the actors . . . we could name writers who once upon a time carried with them our hopes; now they have achieved success. Each new production shows the progress of their downfall, each success is for them a defeat." This is a formidable indictment of the state of the theatre at the dawn of the century, and we cannot but reflect that, in spite of Copeau's and other like-minded peoples' efforts, this indictment is far from having lost all its topicality and pungency.

Copeau saw clearly that great art cannot be confined to any one single aspect of life, he saw that it could neither be devoted to being moralizing or sociological, nor merely idealistic or realistic. He knew that art must aim at painting resemblances suggesting life in its wholeness, that it must try to extract from things their essential life, and that it must allow speech to rise from them and not speak for them and judge them. Indeed the poet's single concern must be the poem; the rest—social message, philosophy, and so on—can only be incidental to and not the aim of the poem. There is a great deal to be said for Synge's view that "true drama is like a symphony, a beautiful creation which is an end in itself and proves nothing".

What were the means employed by Copeau to deal with the task that he had undertaken? He has expounded his views in a long essay published in the *N.R.F.* of September 1939; the best thing to do seems to me to give an abridged version of his arguments, and here are the main points: "We have no formula, no revolutionary programme (as Antoine and the *théâtre libre* have). We do not know what to-morrow's theatre will be, we only wish to react against the defects of the contemporary theatre and to offer a stage to future talents. . . . Our first aim is to restore prestige to the stage by showing our respect for the classics; we shall try to recapture their original freshness, but we shall never try to trim them in order to suit the taste of the day. On no account shall we ever do that, for to attempt to restore an outward youth to what is eternal, or to give a wrapping of modern verisimilitude to what overflows with truth would be a strange amusement indeed. We shall not indulge in such fantasies. The whole and only originality of our interpretation, if we can show any, shall rest on nothing but a profound knowledge of the text. . . . We could never study too much that aspect of producing which deals with the interpretation of the text. We do not want to attach any importance to anything connected with décor and

88

stage designs. . . . It is not because we cannot appreciate the art of creating a dramatic climate by means of colour, light and shapes; we have indeed followed the experiments by Messrs. Meyerhold, Stanislavsky, Max Reinhardt, Gordon Craig and others, and we realize, as everybody else does, the advantage of décors which tend to suggest things over décors which attempt to give a realistic illusion of things. But those methods are by now too widely accepted, too well-known, for anybody to dare to claim, without ridicule, the merit of applying them. If we apply them, we shall do so with restraint. Above all, we are opposed to systems, we intend to remain faithful to common sense and good taste, and we must aver to being sometimes shocked by the pedantic heaviness of some of the ideas of the masters mentioned above. We find certain attempts to stress poets' intentions with concrete and sometimes naïve means rather offensive to the traditional moderation and subtlety of French taste. . . . We fear that the application of such methods, together with a constant pursuit of the sensational (a fruitless pursuit when applied to the great classical works) might lead to artificial, uncouth and almost barbaric productions. I feel that to allow myself to be carried away by engineers' and electricians' inventions is to grant painted canvas or cardboard an undeserved pre-eminence; in one way or another that means subservience to stage tricks, and whether they are old or new, we repudiate stage tricks. In fact, whether machinery is good or bad, rudimentary or fully developed, artificial or realistic, we intend to grant no importance to machinery. . . . For we are convinced that it is disastrous to load dramatic art with a burden of external complexities such that in the end it strains and dilutes its strength, encourages the picturesque, and transforms drama into fairy-tale. We do not believe that in order to represent man in his wholeness we require a theatre in which the décor can rise from the stage instantaneously; we do not believe that the future of our art is a question of machinery, and we shall endeavour to express truth through the feelings and actions of the dramatic characters."

Here was a man of extraordinary integrity, a man who had vision and strength of purpose, and who knew what poetry was. He had in him a grain of that quality which makes saints and great men, he knew that in order to rise, one has to divest oneself of all human trappings and ambitions, that it is by laying one's soul bare, by kneeling humbly in a state of innocent expectation at the feet of Truth or Poetry, that either may come and may live through a being. He knew instinctively that neither poetry nor truth can ever be reached by naked egotists eager to wear them as triumphant feathers. He knew that possession is only the illusions of one's own predatory self, and that in order to reach the possibilities of Truth, one has to cease desiring it. Copeau had the soul of a poet, and when he approached the Greeks, Shakespeare or Racine, he approached them with reverence and with the conviction that their words contained poetry which no human device could improve. He knew that their words trailed with them music and memories of times older than man, reaching beyond man, since they are the unchanging sources of music and memories. If he could not see:

> The cloud-capp'd towers, the gorgeous palaces,
> The solemn temples, the great globe itself,

he knew that Prospero's master alone could see such things, and he was fully aware that no amount of stagecraft and device could add to such visions. He did not attempt to improve on Shakespeare or Sophocles, to bring them up-to-date, or to clean them up. He left that mighty task to Cocteau and others; he followed the example of the angels.

What has been the outcome of his teaching, of his strong influence and of his outstanding example of artistic scrupulousness? When he died, in 1949, Jouvet said: "There is not a writer, nor an actor who does not owe something to him; I owe everything to him." Dullin and Barrault said the same thing. Jouvet and Barrault have maintained alive in France some of the traditions of Copeau. Their companies, from the actors to the stage-hands, have been models of friendship. Both have maintained very high standards for actors' training and for production, and in spite of the fact that they have felt, in various degrees, the impact of the Russian ballet on scenery and acting, they have both maintained their faith in the text.

On the other hand, one cannot help noting how far staging has strayed from Copeau's artistic views. German and Russian influences now hold sway on the French as well as on other stages. Cocteau, besides rejuvenating old myths and masterpieces, revels in machinery with simultaneous décors, with talking horses, men floating in the air, and other devices which are in their place in the cinema but have nothing much to do with the stage. In France, as in this country and in others, many producers are too intent on shining by any kind of means, including fantastic settings, strange groupings and a diction and timing which must bear the indelible mark of their personality. Nowadays we must talk of Mr. X's *Henry IV* or *Hamlet*, or Mme. Y's *Phèdre*. I belong to that category of people who still like to see Shakespeare's *Henry IV* or *Hamlet*, and Racine's *Phèdre*, and more often than not I would gladly give away any of those slick productions which bear the imprint of the producer's strenuous brain-work, for a straightforward production by E. Martin Browne or John Gielgud.

In spite of his sumptuous settings, Jouvet never went as far as Barrault in his love of machinery, and on the whole he retained a great deal of Copeau's rigorism, of his priest-like attitude to the theatre, and if he lost his master's austerity, he retained his love of truth and his faith in the sacred mission of the theatre. Nobody has done more for Molière than Jouvet, and Molière has in no way suffered in the process. If the scenery has been stylized, the scrupulous respect of the text, the high quality of the acting, made of those performances theatrical highlights of our time. Anybody who has seen Jouvet in the great parts created by Molière will agree that he well deserved to be styled "a classic rejuvenated".

Nowadays the influence of the ballet on the theatre is such that some producers set their actors dancing with their lines and attempt to replace words by movements. Jean-Louis Barrault goes sometimes too far in that direction. The influence of the *commedia dell' arte* and of the Nietzschean conception of tragedy and dance has led him along a path which tends to stray away from poetry. Dance is one thing, poetry is another; they are both forms of art, but they are not interchangeable, for they are fundamentally different. One cannot dance the battle of Actium as he tried to do in the course of his production of *Antony and Cleopatra* at the Comédie Française in 1945; gestures and miming in such a case, unless they are part of stage rhetoric, can only limit the evocative power of the poem. Every art has its own province and it is not improved by being combined with another. The Wagnerian mixing of the arts is deadly to the theatre. Dance is based on music, poetry is not, at least not on instrumental music. Good poetry, dramatic or lyrical, does not require music. To attempt to put a good poem to music is to court head-on collisions, the outcome of which will not be harmonious marriages, but mutilated individualities. Some evanescent, slightly inchoate poems of Verlaine have proved ideal material for music and they have been transformed by its help in the same way as Debussy's music transformed Maeterlinck's lifeless text of *Pelléas et Mélisande*. But Donne's or Shakespeare's sonnets are as little in need of music as was *L'Après-midi d'un Faune* by Mallarmé who aptly replied to Debussy, who had asked his permission to put it to music, that "he thought he had already done so himself". Debussy's *L'Après-midi d'un Faune* is certainly excellent but so is Mallarmé's, which has no need of extraneous support. In fact each remains in its own domain, both of them leading their separate lives in the same way as Shakespeare's *Macbeth* is separated from Verdi's *Macbeth*.

If Barrault was rather unwise in attempting to mime what cannot be mimed, his superb gifts of mimicry and his physical capacity to express emotion have all the same been put to excellent use in the service of both Shakespeare and Molière. His Hamlet, shorn of the poetry and of the ineffable music of the

Shakespearian line, is nevertheless the most vital and the most striking of modern times, Gielgud's Hamlet excepted. Gielgud can combine a unique vocal range with the most acute sensibility. Barrault has a remarkable intellect and artistic integrity; he has brooded lengthily over the case of Hamlet, and he compensates by dynamism and mental complexity for what he lacks in passion and sensibility. His *Scapin*, which enabled him to make full use of his *commedia dell' arte* propensities and his dehumanized form of acting which is the best way of rendering the super-human aspect of a type, was something memorable.

Finally I come to Barrault's single-minded task, which lasted over a decade, for the making of Claudel's theatrical fame. Whether Barrault is attuned to, or is in full accord with the deeply religious inspiration and the impact of Claudel's plays is some-thing difficult to say, and anyway irrelevant to the problems under examination; what is evident is that there must be enough imaginative affinity and sympathy between the two, for Barrault to have succeeded in bodying forth so many of Claudel's visions. *Le Soulier de Satin* seemed on the page an intractable text, but Barrault has made of it an unquestioned theatrical success, and one of the theatrical events of our time. My only regret is to have never had the joy of seeing such a performance; but I have seen *Christophe Colomb*, a far less rewarding piece of writing than *Le Soulier de Satin*, and Barrault's production is one of the most impressive stage creations I have ever witnessed. The inner or essential structure of *Christophe Colomb* is the same as that of *Le Soulier de Satin*; it conforms to the architype of Christ. After the discovery of new worlds, after victory and glory, comes humiliation, destitution, nakedness and death. Barrault has contributed here and there graftings from Claudel's other works, and with the support of Milhaud's moving music, he has given full scope to the versatility of his talents—choruses, snatches of film projected on a sail overhanging the stage, Brechtian effects of alienation suggested by Claudel before Brecht even began to write—all these effects combine to show once more that Barrault is now the most gifted of actor-directors in the theatre. For ten years he maintained at the Marigny standards and traditions of which his revered master Copeau would certainly have approved, and his contribution to the theatre is anything but finished. It is just a pity that he no longer has a theatre of his own, or that he is not in charge of one of the great state-subsidized theatrical organizations of France.

CHAPTER 6

Language and Myth
in Modern French Poetic Drama:
Jean Cocteau

THE language of poetic drama can oscillate between the direct-ness and clarity of that of Racine, and the Shakespearian formula of closely packing images and metaphors into moments which are within character and also transport character beyond time; but both types of language must have the external appearance of a common norm generally accepted by the age in which they are used. The alexandrine was the norm of the theatre in Racine's age, just as blank verse was the norm in the Shakespearian age. It seems to me that if the poet has to try to compete with the novel and the cinema, which now dominate the scene, he will have to do so on their own ground, that is by using themes which are perennially human, and a language which can often enough rub shoulders with the bare, direct dialogue of the novel, the speech form of the cinema or that of the plain man in the street, and yet a language suffused with a strength and rhythm which at any given moment can, by an increase in tension, a powerful image or a metaphor, be trans-substantiated into the language of poetry.

Apart from the novel and the cinema, there are two other arts whose developments have an influence on poetic drama. I mean opera and ballet. The growth of opera has precipitated a certain amount of dissociation between lyricism and drama, and the untrue and unwelcome distinction between lyricism and drama outlined by William Archer has gained a wide measure of popular acceptance. The growth of ballet has perhaps been responsible for a greater interest in formal beauty, but it has also been the source of certain analogies between ballet and poetic drama which do not stand the test of examination. It has been said that, just as the choreographer leaves a certain amount of initiative to the ballet-dancer who creates poetry by movement, in the same way the poet should leave a certain amount of initiative to the actors by providing them with certain choreographic guidances, and the poetry would therefore be born from the performance. Ballet has also had a marked influence on acting by stressing the importance of movement and the Nietzschean concept of tragedy and dance. But possibly the greatest impact of ballet is on staging, and also in fostering confusion between poetry and the poetical. We are living in an age of confusion of genres and looseness in terminology; people talk freely of a dancer being a poet. He may be a poet if he writes poetry, but he certainly cannot write it with the arabesques of his legs and arms; what he can do is to create in the spectators who have sensitiveness and imagination a "poetic" state, and if any one of these spectators is a poet, he will transmute the experience undergone into poetry. Poetry is not a state, but a crystallization of such a state into an object or a form; a dancer may have the most poetical soul alive, but cannot be a poet merely by his dancing, because poetry is oneness; it implies a synthesis, an imaginative unity which can only be born from one single mind, and not from a collaboration of people, such as playwright, producer, stage designer, actor and public. Scenery, star-acting and incidental music can create an impression of poeticality, but cannot create poetry, unless the poetry is already in the words.

The difference between poetry and prose is less fundamental than that between poetry and verse. There is, for instance, far more poetry in a few pages of Rousseau and Plato than in the whole verse output of Voltaire or Gide, but the points where prose rises to poetry are rare, and they imply a much greater effort than the one required to pass from verse to poetry. Although verse is only the outward shape of a substance, it is a shape which has been originally moulded on a substance which has existed and can exist again, and while one cannot confuse one with the other, when the substance fills the shape or form we have poetry. Prose can and does rise to poetry when the writer can no longer express logically what engages his conscious self, and when, therefore, highly imaginative and musical language becomes the whole self in a moment which transcends time; but these moments are few, and the aim of prose is to convey meaning and not to be, like poetry, a means to create or to re-create experience. Poetic prose there is, but a poem requires a sustained, rhythmical pattern and an organic oneness which we do not find in prose, for if we did it would then be poetry. Verse form does not make poetic drama: the example of Gide or of some plays of Rostand is there to prove that point. On the other hand, prose plays cannot on the whole be poetic drama, and, as T. S. Eliot wisely remarked about Maeterlinck's theatre, poetic drama in prose is bound to be too "poetical". Verse, whatever it lacks, has a definite rhythm and pattern, and when the tension rises within that rhythm and pattern it becomes poetry. Prose also has a rhythm and pattern, but they are both ancillary to meaning, and they vary from the strong emotional beats of Rousseau and Burke to the nimble butterfly-flights of Voltaire or of Robert Louis Stevenson.

English is an accented language, and the rhythm of its poetry, freed from classical prosody, is easily recognized, being on the whole either iambic or trochaic. The iambic rhythm is also the rhythm of normal prose, and the transition between prose and verse is far easier in English than in French; besides that, one can also pass easily from iambic to trochaic and dactylic rhythms.

Rhythm is the internal pattern of the emotion which underlies speech, and one can find it both in prose and in verse. But emotions and their effects have an extremely individual quality, which can only be conveyed to others by making use of certain accepted and recognizable conventions of speech. When one deals with a language which is accented, one can, through the various combinations of feet, convey, even in free verse, the rhythmical pattern of an emotion, and that, combined with, or rather fully integrated into, the metaphorical, and image value of words, can make poetry.

The French language, lacking these definite elements of rhythm, has to rely more on strictness of metre, rhymes and internal pauses in order to counteract a fluidity which tends towards eloquence. The alexandrine has a very great internal melodic range, but it has, because of the rhyme and the syllabic structure, a stiffness which does not break easily into prose.

The use of myth as a means of producing "poetic drama" has become quite a widespread practice among contemporary French and also English dramatists. The greatest dramatic poets of the modern world, Shakespeare and Racine for instance, have returned again and again to the mythical and legendary sources of poetry, and the end of the nineteenth century witnessed a great renewal of interest in Greek tragedy and mythological subjects. There is therefore a long tradition of poetry through myth, and one can easily understand why, in twentieth-century France, dramatists may have been strongly tempted to follow the example of Racine and others and try to create poetry through myths. But they seem to overlook the important fact that Racine was a genius comparable to Sophocles or Euripides, and that he only used aspects of myth which had not been fully dealt with in the great Greek tragedies. He did not attempt to write another *Antigone* or *Oedipus Rex*, or to modernize existing Greek tragedies; he wrote *Andromaque*, *Phèdre*, *Iphigénie*, and though these themes had been used by Euripides, he imposed upon them a new pattern and in fact restored to them a great deal of the pathos which was originally attached to them, and which they had lost in Euripides' psychological tragedies tending more and more towards the modern concept of drama. Modern playwrights like Anouilh, Cocteau and Giraudoux, proceed in a different way; they take over existing plays such as Sophocles' *Antigone* or

Electra, and modernize them by infusing topical feelings and preoccupations into the characters, whose language becomes realistic
and made to exteriorize the idiosyncrasies of the social group to
which they belong. The linguistic up-to-dateness is mostly used
for comic effects. I cannot help feeling that Sophocles' Antigone
could still speak to us in her Grecian clothes and in her Attic
setting with more power and poignancy than when dressed by the
fashion houses of Paris and trailing behind her the atmosphere of
the banks of the Seine, whether it is Anouilh or Cocteau who is
responsible for the transformation.

With Anouilh's *Antigone*, which we shall examine at greater
length later, we have an attempt to shift the emphasis from the
pathos of Antigone's situation to that of Creon as prisoner of his
function of ruler. That enables Anouilh to give to his drama the
atmosphere of fierce intellectual inquisitiveness which has been
that of France during the last decade; it enables him to transmit
to us the view, all too familiar, that it is more difficult to live than
to die; but the heat of the disputation between Antigone and
Creon dispels that atmosphere of doom and inevitability which
marks the greatness of Sophocles' play, and leaves us with
precious few things to hold on to. We have the irritating, off-
hand, rather slick ways of the chorus which, knowing all, explains
in advance everything that is going to take place; we have the
obvious ambiguities about the situations and the feelings of
Frenchmen under German occupation. We have the usual
sentimentality of the love scene between the two lovers, the
realistic language, the mental attitude of barracks life, and we have
the trivial transposition of Oedipus' relations with his sons into a
scene of melodrama, something which only increases the atmosphere of cynicism and Machiavellian expediency. Admittedly,
this *Antigone* has a personal twist—a kind of emphasis on uncompromising idealism, ending in nihilism, which gives the play a
certain topicality. In Sophocles' play, Creon is a tyrant (in the
modern meaning of the word) who on the whole governs according to the wishes of his people. Although rebellion must be

punished, his attitude towards the sacred ritual of the burial of the dead is an inexcusable sacrilege. Antigone loves her brother, but above all, as a true daughter of Hellas, she fears the gods, and she feels that she must, whatever the human laws may be, respect divine law; if not, her soul and her brother's soul will be damned for eternity, and what is death compared with eternity? In Anouilh, the mystery has been dispelled, the immense figures which cast their shadows on the human plane have disappeared, we are strictly on the plane of the contingent, and intellect and dialectics assume pre-eminence over imagination and poetry. Creon is made to appear as "un meurtrier logique", the prisoner of a concept which crushes his sensitiveness but which he must nevertheless respect, for it involves the very fabric of the society in which he lives. Antigone is in some ways a possessed person, somebody who cannot compromise, who is at heart dissatisfied with the laws of society and cannot accept them. She is looking for death, and her action is neither an act of sisterly love, nor an act of religious reverence, but the gratuitous gesture of a young revolutionary who, in the Dostoevsky manner, feels the need for "experience", for revelation through action which is, in the end, the only positive gesture of a nihilistic conception of life. She is the expression of her age, that age which, deprived of the absolute of faith, seems to believe that the only place where an idealistic soul may find peace is in the absolute of nothingness. This is a conception which swamps most of Anouilh's play and merely echoes, through remarkable dramatic skill, Dostoevsky, Novalis, Gide, Sartre and others who followed the Nietzschean night of the death of God. This apart, there is too much political wisdom of a cynical kind and a too frequent use of the worn-out device of soldiers discussing some of their idiosyncrasies in their own special language, a device which has become one of the stock tricks of many modern dramatists. M. Anouilh is both too wise and too modest to call *Antigone* a poetic drama.

The problem is different with Cocteau, and if Giraudoux's name is briefly mentioned in this context, it is only because of the fact that some of his statements on the theatre seem to echo those of Cocteau; yet we must not attach too much importance to them, for although Giraudoux was one of the most important dramatists of our time, he was not on the whole a sound literary critic. As a playwright, we shall see later that, although he had certain definite poetic gifts—such as fantasy, wit, a kind of whimsicality which could detect the quaintest aspects of things, and at times a dazzling brilliance—in the end he was not altogether a poet. He had fancy, but not truly imagination; he could arrange, adorn, bring side by side in unexpected ways the real and the unreal, extract the fantastic from the real, or give a stirring topical flavour to old mythical or legendary situations, but he could not produce and never produced one imaginative synthesis which could truly be called poetic drama. He was well aware of the importance of style, yet his love of words often ends in sheer jugglery and hollow paradoxes. If there is one play of Giraudoux's which is hailed as poetic, it is *Ondine*, yet, in spite of the fact that one could be momentarily won over by it and spend a delightful evening watching a performance of that play brilliantly produced by Jouvet, who also played the leading part, one could not help being every now and than startled by the pseudo-poeticality of the text and by the extraordinary conglomeration of devices which the author has used. It is, in fact, above all a pantomime packed with miraculous happenings; even time and the elements have been tamed and deftly handled through prodigies of "machinery". There is wit, there is a fascinating blend of comic and heroic, of fantastic and trivial—as when the armour-clad knight explains to Ondine that the two plagues of a knight's life are rain percolating down the neck and an inaccessible flea—and there is the weird atmosphere created by such pieces of dialogue as:

AUGUSTE: Que peut-elle bien faire encore au dehors dans ce
    noir?
EUGÉNIE: Pourquoi t'inquieter? Elle voit dans la nuit.
AUGUSTE: Par cet orage!

EUGÉNIE: Comme si tu ne savais plus que l'eau ne la mouille
pas.

But all that is not enough to make poetry.

From Giraudoux's criticism we shall extract only a few
sentences which partly illustrate his failure to achieve eminence
as a poet-dramatist and also explain the passing association of his
name with Cocteau's in this chapter on poetic drama. These
sentences occur in one of his essays entitled *L'Auteur au Théâtre*;
they come after a rather naïve interpretation of the great age of
Spanish drama and the age of Louis XIV, and they run like this:
"The author does not exist in the theatre; he is only a voice, and
not his own." And further on: "There is no plagiarism, because
there is no property in dramatic art—attribution is the only kind
of paternity the author can claim." This is the kind of statement
which any producer intent on considering the author as a mere
script-writer could have made. In Giraudoux it may only be a
sample of his humour or love of paradox which should not be
taken seriously; yet if it were serious, it certainly shows the kind
of confusion which prevailed in his mind. *L'Annonce faite à Marie*
is surely as much Claudel's as *The Cocktail Party* is T. S. Eliot's,
and both are in the end neither more nor less "objective"
than *Paradise Lost* or *The Ancient Mariner*. Giraudoux obviously
laboured under the illusion that poetry could be the result of
"co-operation between author, producer, actor and audience".

Now this is to my mind exactly the kind of confusion made by
Cocteau, and if I take him as the true prototype of that kind of
confusion, it is because he is the only one who constantly insists
on the title of poet, and also because, in spite of his achievements,
I remain unable to find in his dramatic work a definite basis for
such a claim. His didactic pronouncements closely resemble those
of Giraudoux, with the only difference that they require to be
treated with the utmost earnestness, for they definitely have the
character of "manifestoes".

Let us take for instance his Preface to the 1928 edition of

Language and Myth: Jean Cocteau

Les Mariés de la Tour Eiffel and *Antigone*. There we find *Roméo et Juliette* described as "un texte-prétexte". With regard to *Antigone* he says: "I have tried to give a bird's eye view of *Antigone*, so great beauties disappear, others are brought out; perhaps my experiment is one way to bring to life the old masterpieces." Or again, about *Roméo et Juliette*: "I wanted to operate upon a drama of Shakespeare in order to discover the bones under the adornments; I have therefore chosen the most adorned, the most beribboned." There is no need to stress the lack of foundation of such assertions; they merely show Cocteau's inability to appreciate the poetry of Sophocles or that of Shakespeare. The final result is that his *Antigone* is a public square conversation-piece deprived of any atmosphere or pathos; as for his *Roméo et Juliette*, one must read it in order to realize how Cocteau, "in search of the bone", has reduced the most moving poetry to an ossuary. The 1922 preface of *Les Mariés de la Tour Eiffel* contains Cocteau's famous exposition on "la poésie du théâtre": "L'action de ma pièce est imagée tandis que le texte ne l'est pas. J'essaie donc de substituer une poésie de théâtre à la poésie au théâtre. La poésie au théâtre est une dentelle délicate impossible à voir de loin. La poésie de théâtre serait une grosse dentelle, une dentelle en cordages, un navire sur la mer." But what about the lace that Shakespeare or Racine produced? As T. S. Eliot once so aptly said: "that was lace with the strength of rope", while M. Cocteau's rope is only rope, something which merely holds together, more or less adroitly, things which show at times a strange heterogeneity. How much wiser that great man of the theatre Copeau was, when he expressed his impatience with all *a priori* and artificial classifications such as poetic theatre, realistic theatre, moralizing theatre, etc! Drama, according to him, dealt with life, and therefore could not be reconciled with any *a priori* specialization; and his conclusion is worth quoting: "Let us talk about a poet-dramatist", he said, "that is the title we may dream of, but the words 'théâtre poétique' seem to me an expression which has no meaning." That is exactly what I think about Cocteau's expression, "poésie de théâtre". What Cocteau clearly means is that the kind of poetry he is after is not poetry contained in words, but poetry created by all kinds of devices, some of them admittedly apt and purposefully used in the theatre. Later on, in the same preface, he says: "Thanks to Diaghilev and others, we witness in France the birth of a genre which is neither ballet nor opera, and it is in that direction that the future lies." At least, that was the future as Cocteau saw it. The production of his plays and other forms of entertainment, in the course of which he brought together famous painters, musicians, choreographers and dancers, shows the kind of synthesis he had in mind. His ideal—very Wagnerian indeed—was that a play ought to be written, staged, dressed and provided with musical accompaniment by one single man; but he added, "that perfect athlete does not exist". One must concede that as a film producer, with all modern scientific apparatus at his disposal, Cocteau has certainly done his best to achieve that ideal—but that is another matter.

In my view, his "poetry of the theatre" is an aesthetic emotion of varying intensity, but it is not poetry. A certain atmosphere or a climate created by all sorts of devices, ranging from chiaroscuro lighting to fantastic supernatural shapes, may or may not create an emotional state conducive to poetry, but it is certainly not poetry. The whole thing is likely to remain in a kind of inchoate state in which feelings, shapes and thoughts are different from what they normally are; but unless these things coalesce into form or, to be precise, into words, there is no poetry. Cocteau himself seems to me to be the prototype of the writer who gets into such states of exhilaration in the course of which the human being hovers half-way between the real and the unreal, in a world where all sorts of unco-ordinated ideas and feelings float swiftly across the mind, yet lacking the vision which discriminates and fuses together these elements of chaos into the consistency and coherence of organic life. All men are filled with poetic possibilities, but the lightning force which fuses all these possibilities into existence and timelessness is very rare. Cocteau has at times felt that force, though it never lasted long enough to enable him to write a full poetic drama. More often than not he has taken the shadow for the substance, and he has failed to see that no amount of staging, acting or other devices can produce poetry, unless there is poetry in the words. Surprise, for instance upon which Cocteau relies so much, is, true enough, an element of poetry; a poem must be something new; the words, the images, the rhythm used must have that vitality which makes of each poem a new experience; but surprise is only a means to an end, and by itself it is no more poetry than a poetic theme is poetry. This phrase— "the poetry of the theatre"—which has achieved such fame, is a confusing phrase, which seems to me to be typical of many of Cocteau's unfounded claims. There is, and there was before Cocteau, poetry in the theatre—the whole body of poetic drama, from Sophocles to Shakespeare and Racine, is poetry in the theatre; there is a poetic atmosphere of the theatre; but there is not, strictly speaking, a poetry of the theatre, except in the way in which travel or film advertisements talk of the "poetry" or the "romantic appeal" of Capri or any other famed beauty spot. Whatever is unreal is not *ipso facto* poetry, and poetic themes, like the old myths and legends, together with certain devices, cannot by themselves produce poetry.

Let us not dwell too seriously on Cocteau's assumptions stated in his 1928 preface to *Oedipe-Roi* and *Roméo et Juliette*, that "he could smooth and clear away the dead débris and the dust which clog certain masterpieces"; the mere thought of Cocteau clearing up *Antigone* or *Oedipe-Roi*, as certain museums have cleaned their Raphael or Da Vinci, will bring up at once the incongruousness of the whole idea. Rembrandt's *Night Watch* has been cleaned, but it remains a Rembrandt, which does not have to compete with Mr. X's (the cleaner's) *Night Watch*; but if Cocteau proceeded with his plan—or threat—we should soon have *King Lear*, *Hamlet* or *Phèdre* spruced up for contemporaneity by Mr. Cocteau—something to look forward to, indeed! For, judging by the results left by his deft hand and mercury-like mind on *Oedipus*, *Antigone* and *Romeo and Juliet*, we can only wonder who, knowing anything of the original, could ever think of reading the revised versions. I hope we may be spared further rejuvenating operations. I hope that these revered creations will be left as they are, without any grafting or polishing up; if not, we might see King Lear reviewing the Greys before setting off to carve out his kingdom into three or four portions, and Cordelia arriving by helicopter, heading an airborne landing of her husband's forces in the south of England! One has only to think of the bustle and flash of uniforms which Cocteau has been able to pack into his Ruritanian romance between a queen and a peasant poet, to realize what kind of thing may be born from such attempts. We should of course remember that he will not always find actresses like Edwige Feuillère or Eileen Herlie to retrieve his melodramatic failings; for melodrama, which is more a matter of atmosphere than characterization, is a genre which compels the actor to use to the full his creative powers.

But let us take two plays in which Cocteau tries to give us his own version of two of the most famous myths of the life of man—the myth of Oedipus and that of Orpheus. In *La Machine infernale*, Cocteau has taken the myth of Oedipus, not as Sophocles did, at the point when, after many years of married life, Oedipus is about to be hurled headlong into well-nigh unbearable suffering, but when he reaches Thebes with hopes stretching wide before him. Cocteau concentrates chiefly on the meeting with the sphynx, life in the palace, the marriage and the bridal night. The undoing of Oedipus only occupies approximately a tenth of the play; coming after some very amusing chit-chat, it is divested of its emotional context, and is a kind of Parisian drawing-room comedy which makes us expect at any moment the ring of a telephone bell calling away Tiresias to his patients, or the horn of a motor-car waiting at the door to whisk away Oedipus, with Antigone at the wheel. The play begins with the two soldiers' colloquial dialogue on the battlements, in a scene strongly flavoured with reminiscences from the ghost scene of *Hamlet*, and perhaps also, in the case of the sphynx, from Pierre Benoît's famous book, *L'Atlantide*; the dialogue stretches into a conversation piece when the captain joins the soldiers in a realistic display of modern barracks jargon which Courteline could have written or envied. The Hamletian atmosphere of the ghost dissolves into sheer burlesque, and in no time we have a sample of Cocteau's resourcefulness, in his display of all the well-known tricks of comedy; we have the influence of drains on ghosts, the strong foreign accents in the speech of royalties—the kind of accent which enhanced the fame of Elvire Popesco on the stage and in films; then Tiresias becomes Zizi, the old uncle or the aged physician who is trying to cope with the moods of a restless widow—so that we find ourselves right in the middle of a typical *comédie bourgeoise*. What this has got to do with poetry, or, for that matter, with the myth of Oedipus, is a question which need not be asked, for poetry has certainly no place here—unless one might be tempted to find something poetical in the more than obvious use of the incident of the scarf and the brooch as omens of what is going to follow seventeen years later, or in the very transparent symbolism of the dream. The clowning continues with the queen stroking the young soldier's muscles, and producing a kind of farcical and vulgar ambiguity destined to call forth easy laughter. The language fits the gestures: "La reine te pelote; tu veux t'envoyer la reine" are colloquial expressions unredeemed by the samples of pedestrian wisdom which follow, and by the blatant ominousness and ambiguity of words such as: "This brooch which strikes everybody's eyes, and also pierces everybody's eyes"—where a cheap effect is obtained from the dual meaning of the word "crève". The second act is entirely taken up with the sphynx, who is a woman. There is some fantasy chiefly in the Matrone's speech, but there are too many obvious allusions to the contemporary political situation, and too many clichés smudged with the ink of the penny press. The play proceeds along the facile expected path, with love dripping down from every leaf of every tree. Not even the sphynx-Antinea could have resisted the attraction of young Oedipus, and without her ward Anubis she would have fallen head over heels for his charms. As it is, she can only present Oedipus with a belt which will bring him serious troubles later; but then belts have always done so, both in mythology and in legends. From there we move on to the problem of love in bedrooms, as it is generally described in all juicy love-plays of the 'twenties, and we are treated to a display of coquetry and coyness in a setting which does not lack the expected ominousness; and the symbolism, or whatever one likes to call it, is heightened by the fact that the scene closes with Jocasta being so upset that she goes on mechanically rocking the cradle while Oedipus is asleep on the bed. Here is skill, here is even poetry, some people might say, and I am prepared to grant that the monologue of the sphynx is very poetical indeed; but what is more important is that we have not yet reached the bottom of Cocteau's conjuror's hat. After endless digressions in an atmosphere of *comédie de boulevard* between Jocasta and Oedipus and between Oedipus and Tiresias, there still remain some truths to be foretold in the same obvious and rather trivial way; so we have the grotesque pseudo-symbolism of Oedipus, in pains, reading his fate in Tiresias' blind eyes; after that he subsides into singing the praises of women over thirty, and the play draws to its end among tricks of varying relevance and usefulness. We have the dream of the drunkard who sings a song which echoes the queen's words, we have the mirror and the apparition of the dead queen, and unfortunately we have the emotional tension of the end, marred by Cocteau's irrelevant rhetoric: "Le devoir, il ne t'appartient plus, il appartient au peuple, aux poètes, aux coeurs purs." This play shows Cocteau's inventiveness and gifts as a producer and film-director, but if it were described as poetic drama, then anything could be poetic drama—the flying trapeze, the girl who jumps through the hoop, or the dancing horse: all are feats which have that important element of surprise advocated by Cocteau. As for the hushed silence which the play produces, there are moments in the circus when the heart throbs as fast as when Hamlet is about to strike Claudius, or when Lear walks across the stage with the dead body of Cordelia in his arms; yet, although the heart-beats may have the same speed, the emotions involved and their imprint on the mind and heart are profoundly different.

Orphée is Cocteau's most successful handling of a myth, and his nearest approach to poetic drama. Although the play takes place in a modern setting and with all the stage skill that Cocteau can muster (and that skill is great indeed), the atmosphere of the ancient myth is on the whole preserved, and the play is thus more moving and far more impressive than the *Eurydice* of Anouilh. Anouilh's Orpheus is a wandering minstrel who meets Eurydice, a touring company actress, at a railway station. They meet, they elope, they talk endlessly in cafés and hotel rooms, they part, Eurydice is enticed away by the serpent of the legend, represented here by the company manager, and she is killed in a traffic accident. She is brought to life to realize what they both knew already at the beginning, that the world of death is the only world where they can be happy. Cocteau also has humanized the myth, which therefore loses much of its tragic mystery and also takes on the romanticized colours of the death-wish and the belief that only in the absolute, in the beautiful world of death, can one reach complete happiness. So Death is a beautifully dressed woman, with fascinating eyes, who comes to anaesthetize pain and to bring bliss to men. Who could resist her? Very few indeed; and nobody can be surprised at Orpheus' peevishness towards his wife and his longing to return to such a beautiful mistress. The great journey through Hell, which is part of the original myth, the suffering endured in order to know what cannot be known in the shape of man, the divine song which can rouse stones and trees to dance and women to madness, all that is whittled away and replaced by a horsy muse, a poetry committee of jealous volatile women and a typically French police station. The technical skill of Cocteau is once more impressive; but the elementary wisdom of the horse which, as Jocasta remarked to

Tiresias, requires faith to be believed, the symbolism of the reflected mirrors where one can read one's fate, the handling of the supernatural, doves, Death and her attendants, are neither very original nor poetic. German silent films and stagecraft have gone far enough in that line. One cannot deny the effectiveness of all these assets deployed in *Orphée*, or its novelty and influence since it was first produced in 1925, yet we are bound to say once again that this play, although remarkable theatre, and although it is the nearest approach to it, does not come anywhere close enough to poetic drama as exemplified by the works of poets like T. S. Eliot or Claudel, to mention only contemporaries. In recent years Cocteau has turned *Orphée* into an excellent film; it is perhaps as a film-director that he can make full use of his versatility, his inventiveness and his technical skill.

Myth is, with metaphor, the very foundation of poetry; both involve the source of being and seek to express, in a sensuous way, mysteries which form the texture of life and cannot be apprehended otherwise. Myths are amongst other things the imaginative representations of some central knots of man's affective life; they are obviously the poetic expression of deeply felt upsurges rising from the human soul, and, as modern psychology has shown, they are as old as man. The only way of revitalizing myths is therefore from the source, and not by making old shapes and ancient characters speak in modern ways. The serious use of a myth in modern settings and situations involves an attempt to link together a religious and spiritual element which is no longer ours and is, therefore, difficult to experience, with events and human actions and reactions which cannot fit in it. The result is unconvincing and dangerously near the burlesque, for there is nothing which comes nearer laughter than a seriousness which cannot be grasped, or things which were once awe-inspiring and have now completely lost their aura of reverence. Orpheus' plight, for instance, can only be fully accepted within the atmosphere of Greek life and thought, and not by being transferred into our modern life. The Orpheus of Greek life, with his trail of mystery, is far more convincing than the wandering minstrel of our modern playwrights. The myth of Orpheus and Eurydice still retains for us its former power and pathos, for the mystery which gave it birth is not solved; but we cannot tremble and suffer with Eurydice going up and down in lifts, juggling with telephones and living in luxury hotels; in fact, at times we can hardly repress laughter or irritation.

The only way in which an old myth can be given new life is, I feel, by using not its external form, but the affective tangle which gave it birth, in a modern situation and context, as T. S. Eliot used the myth of the Erynnies in *The Family Reunion*. There we have human beings of our time, enduring the tortures of remorse, the excruciating isolation of self in the state of sin or "impurity" as Orestes endured them, and yet the experience conveyed is as profound and practically as real for us as it probably was originally. If man must rise above the earth, if saintly souls must journey to heaven, let it be by the power of the heart, and the words which can lift us, and not with rope and flying pigeons. It is to the heart that the poet must address himself, and it is with the heart that he must start and not with the golden east or with the machinery of the stage. If Eliot has achieved what remains, to my mind, one of the most remarkable successes of our time in the theatre, it is because he knew where he was going, because he deliberately planned his journey and, with the integrity which characterizes him, refused to put his trust in devices or to attempt to give us the shadow for the substance. As a poet he knows the poetic value of myths, but he knows more than that: he has the true gift of the poet to go to the source, so that the poetry is born from the tensions in the characters or between the characters and is not a matter of external form.

Unless the experience of a dramatic character, whether good or evil, has been imaginatively lived by its creator, unless it has been created through flesh and blood, the character remains outside the realm of our affective life and does not move us. A character, in order to move us and to have our sympathy or repugnance, must make us feel that we might have been like that, that his experiences might have been ours. Characters which have been made of bits and pieces, which have not been fused together by the author's imagination, or which are directly copied from life, or lifted from a myth without transmutation by the author, do not live and cannot move us. Imagination alone can plumb the depths of the heart and descry some of the age-old upsurges which every now and then rock it to destruction, whether the heart beats by the shores of the Pyrrheus or by the banks of the Seine. There only lies the kind of truth which lives on the stage or off the stage, and enabled Racine to give Phèdre, prisoner of the moon, that unfathomable depth of human passion which, from the Minoan palace where she was born, has lifted her, right throughout the ages, on to a height beyond the reach of men and time's changes. There is myth, taken at its source, and offered to men and women who knew of the life of Athens or Rome, and although it bears the imprint of Christianity, it has retained the sense of the "numinous". But what makes Phèdre as alive today as she was at the court of Louis XIV is the poetic revelation of a truth which shakes the husk of names and of ages and reaches the perennial texture of being. There had been indeed many *Phèdres* before Racine's, and many insignificant *Lears* and *Hamlets* before Shakespeare's, but after them it does not seem possible to write a new *Phèdre*, a new *Lear* or a new *Hamlet*. The themes of these plays are as old as social man, and will live as long as life. One may therefore exploit dramatic situations which are similar to that of Phèdre, Hamlet or Lear, yet one cannot write another tragedy of Hamlet, Prince of Denmark, or Phèdre, daughter of Minos and Pasiphae—at least, not in our civilization. That has already been done, and what has been done can neither be undone nor done again without summoning at once what exists already and which therefore destroys by its very existence any attempt at repetition.

CHAPTER 7

Jean Giraudoux

GIRAUDOUX was France's most successful playwright between the two wars, and his theatrical skill has only now been outstripped by Anouilh. Without reading into the word "influence" any suggestion of conscious imitation, but merely accepting the view that what has been done, what truly exists, cannot but have a bearing on what comes after it, one can safely assert that Giraudoux's use of Greek myths and his whimsical blends of fantasy and reality and a kind of baroque style have obviously not been lost for writers as far apart as Sartre, Cocteau, Anouilh and James Bridie. We have seen that with Maeterlinck and with the more successful Rostand, who continues and revitalizes romantic poetic drama, poetry had returned to the stage. We have seen the efforts of Copeau; and there is of course, one must not forget, the most outstanding contribution to poetic drama in France, that of Paul Claudel. But Claudel's success was very slow to come, and in the 1920s and the 1930s he was very far from his present widely accepted fame, for his greatest plays had not yet been performed. After the death of Rostand, realism had regained the ascendancy on the French stage; it was Giraudoux who did for the French stage what the Irish revival did for the English stage. Giraudoux was not a poet worthy of being mentioned with W. B. Yeats or Synge, but he had a poetic mind and he had a good measure of what Coleridge described as fancy; he could see unsuspected similarities in disparate things, and he could bring together widely separated objects or qualities. He had above all a sense of style, which for him, as for Flaubert, was all; and he had, if one can trust his statements about artistic creations, an approach to artistic experience which is certainly poetic and which has been well defined by Croce, Collingwood and D. H. Lawrence. Giraudoux himself has said: ". . . je prends une feuille blanche et je commence à écrire; les personnages naissent au fur et à mesure; au bout de cinq ou six pages, j'y vois clair."[1] This is not a surrender to the subconscious as in surrealistic writing, but a statement stressing the importance of the creative act itself and the absence of conceptualized approach to it. It is a statement which need not be taken literally, for Giraudoux was certainly aware of the theme he was to write about before he took pen and paper, but it merely insists upon the fact that he was aiming at poetic truth born from the interplay of the characters in mutual contact and in action, and not at philosophical or technical demonstrations. This approach to art implies facility of invention, fluency in expression and a capacity to fly with one's own power, unaided by props or devices which Giraudoux did not need. He was not a psychologist in the Ibsenian manner, neither was his poetic vision such as to take him, except very rarely, into realms of deep emotional disturbance and suffering where the characters rise to heroic grandeur; but he had verbal facility together with the gift of vaguely seeing in shimmering outlines characters and situations which acquire striking dramatic vitality on the stage. He is the ideal dramatist for gifted producers and actors, and he had with him as a life-long collaborator the outstanding actor-manager Louis Jouvet, who has left his imprint on his work. The dazzling wit, the whimsicality, the stylistic skill oscillating from preciosity and verbal mannerism worthy of the seventeenth century to the fluid symbolist poeticality, are well known; so are Giraudoux's great gifts as an entertainer. Therefore I shall not concentrate my attention on exquisite pieces of fantasy like *Intermezzo*, *Ondine*, *l'Apollon de Bellac* or *Amphitryon 38*, but rather on the more serious plays in which the struggle against fate or the gods reveals Giraudoux's preoccupation with man's place and plight in the universe and the author's

[1] Fr. Lefèvre: *Une heure avec Jean Giraudoux*, première série, p. 149.

very humane and civilized approach to this ever-debated relationship.

Judith

Flaubert and Maeterlinck had already dealt in different ways with Giraudoux's theme of the salvation of a city or a people through the sacrifice of a young virgin. Flaubert is the only one to have succeeded, for his respect for history, his passion for truth in the present as well as in the past made him take infinite trouble to preserve the atmosphere and the material and spiritual veracity of Salammbô's time. Salammbô is really the daughter of Hamilcar, the worshipper of the moon, and when, after the beautiful initiation scene with the serpent-totem or lares of her family on the moonlit terrace of her palace, she goes to the barbarian Mathô, her action has with it the aura of a ritualistic gesture which transcends her humanity. The reader, suspending disbelief, accepts her as a beautiful and moving creation who lives for the divinity which she worships and will die when the main protagonist of the drama dies, as died Endymion for having been loved by Astarte and having sacrificed to her cult. Events, feelings, all living things must have their true roots in order to come to life and to communicate life. Flaubert had enough genius to be aware of that; Maeterlinck and Giraudoux, who were not of the true explorer-type as Flaubert was, did not go and fetch their goods themselves but rather bought them from bazaars and used them in strange blends of primitivism and modernism, antiquity and contemporaneity; the result of such blends is generally successful if one merely aims at entertainment, but is never so if one aims at seriousness and great emotions.

Judith is described by the author as a tragedy, yet the main character, Judith herself, is not a tragic character; her behaviour, her actions are not the result of inner or external compulsions but are rather brought forth by external events or interventions, such as those of Jean and Suzanne. In the saint or in the tragic hero, essence and existence are as much one as such a perfect unification is possible in time; here, on the contrary, there is not much coincidence between essence and existence, and there is no inevitability of development. Besides that, the language, colloquial and modern, is in contradiction with the theme; it is contemporary, every-day speech, not even refined language but something full of slang expressions and puns, some of them blatantly pornographic and all in all something which contributes to setting the play in our time and in a social context which cannot be that of the Bible. The theme—the salvation of a town or a people through a woman's sacrifice—is Biblical enough and certainly acceptable as such, but it cannot be treated in the language which Giraudoux uses without losing its reality and therefore its tragic pathos. The stress upon virginity increases the gap between the means used, the dramatic verisimilitude, and the theme or story which forms the basis of the work. The virginity is to my mind too blatantly a device used by Giraudoux to put across his ideas about purity and his belief that idealism is not of this world; such ideas are too obviously adorned with a considerable amount of salacious reflexions and saucy suggestions which cannot go amiss with an audience well up in slang or allusions about sex. Judith's character is inconsistent throughout; the device of the end, the idea that God has given her the illusion or the dream of a night of love, is too ludicrous for words and is completely unconvincing as a means to bring to her the belief that God truly wants her to be a saint and that He has preserved her virtue while making her kill "the best of men".

The comments of Holofernes about God and men are truly worthy of Giraudoux. God or the gods are petty tyrants completely lacking in grandeur and attraction when compared with man; they are bogged in smallness and ever engrossed in niggardly games based above all on their jealousy of men's happiness. The pseudo-philosophical statements of Giraudoux are trite, and certainly unworthy of a play which claims to be a tragedy and aims at raising man's deeper emotions—terror and pity. There is here neither: we do not fear for Judith's fate, and we are

not moved by her dialectics or by the device used to explain her
failure to remain a saint. We know that she has enjoyed her mission
and her night which fulfilled her sense of pride and her sensuous-
ness; we know that she has toyed long enough with her virtue
and that she has long been dying to lose it in a worthy encounter.
The twist of the end is too gross to be accepted as a miracle, and
there is much too much concern in Heaven, not about the fate of
a town and its people, but about an erotic young woman's
virginity. In fact, the eroticism of the play detracts considerably
from the height of purity or awe where the play ought to be.
The sacrifice demanded from Judith in Giraudoux's play implies
a metaphysical atmosphere, a climate of vital beliefs totally alien
to Giraudoux's sceptical and sniggering attitude about anything
which is not strictly speaking of the earth. There is no reason why
Judith should bother about God's command, in fact she does not,
she suits herself, and her desire for singularity is only pride and
egomaniacal pre-occupations served by physical charm and
narcissistic frigidity.

The main weakness of the play lies in the theme. Deprived
of the driving force which impelled the Biblical deed—God's
command—Judith looks very much like an enervated, uppish
young lady tired of flirtations with the fops and swains who
surround her and craving for the type of male whom she finds in
Holofernes and which Hollywood provides now abundantly.
He is very much the gallant gentleman who knows his ascendancy
over ladies, and he has obviously more charm, more humanity
than the weaklings who have surrounded and besieged Judith
before his meeting with her. Nevertheless, he does not sound
very convincing when he says that he has succeeded in doing
away with the gods:

De la Grèce aux Indes, du Nord au Sud, pas de pays où ils ne
pullulent, chacun avec ses vices, avec ses odeurs. . . .
L'atmosphère du monde, pour qui aime respirer, est celle
d'une chambrée de dieux. . . . Mais il est encore quelques

endroits qui leur sont interdits; seul je sais les voir. Ils
subsistent, sur la plaine ou la montagne, comme des taches
de paradis terrestre. Les insectes qui les habitent n'ont pas le
péché originel des insectes: je plante ma tente sur eux. . . .
Par chance, juste en face de la ville du Dieu juif, j'ai reconnu
celui-ci, à une inflexion des palmes, à un appel des eaux.
Je t'offre pour une nuit cette ville sur un océan éventé et
pur. . . .

(pp. 155-6)

He offers Judith innocence and physical joy:

Je t'offre, pour aussi longtemps que tu voudras, la sim-
plicité, le calme. Je t'offre ton vocabulaire d'enfant, les mots
de cerise, de raisin, dans lesquels tu ne trouveras pas Dieu
comme un ver. Je t'offre ces musiciens que tu entends, qui
chantent des chants et non des cantiques. Ecoute-les. Leur
voix meurt doucement au-dessous d'eux, autour de nous,
et n'est pas aspirée au ciel par un terrible aspirateur. Je t'offre
le plaisir, Judith. . . . Devant ce tendre mot, tu verras
Jehovah disparaître. . . .

(pp. 157-8)

The gods he has done away with, the "chambrée" are indeed a
very poor lot, a joke easily disposed of for the mere reason that
we never believed in them, any more than we believed in the
slinking, shadowy priests who trade in divinity and divine orders
as other men trade in carpets or peanuts. Giraudoux cannot have
it both ways; having unpeopled the skies, or reduced them to
"une chambrée de caserne", he cannot expect us to be over-
impressed by the messengers of their so-called orders or by the
monster which Judith is supposed to tame or destroy. The former
resembles too much a female ring-master parading and advertising
her power, the latter the circus athlete, the fake giant, too much
used to dealing with hollow weights and not with real ones.
Judith's opinion of God is not meant to make her a saint, but a
rebel completely on the side of men who believe that God or the

gods use them for their sport, something which has nothing to do with divine ways towards a higher though inscrutable purpose:

> Du jour où il m'a choisie, à cause de ma pureté, le regard de Dieu m'a souillée. Car je vais te paraître orgueilleuse, Daria, on ne peut dire cela qu'aux sourds, mais c'est à moi que Dieu en a, et non à Holopherne, et non aux Juifs. Sous les cataclysmes qui soulèvent les races et les hommes par millions, il dissimule son obstination à poursuivre un seul être et à mener un pauvre gibier à merci.

(p. 183)

A pure being or an elect is somebody who according to all accounts has been cornered by God; he is somebody who cannot live and must through death fulfil himself and return to the absolute to which he belongs. Giraudoux's heroine, and later Anouilh's, always prefer death to compromise and to acceptance of the stupidity of life; Antigone behaves towards Creon in the same way as Electra towards Aegisthus. Judith is the only heroine of Giraudoux who is fully intent upon outstanding purity and who, when she fails to achieve it, does not die but goes on living. At the same time, *Judith* is the only one of Giraudoux's plays called a tragedy. It is therefore obvious that for Giraudoux, who believes in purity, tragedy is not in death but in soiled ideals and in a life of compromise. This is an original view of tragedy which, from the Greeks onwards, has always been a progression through sufferings, terror and pathos towards the liberation and the singular joy of death taking on a sacrificial nature. In Giraudoux death is reserved for those who have fallen in love with the ideal, which is in the end death itself. The world these lovers of ideal long for is the world of non-being. The pure, who are the cause of the transmutation from matter to form, are immortal like Ondine, they live on like Electra, or like Lia and Lucile, they die to save their faith. When the pure do not die but compromise and live on, as is the case with Judith, then, and then only, we have according to Giraudoux tragedy. Judith is pure, the purest of the city, and although she could be saved through Suzanne's stratagem, she knows that her hour has come, and she sets off towards Holofernes who is the means to reveal to her, true being. She knows that he is her destiny, what she was born for, and the ideal whose union with her will probably exclude God, as perfect love does in Claudelian theology. Therefore Judith becomes God's antagonist and not God's instrument to save the city, and she kills Holofernes and destroys herself spiritually at the same time. She kills Holofernes not out of hate, as was the hope of the city fathers and the purpose of her mission, but out of love for him, because she knows that she has met in him her ideal, and that ideal is not of the earth. This change in her attitude, this killing for wrong reasons is something which the priests cannot accept; therefore they refuse to let her fulfil herself through death, and they say that in fact God has protected her from Holofernes and that her night of perfect love was really a kind of miracle, God-willed. Thus Judith has lost everything—her pride, her virginity and her hopes; she is left bare after absolute betrayal, deprived of any possibility of salvation, for the hope of salvation through death has been taken away from her through God's connivance with the priests. She has no reason to live, but even less to die; therefore she accepts the tragedy of life, for she has become in the true sense of the word Judith the Prostitute, the one who has no ideal informing her life, the one who is used as an instrument for hedonistic purposes which are not her own. Her first act of prostitution, which she thought was really sacrifice to an ideal, turned out to be God's game; the second act of prostitution, which flows from the disillusionment of the first, is the renunciation of the original emotions which informed her deed; she consents to say that she killed out of hate and not out of love. Lucile, in *Pour Lucrèce*, when she realizes that she has lost her ideal, kills herself and therefore regains purity, but for Judith that is both too late and impossible, for God bars the way. So, in the end, although the city has been saved, purity has died, and this is, for Giraudoux, tragedy.

Jean Giraudoux

Electre

The theme of *Electre* is once more the theme of purity and uncompromising idealism. Electra is obsessed by her mother's guilt and by the idea of revenge; there is nothing else in her head but the burning urge to destroy her father's murderers. Why such an urge, except out of very primal instincts and passionate hatred of her mother, which makes it look as if Electra had from her very early youth a strong father-complex, one cannot see. She does not believe in divine justice, she thinks that the gods, like artists, look at things more from the aesthetic angle or the point of view of effects than from the ethical point of view. She is impelled by inner forces which somehow have such a fierceness and such a complete disregard of other people's feelings, including Orestes', that her purity looks more like sheer hatred of her mother than anything else one could think of. Therefore, though the movement of the play has a rhythm of ineluctability which is that of tragedy, Electra is not a tragic character. She is more a twentieth-century creation than an ancient Greek; the forces which move her are inner, not external forces, and in her case she could easily be put right by a good psychiatrist. She elicits fear, for she is a terrifying character undeterred by anything, but she produces no pathos and she draws no sympathy. The butchering of the two criminals at the end of the play brings upon them pity, and nothing but repulsion and awe towards Electra, whom one would neither like to meet nor like to know that she had any authority whatsoever over the town in which one lived. One cannot say that Orestes is a tragic character either, for he completely lacks grandeur and tragic pathos, though he certainly is the one whose plight and pliability in his sister's steel hands move us most. But in truth, his existence is so shadowy, so unreal as to be reduced to the size of an instrument, an avenging sword at his sister's command. The only dramatic conflict which underlies the play and causes the slow hesitations or brief halts in the tragic course, is that between Aegisthus and Electra. Aegisthus, in spite of the initial flaw of his character, has something very Macbeth-like,

I   121

and it is this something which leads him to a similar situation under the ruthless will of Lady Macbeth-Clytemnestra. He is an intelligent, astute political ruler, who knows exactly how to steer a middle course between gods and men, and also how never to confuse metaphysical preoccupations with earthly paradoxes. He knows that the gods' blissful state is as unconscious of mortals' agitations as a diamond is unconscious of the light that it reflects, and he knows that as long as the ideas of things or of human realities are kept in being, that is what counts. It is not necessary that retribution should be meted out to real criminals, or that corrupt cities should be punished with plagues; no, he knows that as long as retribution or plague falls somewhere on earth, the idea of these things exists, and that is all the gods of this Platonic world want. The best thing for men to do is to avoid any move which might attract the gods' attention, for if they awaken the result might be random blows and calamities about which one knows the beginning but not the end:

> Quoi qu'il en soit, il est hors de doute que la règle première de tout chef d'un état est de veiller férocement à ce que les dieux ne soient point secoués de cette léthargie et de limiter leurs dégâts à leurs réactions de dormeurs, ronflement ou tonnerre.
>
> (p. 42)

Aegisthus is therefore intent on plunging Electra into anonymity: he plans to remove her from a position of pre-eminence as the daughter of all too well-known royal parents, and to make her the plain wife of a gardener. He hopes by that to avert at last destiny's concern from the Atrides. Electra, on the contrary, is intent on pre-eminence and singularity; even if lightning were to strike and destroy her, her city and all, she would prefer that apocalyptic doom to silence and to the acceptance of anything but her own savage terms. She is a Wagnerian character; the *Götterdämmerung* is her dream, and will be her final undoing. She has nothing human; she is a knife looking for a breast, a magnetized piece of iron moving blindly towards its pole, which is formed by Clytemnestra's and Aegisthus's blood. She snarls and chugs at her mother as a fierce dog which will not let go its prey, until death ensues. Nothing can shake her, neither Aegisthus's entreaties about her city which is being destroyed under her eyes, nor his genuine repentance. In spite of what she says, her aim is revenge and not justice; and for the sake of that revenge she sacrifices a whole people, who are completely innocent and whom Aegisthus, who has at last seen the light, wants to save from external and internal destruction.

> Depuis ce qui m'est arrivé, tout à l'heure, à la lisière de ce bois d'où l'on voit Argos, ma parole vient d'au delà de moi. Et je sais qu'elle me voit aussi, qu'elle est seule à me voir. Seule elle a deviné ce que je suis depuis cette minute.
>
> (pp. 170-1)

Aegisthus, who has had a revelation of what purity and innocence are, and who knows that these qualities are part of Electra's essence, implores her to be with him for the duration of the crisis; he begs her to say the word which would confer innocence upon him:

> Si je me suis hâté vers toi, Electre, c'est que tu es le seul être qui puisse me donner sa propre essence.
>
> (p. 181)

He pleads with the urgency of a man who knows that he requires purity to save a people; his pleading has dramatic intensity and seems to hold for a brief moment the flood of Electra's rage, but not for long. For her, time and expediency have no meaning; she is beyond the particular and beyond existence, lost in a world of abstractions and qualities which transcend frontiers and which matter more than individuations:

> Argos n'était qu'un point dans cet univers, ma patrie une bourgade dans cette patrie. Tous les rayons et tous les éclats dans les visages mélancoliques, toutes les rides et les ombres

dans les visages joyeux, tous les désirs et les désespoirs dans
les visages indifférents, c'est cela mon nouveau pays. Et c'est
ce matin, à l'aube, quand on vous donnait Argos et ses front-
ières étroites, que je l'ai vu aussi immense et que j'ai entendu
son nom, un nom qui ne se prononce pas, mais qui est à la
fois la tendresse et la justice.

(pp. 197-8)

In her mind, her mother's and Aegisthus's crime affects the
essence, and that cannot be forgiven; only death can bring about
a change. The culprits must die, even if a whole city dies with
them, for it seems that for Electra only these two rulers matter,
the rest of the inhabitants of Argos are completely insignificant.
She refuses to compromise or to delay for one single moment the
punishment of the crime. Aegisthus is paralysed, he is obviously
not "de la race des maîtres mais de la race des esclaves", for he
could have Electra thrown into prison, but he does not, and that
at the price of a verisimilitude which is brought to mind by the
realistic handling of the theme and the over-strong admixture of
modernity. Clytemnestra completes the general surrender by
confessing her hatred of her former husband, in a movement
which is perhaps rather contrived, but which enables the play to
draw to its close midst utter desolation and madness crowding
round the last descendant of the Atrides.

Electre is an hybrid genre. None of the characters is tragic;
the force which carries the play forward lacks grandeur, and
because of its lack of metaphysical atmosphere is more like an
obsessional fixation than a perennial, harrowing, human problem.
Compared with the hesitations and anxieties of Hamlet, so moving, so piteous in his plight, Electra is a cold, abhorrent creation,
too mechanical to elicit passion or poetry. Besides that, the wilful
anachronisms in speech, or rather the thorough modernization
of the language, give the play an atmosphere of whimsicality and
unreality which, coupled with the lack of metaphysical background, shows that the play is more connected with intellect

than with the emotions. The characters of Agathe and her husband belong essentially to bourgeois comedy, and their interventions in the affairs of the Atrides, culminating in the scene where they wash their dirty linen in public, is a sparkling piece of writing in itself, but is out of key in such a play, even in spite of the fact that Electra points out that Agathe's confessions of her hatred towards her husband give her the clue about her mother's reactions towards her father. Altogether, this is a rather perplexing play, with brilliant passages and long recitatives from the beggar, the gardener and the other characters, the beggar being the most impressive in the exciting part of the chorus. Leaving out the up-to-date expressions and the striking phrase by which Giraudoux seems to have hoped to confer upon his characters an aura of modernity as well as the aura of timelessness, which he tries to obtain by their immersion in problems which are part of man, the language has at times undeniable poetic beauty. Nevertheless, although one may interlace many aspects of life, comic and tragic, in a play, as is done in Shakespearian drama, the language must remain appropriate to the time when the characters live, for discrepancy between time and language used is an effective means of comedy but cannot be used to convey timelessness in a serious play. This play has obviously been a source of inspiration for numerous other experiments in the theatre and in the novel. Electra, by her obstinacy and insistence on purity, is an elder sister of Antigone; the problem of guilt is also the problem of *Les Mouches* by Sartre and of *La Peste* by Camus.

Sodome et Gomorrhe

Sodome et Gomorrhe is to my mind the most boring play Giraudoux has produced. The characters, who are vague, inchoate creations oscillating between allegories, symbols and realities, pour out endless trivial verbiage criss-crossed with interruptions from angels and from famous Biblical personages. There is no plot, and although there may have been some idea in Giraudoux's mind, there is no action. This long argument about relations between men and women is singularly deprived of wisdom, and without the odd twist of precious language or the by now well-tried Giraudoux recipe of mingling fantasy and reality, angels and human beings, it would be well-nigh impossible to descry behind these inflated gongoristic outpourings the author of *Ondine* or of *La Guerre de Troie*.

The theme is, once again, the impossibility of human love. Jean and Lia know that love attained ceases to be love; Samson and Delilah, on the other hand, show that a loveless marriage, given cynicism on one side and stupidity on the other, can work quite well. Lia is Giraudoux's typical idealist; she lives for love, and would rather die than counterfeit it. She insists on theoretical perfection, while Jean insists on practical perfection; each prefers the angel to the other. Lia refuses to fool God and to allow the town to be saved at the price of a lie; she insists that love is more important than life, and Jean, who would have given in, if allowed to do so, dies with her. So we see that in Sodom as well as in Argos an implacable woman intent on purity destroys a city; in both cases, as in most of Giraudoux's theatre, idealism refuses to compromise with reality. Helen, in her dialogue with Andromache in *La Guerre de Troie*, divides the world into two: there is matter and form, appearance and reality, and in this Platonic world of Giraudoux's the two must not mingle. They go side by side, as the shadows and the human beings of Plato's cave. When characters like Aegisthus, for instance, become aware of both aspects of the world, they lose their grip upon reality and they have to die. All characters who fall in love with the absolute or the ideal must die: Hans in *Ondine*, Holofernes in *Judith*, Lia in *Sodome et Gomorrhe* and Aegisthus in *Electre*. Perfection cannot be of this world. In the end Aegisthus understands and approves of Electra; he therefore finds himself in the other camp, he has passed from matter to form, and he realizes that it is better to die for truth than to live without it; he accepts death, and so demonstrates once more Giraudoux's belief, at the cost perhaps of a slight dramatic flaw. Still, what counts is that the ideal must remain unstained and that justice, though it involves death, is conceivable and is of supreme importance. The blend of the two worlds—the world of fantasy and the world of reality—a blend which is so much the crux of Giraudoux's art, is perfectly realized in *Intermezzo*, which is a remarkable theatrical achievement. Isabelle is the young, innocent girl of popular lore and particularly of Giraudoux's theatre; she is young Judith or Ondine, and as long as she remains pure of materiality, free from any contact with men, she has the gift of being able to bring the dead back to life and of conversing with them. This situation gives scope to poetic fantasy, to the very dramatic use of a ghost, and to irrepressible fun and satire on society which Giraudoux handles with his usual dexterity. The character of the human lover (Le Contrôleur) is a remarkable creation who convincingly succeeds in wresting Isabelle's heart from the grip of the ghost or the ideal. The children—Isabelle's class—with their freshness and their ballet-like movements, add to the exhilaration of a play in which the characters merge into types and trail behind them memories of *Midsummer Night's Dream* or of the *commedia dell' arte*: Scaramouche (the ghost), Pantaloon (the inspector), the Doctor (the apothecary), and even Harlequin and Brighella (the two burlesque hangmen) are all present in disguise.

Pour Lucrèce

Pour Lucrèce is an homage to fidelity, and above all fidelity to one's ideals. Lucile, the heroine, when she realizes that she has lost her ideals, chooses death to reassert their value, for she realizes that what matters is not whether she has been seduced or not, but the fact that she has behaved as if it were so and therefore she has showed that she has lost faith in herself. The action of the play takes place in Aix-en-Provence in 1868 or thereabouts; the substratum of realism is maintained throughout, and although the characters tend towards types and *personae* more than towards realistic representations, there is enough psychological truth in them to make them acceptable and real as imaginative creations

capable of engaging our attention, our sympathy or our antipathy. There are four main characters, and each could be summed
up in one single sentence. Lucile, the Procurator-General's wife,
is a paragon of virtue; Marcellus represents vice, he is the rake,
Don Juan or Valmont, ready for anything; Paola is a loose woman,
a lover of men in general, therefore always in search of change;
Armand is an idealist who has put his trust in his wife, Paola, and
who is completely shattered the day he realizes that she has been
and is false to him. Lucile, the pure, has a kind of second sight, a
visionary gift which enables her to detect around her any evidence
of infidelity. Eugénie, her friend, pleads in vain for indulgence
for a more compromising attitude, telling Lucile that all was well
in Aix before she came:

> L'amour était sur Aix avec ses privilèges, la confiance des
> maris, la cécité des mères, avec ces orages des mois calmes,
> de juin, de septembre, qui apportent le pathétique aux lieux
> passionnés.
>
> (p. 22)

But for Lucile love is something different; she has the capacity of
descrying behind masks the true reality, and she therefore sees
the bestiality and baseness of human behaviour. She has brought
with her, as Eugénie points out, the awareness of original sin,
and she refuses to play the game which all the others play. She is
here to say "no", and not "yes"; her view is that God looks after
our souls, so it is up to us to look after our bodies. Given such
premises, we know at once what kind of conflict we must expect.
Armand and Paola are sitting at the same café where this conversation between Lucile and Eugénie takes place. Lucile refuses to
acknowledge Paola's presence; Armand, knowing and respecting
Lucile's virtue, comes to speak to her; Lucile refuses, and by so
doing reveals to him his wife's infidelities. Paola swears revenge,
and as Lucile, in order to avoid a scandal, has at last accepted to
speak to her, she pours a sleeping powder in her glass and
Babette, the procuress, helps her to take Lucile away. Next day,

when Lucile recovers consciousness in one of Babette's houses, they make her believe that she has been seduced by Marcellus. Lucile believes what she is told and goes to Marcellus, whose wife she says she has become through sexual union, to entreat him to kill himself and to liberate her by leaving her a widow. Marcellus then tries to seduce her, but Armand arrives; Armand has recognized in Lucile the virtue he longed for and sought in vain in his wife, so he offers to avenge her honour by a duel with Marcellus who, as a gentleman, accepts the challenge. Marcellus dies, keeping his secret and therefore proving that he has really fallen in love with Lucile. Armand also is hopelessly in love with her, but when Lucile is told that she has been tricked, that the physical rape which could have tainted her body but not her soul has not taken place, she realizes that she has lost faith in herself and in her purity as the result of a hoax; she knows then that there is nothing else for her to do but to kill herself, for she has not been violated but has violated herself, as Paola says:

> Elle n'est plus la pureté, puisqu'elle n'a rien deviné à sa pureté. Parmi les autres, elle se vante de reconnaître celles qui ont embrassé à l'aube, lu le mauvais Musset pendant la sieste, ou péché à cinq heures. Elle n'a pas deviné qu'elle n'avait pas embrassé, pas aimé. La pureté se serait moquée de notre farce.
>
> (p. 176)

She has made a hero of Marcellus, who has then left her with nothing but her illusions:

> Il vous laisse étendue, niaisement et ridiculement étendue à terre, maintenue sur le dos par un démon, que vous n'avez pas reconnu dans la nuit, et qui vous répète sans relâche, depuis ce matin, tous les gestes et les mots de l'amour, toutes ses voluptés et ses hontes, et qui n'est que vous-même.
>
> (p. 178)

Lucile knows that her only salvation lies now in her refusal to accept a life which is ignoble and vile, and therefore she must get out of it; she realizes that she could not bear to live on with her husband, whom she deludes, thanks to Babette's connivance. She is aware that "les héros sont ceux qui magnifient une vie qu'ils ne peuvent plus supporter".

LUCILE: . . . Le monde est pur, Paola, le monde est en beauté et lumière! Dites-le moi vous-même. Je veux l'entendre de votre bouche. . . . Dites-le moi vite.

ARMAND: Mais dis-le donc!

PAOLA: Il l'est. . . . Pour une seconde. . . .

LUCILE: Cela suffit. . . . C'est plus qu'il ne faut. . . . Merci. . . .

(pp. 189–90)

Lucile is satisfied, and even Babette consecrates her action by saying:

La pureté n'est pas de ce monde, mais tous les dix ans, il y a sa lueur, son éclair. Sous l'éclair de pureté elles vont toutes se voir maintenant dans leur manège et leur turpitude. . . . C'est pour cela que la plus coureuse d'entre nous peut entrer vierge au paradis, pas seulement parce qu'elles oublient tout, la vertu d'une femme c'est celle de toutes les femmes, dans l'univers entier et dans le ciel elles sont pures de ta pureté en ce moment.

(pp. 192–3)

So Lucile dies, so as to recover her purity, which she could have kept, rape or no rape, if she had not been proud, if she had not preferred

. . . cette noce et cet artifice au malheur, qui toujours est simple. Paola voyait plus juste. Madeleine n'a épousé aucun des mille chameliers. C'est par orgueil que j'ai voulu passer une robe blanche au-dessus de l'ignominie.

(p. 160)

Marcellus dies too, for having, like Hans, Holofernes and Aegisthus, fallen in love with the absolute; and Armand, who understands Lucile and is her ideal, remains alive to perpetuate this ideal and to be a witness of the vision which has taken place. His life from now on will be illumined by this strange, fleeting vision of happiness:

ARMAND: Aujourd'hui, cela a tué. Je parle de l'inoffensif. Cela a saccagé sa vie. Cela vous a vue. Cela est heureux.

LUCILE: Merci. . . . Lionel peut revenir. . . . Adieu. . . .

(p. 167)

Pour Lucrèce is Giraudoux's last play, a play which was only performed in 1953. It shows that his great gifts had remained unimpaired and his ideals unchanged; this combination makes of him one of the important playwrights of our time. If other plays like *Amphitryon 38*, *La Folle de Chaillot* and *L'Apollon de Bellac* have not been mentioned here, it is only because, although they add to his reputation, they do not illustrate any new aspects of his talents. Nevertheless, the extraordinary humanity and the blend of social satire and fantasy of *La Folle de Chaillot* should not pass unmentioned, for they show a Giraudoux who, for all his concern with purity and the Hegelian absolute, could be profoundly moved by the sufferings and the destitution of the downtrodden masses who compose the greater part of mankind.

La Guerre de Troie n'aura pas lieu

I have left for the end a play of an undying topicality; the theme of *La Guerre de Troie* is the inevitability and the misery of war. The action of the play is well grounded in situations and in characters which, if they are not strictly speaking historical, have enough legendary and literary evidence to have historical value. The play is in fact a judgment upon history; it makes clear that, whether in Homeric times or in our times, men may dream of what they long for but their actions are only the result of forces which are beyond them. They are only a means of knowing what they are, but they are not an expression of individual will. Helen is no more the cause of the Trojan war than the Austrian Archduke's death in August 1914 was the cause of the First World War; she is a signal, a means of crystallizing certain emotions necessary to war, and she is above all an instrument of fate or of the gods, who seem to be unable to accept human happiness and who perhaps believe that human misery and suffering are the only sport which can relieve the boredom of Heaven. If the characters of the play are legendary, the action on the contrary unfolds on a plane of naturalistic and psychological truth, tinged here and there with the supernatural through the rather unfortunate appearance of allegorical figures like Peace and Iris, the messenger of the gods.

Helen is not only the instrument of fate, she is also the hedonist who takes pleasure where she finds it, and she accepts with indifference the beauty which has been given to her and the misery and suffering which surround her. She has no pity for others because she has no pity for herself; she can cast a cold eye upon all things. She knows that mankind is divided into two groups, and she knows to which group she belongs:

> Je ne passe point mes nuits, je l'avoue, à réfléchir sur le sort des humains, mais il m'a toujours semblé qu'ils se partageaient en deux sortes. Ceux qui sont, si vous voulez, la chair de la vie humaine. Et ceux qui en sont l'ordonnance, l'allure. Les premiers ont le rire, les pleurs, et tout ce que vous voudrez en sécrétions. Les autres ont le geste, la tenue, le regard. Si vous les obligez à ne faire qu'une race, cela ne va plus aller du tout. L'humanité doit autant à ses vedettes qu'à ses martyrs.
>
> (p. 144)

Andromache, the ideal wife, the loving mother, the white-armed Homeric spouse whom Hector admires, is deeply human, aware of the priceless worth of life, and is only prepared to risk it if asked to do so in defence of very high ideals. Her plea to Helen is just like tears on marble; Helen does not see any sense in love or in worrying about posterity; she is Helen, that is enough, and the world and history will do the rest. Hecuba is on the side of wisdom. Priam is the typical old man enjoying the vicarious excitement of talking about beauty, sacrifice, noble courage, like the other old men who rush up and down the ramparts to watch either the legs or the face of Helen. In our time he would be a faithful reader of the spicy sex stories which adorn some of our Sunday newspapers or of the "feelies" of *Brave New World*. Paris is inconsequential; he is a bed-warmer, a professional fornicator to the same degree as Oiax is a wine-bag and Demokos a prostitute-poet who would gladly start a war in order to write a song or burn a city in order to paint the picture of a fire.

The two most important characters are Ulysses and Hector; they are both faithful to tradition and extremely human, Hector much more than Ulysses, whose wisdom and scepticism about men and the gods enable him to look upon human affairs with cold detachment and dignified public-school phlegm. His arrival on the scene as one of the protagonists of the play increases the tension and at once transforms the excitement of the public inquest on the Paris-Helen relationship into the moving atmosphere of the most impressive dialogue of the play, the one which opposes him to Hector. His wisdom is magnificent, he is to Hector what an adult man of the world and a gentleman is to a young man with a passionate heart and strong ideals which still hide reality from him. In his words ring echoes of historical truths and historical scenes—Stresa and Locarno—while certain names surge to mind—Briand, Streseman, France, Germany:

Il est des peuples que tout désigne pour une guerre, leur peau, leur langue et leur odeur, ils se jalousent, ils se haïssent, ils ne peuvent pas se sentir. . . . Ceux-là ne se battent jamais. Ceux qui se battent, ce sont ceux que le sort a lustrés et préparés pour une même guerre: ce sont les adversaires.

(p. 185)

133

They are the gladiators to be sacrificed in the arena of the watching world. Ulysses knows everything, even the infinite distance which separates a promise from its realization, a council-room from the waiting ships, and he acts as he does not so much out of idealism, nobility or some similar concept, but merely because "Andromaque a le même battement de cils que Pénélope" (p. 194). Hector is nobility personified; he is the loving husband, the loyal friend, the soldier brave as the most brave, but who has been shattered by the horrors and the sufferings of war. For him there are no enemies, there are only men pitted one against another in a monstrous struggle and in the end folded in the same silence. Heroes, cowards, victors, vanquished, are vague words whose meaning changes; there are for him only two categories— the living and the dead, those who still can use their senses and those whose limbs are kneaded in clay; and there is the pity men must feel for so many lives, so many hopes undone. If Hector lacks the wisdom and the statesmanship of Ulysses, his humanity, his love of men irrespective of nationality, his capacity to swallow his pride and to endure for others make him the most moving and lovable character of the play, and when at the end the doors of the temple of war slowly slide open, one can already vaguely descry in the distance the dark wings which will soon lift this moving sacrificial being into death.

This is a most moving and beautiful play, the best work of Giraudoux. Here we have passionate idealism and nobility of purpose embodied in human beings who, whether Greeks or modern, hate the horror and the futility of war and struggle desperately to save mankind from ever-recurring fratricidal struggles. Tossed about between the savage irony of Hector's remarks:

Si toutes les mères coupent l'index droit de leur fils, les armées de l'univers se feront la guerre sans index. . . . Et si elles lui coupent la jambe droite, les armées seront uni-jambistes. . . . Et si elles lui crèvent les yeux, les armées seront

aveugles, mais il y aura des armées, et dans la mêlée elles se
chercheront le défaut de l'aine, ou la gorge, à tâtons. . . .

(pp. 20-1)

and the comical obtuseness of the legal adviser, Busiris, who can
find an explanation for everything, or the crude yet psychologically sound pride of the sailor who defends his master's prowess
at love-making, we reach the pathos of the great scenes between
Helen and Andromache, and Ulysses and Hector, or the scene
of the closing of the doors of the temple of war, scenes whose
beauty is unsurpassed in the modern theatre. Here are, with some
of Owen's poems, probably the most moving words which have
been written about the pity of war:

> Aussi qui que vous soyez, vous absents, vous inexistants,
> vous oubliés, vous sans occupations, sans repos, sans être, je
> comprends en effet qu'il faille en fermant ces portes excuser
> près de vous ces déserteurs que sont les survivants, et res-
> sentir comme un privilège et un vol ces deux biens qui
> s'appellent, de deux noms dont j'espère que la résonnance ne
> vous atteint jamais, la chaleur et le ciel.

(pp. 129-30)

The desperate struggle of Hector to save peace at all costs is
heartrending, yet nothing can prevent war; fate, or the immutable laws of human nature, seem to require every now and then
vast blood sacrifices to enable life to go on. Helen is not the cause
of war, she is the instrument of fatality, she is the spark which
sets the fire going, the spring which sets the snare in action. In the
words of Ulysses:

> Nous parlons d'Hélène. Vous vous êtes trompés sur Hélène.
> Pâris et vous. Depuis quinze ans je la connais, je l'observe.
> Il n'y a aucun doute. Elle est une des rares créatures que le
> destin met en circulation sur la terre pour son usage personnel.
> Elles n'ont l'air de rien. Elles sont parfois une bourgade,
> presque un village, une petite reine, presque une petite fille,

135

mais si vous les touchez, prenez garde! C'est là la difficulté de la vie, de distinguer, entre les êtres et les objets, celui qui est l'ôtage du destin. Vous ne l'avez pas distingué.

(p. 189)

The Trojans have laid their hands upon the only thing that they ought not to have touched, so their country will once again be ravaged by war, irrespective of the destruction or the irretrievable sorrow which will strike those who have hated war and those who welcome it, Hector and Andromache, the poet, the old men and the drunken warrior. And one is left with the feeling that the world will ever go on, between long nights and brief dawns, along roads soaked in blood and making more vivid the poignancy of flowers and of tender human feelings, until mankind is no more. The play suggests to us a profoundly humane Giraudoux pouring his generous sympathy over men's plight and mingling lyricism and irony on the verge of the grave towards which man is mercilessly, pathetically drawn by forces beyond his control. This is the Giraudoux we wish to remember, for his insight and his poetic creations have added something to the nobility of man.

Giraudoux's drama is, strictly speaking, religious drama without religion. His conflicts, set in a creation whose endless diversity is bound together by the principle of unity, always involve man against the cosmos, the common humanity which surrounds him, or the gods. Giraudoux's world is a kind of Gothic cathedral without divine presence and in which every created thing is part of the ultimate reality, depicted with loving care and a baroque sense of detail and decoration. His religion is the pantheism of Spinoza tinged with Leibnitzean optimism. In his world man is intimately connected with, and an integral part of, the cosmos, and whatever he does has repercussions and echoes in it. Auguste, Ondine's foster father, bursts out in anger, and a thunder-clap punctuates the end of his speech; Siegfried arrives in Landhurst, Germany, on 21st March 1922 at exactly twelve midnight, just like spring; *Intermezzo* abounds in correspondences between man and nature. The gods, or the powers that be, of this pre-established universal harmony only deal in archetypes or ideas, and not in particulars, therefore they are unable to notice men's petty agitations. The result is that as long as the general equilibrium of human life is not disturbed, the gods remain unconcerned in their supra-human consciousness. The means by which the equilibrium is maintained do not matter, for the human words: "innocent or guilty" have no currency in the world of the gods, unless they are applied to the archetypes or to the chosen few or elect whose mission is to shatter silence so as to awaken the gods and to bring tragedy into the world of men. These gods, and their relations with men, are best described by Aegisthus in *Electre*:

> Je crois aux dieux, ou plutôt je crois que je crois aux dieux. . . . Je les imagine, non point occupés de la tare qu'est l'humanité, mais parvenus à un tel grade de sérénité et d'ubiquité qu'il ne peut plus être que la béatitude, c'est-à-dire l'inconscience. Ils sont inconscients au sommet de l'échelle de toutes les créatures comme l'atome est incon-scient à leur degré le plus bas. La différence est que c'est une inconscience fulgurante, omnisciente, taillée à mille faces, et, à leur état normal de diamants atones et sourds, ils ne répondent qu'aux lumières, qu'aux signes, et sans les com-prendre. . . . Il n'est pas deux façons de faire signe, Président: c'est se séparer de la troupe, monter sur une éminence, et agiter sa lanterne ou son drapeau. On trahit la terre comme une place assiégée, par des signaux.

(Act I, scene iii)

The bulk of men, engrossed in their daily tasks and preoccupa-tions, have no notion of the mysterious workings of the various forces of the universe, and of the part they play in these forces. Their rulers, whether they are called Aegisthus or Hector, are aware of the existence among their people of pre-ordained or elect individuals who can attract the gods' attention, and with it bring catastrophe upon the people to whom they belong. Their duty and policy as rulers consists in trying to prevent these chosen few from becoming aware of their singularity and from summoning the gods' wrath down to earth. The elect, born for their appointed tasks, which is to redeem through fire, are generally young women called Electra or Judith, who have not learnt to compromise with life and to accept a soiled reality. They are generally virgins who retain their mysterious power of vision and of apprehending through reality as long as they remain uncontaminated by men, or they are, like Helen or Lia, so irrevocably axled on their destinies that men have no meaning for them and leave them untouched. Paris matters no more than Menelaus; Helen, intent on her destiny, does not see either; and Lia, obsessed by her ideal, could never find it amongst men. Men and women cannot change the course they have been set upon, for they are part of a deterministic pattern, but once light has dawned upon them and once they know what they are born for, no human consideration can prevent them from realizing themselves. They are in fact beyond human good and evil, in a state of purity, innocence or grace which connects the temporal with the eternal in instants in which existence and essence are one, as in the case of the saint, and which reveal to the individual the immutable order and the distance which separates him from it. The aim of existence is to reach, through individuation, the knowledge which is the fulfilment of essence. The capacity to know at such a level is given to few, and finally rests not on analytical processes, but on pure intuition which connects with essence. The individuals of good intellect, like Holofernes and Ulysses, can free themselves from the fear of the gods, and therefore create possibilities of happiness, but they cannot alter destiny. Holofernes can give Judith a glimpse of the world as it might be without original sin or the fear of the gods, but he can no more than the gods deflect fate, which is that he should die by Judith's hands. She kills him for wrong reasons, that is to say not as part of her appointed mission, but for her own Promethean reason, which consists in trying to steal a spark of fire or bliss from Jehovah, even at the price of death. The gods, whether they are called Jehovah or Jupiter, behave towards human beings with a kind of ruthlessness and cunning which shows that men can only have learnt that from them. Judith and Lia are as much pawns in the hands of Jehovah as Alcmena or Ondine in the hands of their pagan gods, and it is worth noticing that in each case divinity fails to reach its goal. Jehovah fails with Judith and Lia, Jupiter does not succeed in winning the love of Alcmena, and Ondine fails to hold Hans, who prefers a mortal.

There are few authors to whom one could apply with greater veracity than to Giraudoux, Buffon's dictum, "Le style est l'homme même", or Croce's definition of art as intuition-expression. His style or expression exteriorizes his concept of the universe as a network of pre-established harmonies, whose discordancies, when caused by anthropomorphism, are constant sources of laughter and irony. When, for instance, the inspector in *Intermezzo* kills a caterpillar which is bothering him, he starts an uproar from the little girls who complain that only blackbirds can do such a thing because they eat caterpillars, while in the case of the inspector, who does not, his gesture is sheer wantonness and infringement of the order of nature. Giraudoux's characters display most of the time a kind of empyrean vision which expresses itself in wide-ranging metaphors and terms of reference which, though they become at times sheer preciosity and displays of verbal paradoxes and facetiousness, imply a constant awareness of the oneness and interrelationships of the cosmos, and if not imagination of a high order, certainly brilliant fancy. His characters are both individuals with singularities which can be either amusing or terrifying, and expressions of cosmic or historical forces; they blend conformity to the category or the group to which they belong, with the unicity which is the essence of their existence set in a world of immutable laws. Their conflicts always involve the destinies of the people or peoples with whom they are connected; Judith, Lia, Electra, etc., control the destinies of their people, and Siegfried's personal problems are set against the background of the historical conflict between France and Germany, and derive from it, forces which heighten the tension to heroic proportions.

The poeticality of Giraudoux's writing is essentially a matter of correspondences and interplays between particulars and universals, in a world of complex interpenetrations between man and the universe. In such a world one is continuously tossed about between the real and the ideal, and between the anthropomorphic vision and the vision from the plane of eternity. His preciosity is not a style or an attitude adopted in order to follow a fashion, but something natural to his mind and sensibility, and the means of reconciling his concern for man with his pantheistic concept of the universe.

CHAPTER 8

Jean-Paul Sartre

PHILOSOPHER, essayist, novelist, playwright, Sartre is probably the most widely known and the most controversial of contemporary writers. His philosophic system may creak and break down at many points, his literary essays may be marred and scarred by the weight of the thesis which he tries to clamp down on elusive personalities like that of Baudelaire, but nobody will deny Sartre a powerful intellect and a psychological insight into character which give his novels and his plays their strange tenseness and their strong impact. He is, like his outstanding French contemporaries Malraux and Bernanos, a moralist, somebody engaged in warning man of what he ought not to do, or in telling him what to do in order to lead a life worthy of the name of man and to reach some kind of fulfilment in the midst of an absurd world. For Sartre, man's problem consists above all in being aware of the absurdity of life and in assuming in full consciousness, complete responsibility for every one of his acts. This conscious awareness of one's responsibility in action commits man to the human situation, does away with hypocrisy and bad faith, and gives his life the hallmark of authenticity and individual responsibility. While Malraux brings out the tragic element of life and outlines man's greatness and nobility against a background of absurdity, fears and finitude, Sartre outlines man's growth towards consciousness and freedom against a background of hypocrisy, amorphousness and the baseness which constitutes everyday life.

Sartre's plays and novels are embodiments of his philosophical ideas, and therefore it might be useful to cast a brief preliminary

141

glance at some of the principal philosophical tenets which are the mainsprings of the actions of Sartre's characters in his plays and novels. They centre around the most important, probably the most hotly debated problem in philosophy—consciousness. Without going as far back as the father of philosophy—Plato—one might merely remember that Descartes, one of the landmarks of philosophy, separated consciousness from the outside world and the spiritual from the material universe. St. Thomas Aquinas had previously stated that knowledge takes its beginning from the senses and the idea of starting from a thinking substance in order to prove one's existence and that of the outside world would have been completely alien to him. But in the seventeenth century his influence which had been linked with scholasticism was on the wane, and it had been replaced by that of Okham and Bacon. Nevertheless, the Cartesian division between spirit and matter was not maintained for long. Bradley, Hume, Kant, Schopenhauer, all proceeded to deny such a separation between the perceptual world and human consciousness. To Kierkegaard, the famous "I think, therefore I am" was a contradiction in terms, and stressing once more the Kantian interpenetration of reality and spirit and the necessity for thought to follow the flux and reflux of life, he endeavoured "to allow thoughts to emerge with the umbilical cord of their first fervour". Gabriel Marcel, echoing him, said: "One cannot speak of existence apart from objects presented in immediate relationship to consciousness." It is this relationship to consciousness which confers existence upon reality, for, according to existentialist thinking, in order to exist one must choose what one wishes to be; things by themselves cannot choose, therefore they do not exist in themselves; they are, but they only exist through human consciousness. Heidegger said: "I am the being by which there is being." Existence is a perpetual transcendence, and is realized through free choice. The atheist existentialists—a terminology which existentialists like Marcel condemn as being meaningless—base existence on free choice, but do not use the word "transcendence". They talk about *becoming*, and Sartre says: "It is in becoming, for me, that the world receives significance, becomes intelligible and contributes to the true being; . . . the only world that exists for me, is the world of my consciousness"; and, echoing Heidegger, he continues: "It is the uprising of the for-itself (*le pour-soi*) that is consciousness, that brings it about that there is a world."[1]

The vital question therefore is: what is consciousness? Satre's subjectivism is derived from modern phenomenology, whose foremost exponent is Husserl. The latter, accepting the Kantian separation of reality into phenomenon and noumenon, placed in parenthesis or in suspense the question relating to the being of things, and confined himself to studying what he called the phenomenological essence, that is to say the varying structure of consciousness in relation to things. Heidegger, his successor in the chair of philosophy in the University of Freiburg, discarded the parenthesis and declared that man knows only one kind of being, the phenomenon, and he therefore makes of phenomenology an ontology. For Husserl, consciousness is consciousness of something part of the phenomenal world, and by itself it is merely a latency or an indefinable movement towards this something which makes being. For Heidegger, consciousness or being emerges from nothingness, which seems to acquire ontological value. Sartre discards Husserl's movement, goes further than Heidegger, and says that consciousness is consciousness of reality, and that without it, consciousness is nothing; it is a vacuum, or a hole to be filled by outside reality. The fallacy of such a concept is evident, and it spreads to many aspects of the relationship between consciousness and reality. First of all, a hole or a vacuum implies boundaries. Secondly, movement of any kind takes place through, and creates, energy, the coming of the outside world into consciousness implies some kind of energy, which must emanate either from the phenomenal world forcing itself into the vacuum so as to create consciousness, or, if one may excuse the contradiction in terms, from that vacuum towards the

---

[1] *L'Etre et le Néant*, p. 305.

object which will create consciousness. The theory of the vacuum is the least tenable, for while it is obvious that the consciousness of any given thing is something different for every person, it looks as if there was some kind of modifying element in every individual, this modifying element being the "I" of Husserl. The phenomenal world is never registered photographically by the "I", but in some ways, processed; therefore one is bound to accept the idea of the existence of some kind of energy as being part of the hole or of the vacuum which Sartre posits. Besides that, one cannot say: "I am nothing", for *nothing* with the verb *to be* becomes a predicate just as valid as *something*; it becomes: "I am no-thing", I am therefore the readiness to be any thing—a very God-like situation indeed. Neither can one be "out of the world, out of the past or out of oneself";[1] all these predicates are only applicable to God, but not to man, for only God is eternal present or time-lessness, and capable of withdrawal, while man is time, finitude and change.

The non-awareness of consciousness can be equated with nothingness or the void only if one gives to nothingness a purely negative meaning. Nothingness is what is not, that is to say not an *ens*, but merely the virtualities of being denied perhaps in time but not in the absolute; it is the temporary negation of what is not yet, but not a positive entity. Nothingness or non-Being is there-fore an attribute of the absolute, but not an absolute; it is a term which is only valid in relation to existence, for the absolute, Being, is all, and non-Being is only what is not but could be or might be. Consciousness of nothing could only be consciousness of a non-realized thing, or of the contours of a thing which is not yet or is no longer present, but which is casting its shadow into consciousness, in the same way as the sun, during an eclipse, temporarily casts the shadow of the moon on to the earth, until light and the orb soon emerge and bring with them joy, the joy and the plenitude of consciousness which is also the joy of creation.

[1] *Le Sursis*, pp. 85 and 238.

Sartre, who, in the wake of Dostoevsky, insists on the gratuitousness of action, is probably aware that true being is what it is, and that it cannot be willed or anticipated according to preestablished codes of social or individual behaviour. Where Sartre founders is when he attempts to reconcile his spontaneity of action, or unwilled emergence of true being in existence, with beliefs in individual freedom and individual choice. On the one hand, man is according to him supposed to do things without any anticipatory thoughts or choice, and he only knows what truly is once there has been something; on the other hand, Sartre keeps on talking about man choosing himself and choosing for others. What he truly means is that there is not, on this human plane of his, a knowable pattern to which man can refer himself and from which he can claim logicality of behaviour and consciousness of motives; there is only action and being, and, through being, consciousness. Pursuing a development which Sartre's atheism would not follow, one could say that consciousness is Being known existentially, that is to say known as past, but not as present or as future, except perhaps through certain levels of revelation varying, according to grace and vision, from the human to the suprahuman; but such a power to descry the indefinable time-lag between essence and individuation or between noumenon and individuated phenomenon, is only given to few, and has a very limited range. The vision which can see all things in their essence, finality and Being, is that which is, beyond human comprehension. On the human level, consciousness is that which is, and therefore it must not be conceived as a so-called guiding light, something which is merely a conceptualization according to individual egos. True consciousness, the existential awareness of being revealed through genius or other myth-makers, is what is according to laws which elude us and which we can only attempt to probe, starting from consciousness or appearance in existence; it is what a human being truly is and what he reveals, in the same way as the shape and colour of a plant are truly what the plant is.

This is not the Cartesian concept of an hypothetical "I" performing an hypothetical operation called thinking, and making of that operation a proof of existence. "I" can only be given reality by the verb, and the verb *to think* cannot grant primary reality to "I" unless "I" already is, that is to say unless there is some proof of existence other than thought. For thought presupposes the existence of certain means, such as an "I" or energy, and the phenomenal world together with concepts and notions at the cosmic and microcosmic levels. Thought is therefore a secondary and not a primary process, the primary process being the intuitive awareness of Being, the source and aim of creation.

Consciousness for Sartre does not choose itself, except in choosing what the world shall be for it, that is to say by creating its own world for itself. This is of course something which implies the emergence of a new reality, the reality of the mind, born from the marriage of the outside reality, which for Sartre is by itself meaningless and predetermined in its causality, with a person which is continuity, change and freedom. It is difficult to see how consciousness could be entirely free from the determinism which affects nature, without returning to the pure subjectivity of Descartes; man is part of the world and composed of elements which, as far as one knows, are also part of the world, and are therefore submitted to the same laws, the full causality of which seems to defy the human mind and human knowledge. The whole of Sartre's theory about consciousness and free will bristles with contradictions and overflows into the determinism which he seeks to avoid. "We choose according to our ends", he says. But how do we choose our ends? "The choice of our ends", says Sartre, "is absolutely free, made without any basis ... it is founded on no reason for the good reason that all reason comes into the world by free choice."[1] Instead of original sin we have original choice, beyond consciousness and therefore beyond liberty. Man is born with his liberty, which is Adam's sin; he is condemned to choose, and if he refuses to choose, he still chooses; he is no more

[1] *L'Etre et le Néant*, pp. 558 and 567.

146

free than any other of Adam's sons. "For a free being not to engage himself", says Sartre, "is only another form of engaging." Pascal had explained that before, and with more *finesse* and truth, in his famous *pari*. This philosophy that a man must choose in a spontaneous, irrational way is in the end a philosophy of inevitability which is by no means mitigated by Sartre's assertion that man is always in search of some kind of external solidity to fill up his consciousness. Everybody wants to exist, not in himself, for he is afraid of discovering the vacuum which is at his centre, but in others, in social respect and love from others, and for Sartre all these desires are mere weaknesses, "futile passions", based on the fact that man dare not look at his emptiness. Again, Pascal had said that before, when he remarked that men's troubles are mostly caused by the fact that they are unable to face solitude and solitary reflections. The aim of Sartre's ethics seems to be to compel man to face the boredom, the *ennui* which terrified Baudelaire, and to reconcile himself to the ugliness of life. It is the acceptance of things as they are which becomes a choice, and it is that choice which contains possibilities of fulfilment and happiness. "In Thy will is our peace", said Dante. Christian thinkers, from the beginning of Christianity to Newman, have repeated that man has free will to do God's will—something which obviously brooks of no alternative; when he does so he is happy, when he does not, he is unhappy, and he can no more change God's will than Sartre's hero Roquentin can change his town of Bouville. The real is the unavoidable, and any attempt to avoid it is bad faith; yet it seems obvious that if there is something unavoidable, all is bound to be unavoidable, for unavoidability is an absolute—unless of course one says that x is unavoidable on the moon but not on earth, that is to say, unless one can circumscribe its causality by boundaries which in fact defy the human mind. "The way to accept reality", says Sartre, "is to give it a meaning"; Christian and other religious thinkers have preached that for thousands of years, the meaning that they were after, being of course, not a solipsistic self-extension, but a revelation or manifestation of the spirit which informs creation.

Sartre says that "only things are sincere, because they are what they are; man is defined by the fact that he never coincides with his real self or *pour-soi*." Sartre means that he has no himself, he has to create himself. "Man", he says, "is the sum of his actions." This, obviously, is only partially true; mankind is something more than an unrelated conglomeration of sums representing individuals; these various sums have common denominators, and beyond the individuations which characterize human beings they all meet in a pattern, and as part of a force which makes mankind and creation. There is here a confusion, more wilful than otherwise, between the concept of man—something which is in various ways part of every thinking mind—and the creation through human existence of what is called a human person and which Sartre calls essence, something which, since the word "person" implies a religious belief, could be described as the graph or the handful of ashes left behind by a human life. There is nothing more contradictory than Sartre's various assertions about freedom. He posits it as a kind of absolute with no other concept to stand up against; yet one can only be free in relation to certain opposing forces, and since God does not exist, the only opposing elements are nature and other beings. Nature is neutral, made to be made use of; other men are enemies ever engaged in realizing their "project" in conflict one with the other. Life is not a brotherhood, or "being with", but a jungle, a free-for-all. Love in the Sartrian world is the desire to possess the other so as to use him as a kind of appropriation, as an object or *en soi*. "The lover aspires to see the 'thou' of another lost in his own 'I'; to love is to wish to be loved, and also to wish that the other should wish us to love him."[1] "My original fall", says Sartre, "is the existence of other people; original sin is an entry into the world in which there are other people".[2] Man, enclosed in his own existence, cannot make himself understood or understand others; whom then is man responsible to? What is man free from? Sartre does

---

[1] *L'Etre et le Néant*, p. 444.   [2] *ibid.*, p. 481.

not say; it is all absurd, like everything else; "man must choose", says he, and this choice is a cause of great anxiety, for "by making his choice he is forced to decide upon the meaning of existence, both within himself and everywhere outside himself".[1] How such a choice can affect the general meaning of existence, since Sartre does not believe in such an essentialist concept, or how one choice can affect the others, all based on the same gratuitous individualism and "necessity to be perpetually renewed",[2] is difficult to understand. Besides that, liberty seems to be for Sartre an entity, something which can be "grasped", "isolated", and so on—while liberty is a quality of human behaviour and experience, and can only exist against a background of order, whether social, materialistic or metaphysical. It is true that values are created by actions and experiences, but it is at least reasonable to remember that these aspects of human behaviour take place in a world which, since it is a human world, has a sense of morality and therefore has, at the conscious or subconscious level, an awareness of values or of denial of values. In brief, there is no pure act, except by God. An act is part of a pattern of conditions and causes involving values from the very moment when Adam's solitude was broken by Eve's presence, or from the moment when they broke the perfect harmony of Eden.

Let us now pass from the theory to the practice and see, by a brief examination of the main plays, how Sartre has reconciled or failed to reconcile philosophic notions and drama.

Huis Clos

In *Huis Clos*, Sartre's first important play, the three protagonists, Estelle, Inès and Garcin, have been brought together in a hell where there are no hangmen, devils or fires, which would be unnecessary, for it is they who will provide their own hell; each one of them will be hell for the others in the Sartrian world in which "l'enfer c'est les autres". This fantastic picture of a strange underworld made to illustrate Sartre's view that we only live by

[1] *L'Etre et le Néant*, p. 642.   [2] *ibid.*, p. 560.

and through others, undeniably has moments of extremely disturbing force, particularly when it deals with the crudity, the baseness and the bestial aspects of human life at a realistic level, that is to say at a level where one accepts the characters and their actions as part of this world. Yet they somehow fail to move us and to carry conviction when they become part of the extremely well-contrived vision of hell which Sartre offers us; that vision remains in the end a masterly game, but nevertheless a game, for after all, if knives can only be symbolical and have no chance of penetrating unreal bodies, it must be the same for love in its physical aspect and for all the jealousy that it entails. Bodies cannot be bodies for love-making and not for knives. The realistic picture of depravity and mud-laden behaviour is extremely powerful and disquieting, but the end is unconvincing, and so is the idea that human beings can be condemned to an eternity of mutually imposed suffering. One might also mention the fact that the idea of eternity is something completely alien to Sartre's philosophical thought, and even add that by presenting consciousness without body he gives it a life of its own, contradicting his stated view that it is merely an epiphenomenon. In the same way, Inès' statement, "Il n'y a pas de hasard"—a belief which is fundamental to the structure of the play—contradicts Sartre's views on freedom, for no hazard means no freedom; and what is true for hell is true for life, at whatever level one may accept the concept of hell.

Les Mouches

The characters of *Les Mouches*, his next play, first produced in Paris in 1942, are those of the old *Oresteia*, but the theme, the atmosphere, the emotions and thoughts involved are completely different, and bear no resemblance at all to the work of Aeschylus. The play is above all a means to expound Sartre's philosophy of freedom. It begins with Orestes' return to his native town which he finds plunged in remorse, self-flagellation and complete abasement in expiation for the murder of Agamemnon which took

place fifteen years previously. Jupiter, one of the protagonists of
the conflict, appears very early on the scene and is present throughout most of the action. He has the outside appearance of a rich
merchant who, at the outset, engages Orestes and his tutor in
lively conversation, and in no time, as befits a god, offers Orestes
advice and the pleasure of his company. Orestes is in obvious need
of it, for he does not understand the wailing, the buzzing flies,
the walls daubed in blood or the cowed appearance of his people
fully engaged in outdoing one another in acts of abject repentance. There is nothing in the air but repentance and loud confessions of true or imagined crimes; the more one confesses, the
better, for then the more they will be loved by the gods intent on
keeping men blind and in slavery. Aegisthus is the only one who,
as befits a king, does not stoop to repent, for he knows that
destiny controls men's actions, and the dead are well and truly
separated from the living:

> Je suis las. Voici quinze ans que je tiens en l'air, à bout de
> bras, le remords de tout un peuple.

$$(p. 71)$$

But he is weary of emptiness, of hollowness under silent skies, and
he says he would gladly give his kingdom if he could shed a tear.
Electra has no sense of remorse, she dreams of vengeance (though
one does not know why), she feels her youth uncontaminated by
the dead, and she thoroughly despises the gods and authority; she
is a rebel, like the Antigone of Anouilh, and she says "no" to
repentance and to mummeries. The insistence on guilt and
repentance which pervades the beginning of the play belongs
more to the time when it was written and produced, in occupied
France in 1942, than to Christian or mythological atmosphere.
Marshal Pétain, who had assumed in his person the destiny of
France, had done his best to cover her head with ashes and
to try to teach her to crawl and to wail her guilt and remorse at
the feet of the German Jove. The emotional heat generated by
such a mirroring of reality is, of course, now mostly lost.

The day after Orestes' arrival in his home town is All Souls' Day in Argos, a day devoted to the dead. The population, with king and high priest at the head, opens the entry to the cave which communicates with the underworld, and the dead have the mastery of the town for twenty-four hours; they have their say against the living. This day's celebration is marred by Electra's refusal to co-operate; instead of wailing and sighing, she comes beautifully attired and performs a dance. After that, she knows what to expect from Aegisthus who is tired of exercising authority. The time is ripe for Orestes' deed, but before it takes place we have, in the fifth scene of the second tableau in the second act, a dialogue between Aegisthus and Jupiter which contains the exposition of some of Sartre's most important philosophical points on the problem of freedom and the relations between gods and men:

JUPITER: . . . j'aime les crimes qui paient. J'ai aimé le tien parce que c'était un meurtre aveugle et sourd, ignorant de lui-même, antique, plus semblable à un cataclysme qu'à une entreprise humaine. . . . Quel profit j'en ai tiré cependant! pour un homme mort, vingt mille autres plongés dans la repentance, voilà le bilan. Je n'ai pas fait un mauvais marché. . . . Qu'ai-je à faire d'un meurtre sans remords, d'un meurtre insolent, d'un meurtre paisible, léger comme une vapeur dans l'âme du meurtrier. J'empêcherai cela! Ah! je hais les crimes de la génération nouvelle: ils sont ingrats et stériles comme l'ivraie. . . . Le secret douloureux des Dieux et des rois: c'est que les hommes sont libres. Ils sont libres, Egisthe. Tu le sais, et ils ne le savent pas.

EGISTHE: . . . Depuis que je règne, tous mes actes et toutes mes paroles visent à composer mon image; je veux que chacun de mes sujets la porte en lui et qu'il sente, jusque dans la solitude, mon regard sévère peser sur ses pensées les plus secrètes. Mais c'est moi qui suis ma première victime: je ne me vois plus que comme ils me voient. . . .

JUPITER: Quand une fois la liberté a explosé dans une âme d'homme, les Dieux ne peuvent plus rien contre cet homme-là. Car c'est une affaire d'hommes, et c'est aux autres hommes—à eux seuls—qu'il appartient de le laisser courir ou de l'étrangler.

(pp. 76, 77, 79)

Here we have a clear sample of the shifty ways of the gods, intent on keeping men in subjugation through fear and remorse so that they may not know that they are free. But let a man like Orestes perform murder without worry or fear, let him perform the gratuitous act without forethought or afterthought, and he will be free; and once he is free, the gods have no power over him, they will be to him as useless and desultory as the world of tall shades and broken dolls which he has left in the nursery. Sartre, intent on showing the paltriness of the gods and the pride of man with his newly-found freedom, glides lightly over philosophical contradictions; man claims to owe nothing to the gods, but when Jupiter asks Orestes: "Qui donc t'a créé?", the conversation proceeds:

ORESTE: Toi. Mais il ne fallait pas me créer libre.

JUPITER: Je t'ai donné ta liberté pour me servir.

ORESTE: Il se peut, mais elle s'est retournée contre toi et nous n'y pouvons rien, ni l'un, ni l'autre. . . . Je ne suis ni le maître, ni l'esclave, Jupiter. Je *suis* ma liberté! A peine m'as-tu créé que j'ai cessé de t'appartenir.

(pp. 99-100)

There is enough here to throw to the ground the whole of Sartre's system, for Orestes cannot deny that the gods created men and created them free. Therefore man is not the demiurge which Sartre would like him to be, nor is liberty a purely existential concept, since it is given as being man's true existence. Jupiter, in spite of his omniscience, is a figure of fun who can only perform certain parlour tricks, but who can be summarily dismissed once the audience which he has amused is tired of him. He is too obviously at the beck and call of the master of ceremonies, and is therefore not part of a dramatic necessity.

Once the deed is done, the third act sees the breaking down of Electra, who cannot accept the responsibility of her freedom and the triumph of Orestes; Jupiter looks a very trivial figure, and fades away in a melodramatic atmosphere. Orestes, armed with his freedom—"tout à coup, la liberté a fondu sur moi et m'a transi, la nature a sauté en arrière, et je n'ai plus eu d'âge"[1]— dismisses Jupiter, who is cowed by this newly born, unbound Prometheus who tells him that the men of Argos are free, and "la vie humaine commence de l'autre côté du désespoir".[2] Jupiter snivels away, while Electra rushes out, shrieking, pursued by the Erinnyes. Olympian Orestes calmly waits and faces the angry populace with the wondrous, soothing story of the Pied Piper of Scyros, then walks away in a kind of fairy-like atmosphere, trailing behind him flies and Furies while the curtain falls.

The impact of the play, like that of Anouilh's *Antigone*, probably varies with the time at which the play is produced. I remember listening to a radio production of *Les Mouches* immediately after the war, and being much moved and excited by the emotional haze which arose round the concepts of state-of-siege, occupying flies and the proud liberator who drives them away beyond the Rhine and Hamelin. Re-examining the play eight or nine years after is quite a different matter, though one should not confuse even pristine excitement with any idea of true achievement, least of all greatness. The play is unsatisfactory on many counts. The philosophical debate, which is entrancing from the intellectual point of view, weighs down the play and

[1] p. 101.   [2] p. 102.

accentuates the allegorical aspect of the characters. Plays, like poetry, are made of emotions, not of intellectual contests which are dramatically worthless unless they generate explosive emotional heat. One can, with goodwill, follow up to a point Sartre's metaphysical disquisition and attempt to base freedom on individual responsibility and gratuitousness, but one cannot understand how this freedom must be proved and established by killing one's mother, to say nothing of her lover. True enough, Orestes is a descendant of the Atrides, that famed family doomed by the gods to atrocious deeds, but then even that kind of fate has to be made partly clear, by behaviour, hesitations and tensions which are completely alien to this Sartrian Orestes. He bleeds his mother and Aegisthus with less concern than a normally kind-hearted Englishman would show about bleeding chicken. There are limits to detachment or pragmatic philosophical demonstrations; the fact is that the murder scene is to my mind so perfunctorily unconvincing that one expects Aegisthus and Clytemnestra to reappear on the stage much earlier than the final gathering of the actors after the last curtain. One cannot quite understand why the hero does not even blink an eyelid or show any sign of regret at what he has done; he does not show anywhere any human awareness of pain, of feelings or other human reactions, he is merely mechanical. Sartre has obviously followed in the wake of Giraudoux, towards the transposition of Greek myth on the modern stage, but he has not only transposed, and therefore lost the necessary atmosphere to a great theme, he has dehumanized to a degree which renders Electra a paltry, namby-pamby character, and Orestes Frankenstein-like, so that in the end the philosophic message remains, but the play as such does not impinge much on human sensibility.

After *Huis Clos*, Sartre wrote two short plays, *Morts sans sépulture* and *La Putain respecteuse*, the latter being a very effective one-act play. Then he wrote *Les Mains sales*, which was produced at the Théâtre Antoine on 2nd April, 1948; the play has four acts, a prologue and an epilogue. Sartre is here batting on the same wicket as Giraudoux and Anouilh—purity. The theme of the play is the incapacity of the idealist to compromise with the world and to find a place for himself in society. Hugo is Antigone or Electra, while Hoederer, the statesman, is Creon[1] or Aegisthus; he uses words which either of them would have used, for the circumstances in which they find themselves involved are similar:

> How attached to your purity you are, my boy! How frightened you are of soiling your hands! All right, stay pure! Whom does it help, and why did you come to us? Purity is an ideal for a fakir or a monk. You intellectuals, you bourgeois anarchists, you use it as an excuse for doing nothing. Do nothing, stay put, keep your elbows to your sides, wear kid gloves. My hands are filthy. I've dipped them up to the elbows in blood and filth. So what? Do you think you can govern and keep your spirit white?[2]

To this Hugo answers:

> I joined the Party because its cause was just and I will only leave it when it has ceased to be so. As for my fellow men, it isn't what they *are* that interest me, but what they may become.

And Hoederer's rejoinder to Hugo would also apply to Antigone:

> I know you, my boy, you're a destroyer. You hate men because you hate yourself; your purity is the purity of death and the revolution you dream of isn't ours; you don't want to change the world, you want to blow it apart.

(pp. 85-6)

[1] *Antigone* by Anouilh (Table Ronde), p. 84: "Pour dire oui, il faut suer et retrousser ses manches, empoigner la vie à pleines mains et s'en mettre jusqu' au coude . . ." to the end of Créon's speech.

[2] The translations of the quotations from *Les Mains sales* and *Le Diable et le Bon Dieu* are by Kitty Black.

—words which are not only true, but carry with them overtones of affection which render Hoederer's death moving and piteous. Hugo needs an ideal, and he cannot find it by himself or in the life of his class, so he joins the Communist Party, the party of purity. He is mistaken, for the party is fully entangled in contingencies and applies adequate dialectics to justify opportunism, so that in the end Hugo, realizing that one cannot act and yet preserve purity, is compelled to join the pure like Electra and Antigone in the only world where they can be pure, the world of death.

The action of this play takes place in Illythia, a country occupied by the Germans while the Russian liberating armies are approaching. Illythia is obviously France, with the Regent as Pétain, the Pentagon as resistance to the Germans without any truck with the Communists, and the Communists exactly as they were in France at the beginning of the occupation. The play opens with Hugo coming to the room of Olga, his former mistress and party associate, after two years' imprisonment for having killed a Party boss, Hoederer. Louis, the Party leader, and rival of Hoederer, is hard on Hugo's heels and wants to kill him because he says that he talks too much. Olga pleads for Hugo's life, and asks for three hours' respite, until midnight, to hear Hugo's full story before deciding his fate. Louis agrees, and we have Hugo's story.

Two years before, there had been a split in the Communist Party's policy, and Hugo, together with his wife, had been sent by Louis as a secretary to Hoederer, but in reality in order to kill him. Hoederer was in favour of coming to terms with all the other forces opposing the Germans, and of working together with them until the arrival of the Russians. Louis was in favour of standing alone without compromise, and of fighting for revolution and power; so was Hugo. But life has its own way; Hoederer soon emerges as a skilful, courageous, wise and humane character who conquers both Hugo and his wife. Hugo finds Hoederer's arguments in favour of compromise at that moment, irresistible;

he can only say that Louis might have turned the tables on the opponent, but we can easily see that he is not at all convinced, and neither is anybody else. Besides that, he has unavoidably grown fond of Hoederer, who reciprocates his feelings and who, in the end, tries to save him at the very risk of his life. Hugo, adrift, incapable of finding his feet in action, tossed between admiration and affection, walks out of the room when he ought to have killed Hoederer, and comes back a moment later meaning to offer him his services and devotion. When he returns, he finds his wife, who has fallen in love with Hoederer and has forced herself in his arms, in a situation which just for one moment enables him to believe that Hoederer saved him not for his own self but because of his wife, merely as a pawn in the game of adultery; so he has a kind of instinctive reflex, he seizes the revolver which was in the drawer, and he kills Hoederer. Yet, as he had taken an unconscionable time to do so, the Party was displeased and uncertain about the final motives which caused the killing. Olga's problem is to discover these motives in order to decide if he is really fit for salvage.

Hugo himself is not quite sure; it is not for nothing that he was called Raskolnikov. He is a kind of Hamlet, incapable of deciding what to do, and action is his only means of knowing what he is. Hoederer knows him well, and says to him:

You wanted to prove to yourself you could be a man of action and you chose the most difficult path; like when people want to get to heaven. . . . And a man must do what he is fit for; so much the better if the job is easy.

Hugo is certainly not fit to be a killer; he thinks too much, and it is extremely difficult to kill in cold blood, or out of any kind of idealism. Killers do their job instinctively, without thinking or analyzing the right or wrong of their actions. In the end, Hugo hardly knows why he killed; he did so in the grip of distress, having lost self-esteem and confidence, overwhelmed by the feeling that he was unworthy of any love, and therefore out

of a sheer reflex to avoid, in a last moment of panic, his final
disintegration:

> I . . . I killed him because I opened the door. That's all I
> know. If I hadn't opened that door. . . . There he was,
> holding Jessica in his arms. He had lipstick on his chin. It
> was all so trivial. I had been living for so long in the depths
> of tragedy. It was to save my tragedy that I fired.
>
> (p. 99)

The Party's orders, like Hamlet's ghost, are not enough to bring
him to action, he only comes to it in a kind of instinctive way.
When it comes to self-analysis and elucidation of motives, two
years' solitary meditation in prison have not been enough to
clarify his mind; the truth only dawns upon him in Olga's flat,
at the end of his story. His wife's sympathy, Olga's interest in
him, and above all Hoederer's affection for him, all point to the
fact that he is a pitiful character, "an uprooted", a human being
with gifts such that, had he been placed in different surroundings,
he might have avoided the agony of self-destruction. There is a
certain feeling of tragedy about him, for he carries with him the
seeds of his own downfall; he could only find his harmony out
of the world, in a community of mystics or pure people.

But that feeling of tragedy is even more marked in the case of
Hoederer. Hoederer is not an idealist, but a man of action who
has at times not hesitated to soil his hands for the sake of the
Party; but beyond the odd stains left upon him by life, he is a
man conscious of his destiny, willing to accept it and to face death
or the solitariness of Moses with the calm control of a man who
knows that his task matters more than his own individual life.
He is not only endowed with a wisdom which asserts itself
throughout the play and which in the end triumphs, but he is very
humane and worthy of sympathy. His eruption in Hugo's flat at
the end of the meeting with the Regent is imprinted with pathos:

> You can quite well turn me out. [*To Hugo*] You don't have
> to see your boss when he's got the blues. [*Pause*] I don't

know why I came. I wasn't tired, I tried to work. . . .
[*Shrugs his shoulders*] A man can't work all the time. . . .
When I was a deputy in the Landstag, I lived with a man
who kept a garage. In the evenings, I used to go into their
dining-room to smoke. They had a radio, the children played
on the floor. . . ."

(pp. 79-80)

Even his previous intervention, when his two bodyguards were
searching the flat and Hugo's clothes, is marked with a sense of
fair play and gentlemanly feelings. And after that, his personality
grows, his humanity prevails; he easily dominates Hugo in a
dramatic argument which everybody, including himself, knows,
involves his very life. The next morning, he is calmly prepared to
gamble his life merely to save Hugo's self-esteem, and to enable
him to find his equilibrium:

HOEDERER: . . . You shouldn't humiliate people. I'll talk to
him.
JESSICA: You'll let him in with a gun in his pocket?
HOEDERER: Why not? I'd like to change his mind for him.
There'd be a dangerous five minutes, not more.
If he doesn't make his attempt this morning, he'll
never do it.

(p. 90)

There he is, at the very peak of his brilliance, after having
displayed heroic quality, profound humanity and refinement of
feelings in refusing to have anything to do with Jessica—and it
is at that very moment that he is killed, merely because a little
woman, who has been bowled over by a splendid display of
altruism and virility, insists on kissing the hero right on the spur
of the moment. She could have waited, of course, but obviously
it had to be that way, for without her there would have been no
shooting, and therefore no play.

The circumstances of Hoederer's death carry around them an
aura of tragedy, and tragedy is a word which carries with it

implications of purity of emotions and feelings which pertain only to good plays; and, in spite of very obvious flaws, this is a good play. The main flaw is, as Mr. Harold Hobson rightly suggests, the weakness of Louis' character; he is less than a shadow. The other flaws, which Mr. Hobson also mentions, are the lengthy scene with the Regent and Karsky, the stilted reactions which follow the bomb explosion, and the overdrawn scene of drunkenness. Against these flaws one has to place the tense dramatic scene of the search in Hugo's flat, the moving debate between Hugo and Hoederer in the flat, and what follows right through the epilogue, which is masterly in tension and pathos. There, the last veils fall from Hugo's vision, and he realizes, painfully, yet with a sudden upsurge of faith, that idealism is not possible on earth, that he has been a murderer for the wrong reasons. He has killed a man whom he loved and who loved him, not out of devotion to principles, but out of sheer impulse or a reflex involving above all his ego. Worse still, the ideal which he was parading has now been repudiated by the Party. Hoederer, who has died for it, is now to become a hero, and for that requires Hugo's connivance, that is to say a second betrayal of his ideal. This time it is too much, the dregs come up to the surface, and by a last effort Hugo tears himself away from the mud which surrounds him and walks calmly into death:

HUGO: [*without taking the gun*]: You've turned Hoederer into a great man. But I loved him more than you will ever love him. If I deny my act, he becomes an anonymous corpse, a wreckage of the Party. [*The car stops*] Killed by chance. Killed for a woman. . . . A man like Hoederer doesn't die by accident. He dies for his ideals, for his policy, he is responsible for his own death. If I recognize my crime before you all, if I reclaim my name of Raskolnikov, if I agree to pay the necessary price, then he will have had the death he deserved. . . . [*Walking to the door*]

> I haven't killed Hoederer yet, Olga. Not yet. I'm
> going to kill him now and myself with him.
> [*More knocking*] . . . (*Hugo opens the door and bows
> slightly*) Not fit for salvage.
>
> (pp. 105-6)

Salvage also implies dustbins and refuse heaps; Hugo could not
accept that, and he frees himself from that fate. One can understand why this play could cause serious qualms to the Communists; not only is their opportunism exposed, but also the
impossibility of avoiding soiling one's ideals. The background of
political realism which underlies the play, the conflicts between
the various resistance movements in France and the Pétain
régime no doubt help to explain the play's popularity when
it was first produced; that element of topicality will certainly tell
against it, but it has nevertheless enough dramatic merits and
psychological insight to survive the test of time.

Le Diable et le Bon Dieu

Le Diable et le Bon Dieu was first performed in Paris on 7th
June 1951 at the Théâtre Antoine; it was Louis Jouvet's last production. Sartre says of the play:

> I have tried to show that Goetz, a freelance captain of
> mercenaries and an anarchist of evil, destroys nothing when
> he believes he is destroying the most. He destroys human lives
> but cannot disturb society or social judgments. . . . Whether
> he tries to achieve the absolute through good or through evil,
> he succeeds only in destroying human lives.

The play is based on the Peasants' Revolt in sixteenth-century
Germany, and the action takes place around the town of Worms.
Two crises shook Germany at that time; the revolt of the peasants, and the beginning of the Lutheran Reformation. The town
of Worms has rebelled against the Archbishop and his priests,
who have been driven by the populace to seek refuge in a mon-
astery. The Archbishop has succeeded in creating a rift between

Conrad and Goetz, two captains of mercenaries attacking the town, and Conrad is defeated and killed. Goetz, the most brilliant captain of his day, remains, and he is about to go his own ruthless way and to destroy the town. He is a formidable, terrifying figure, indulging in evil for evil's sake, with the conviction that hell is his unique domain and that his evil-doing keeps God Himself anxious. As a bastard son, he is rejected both by the nobles and by the peasants; kept in a kind of no-man's-land, he seems to have developed the demonic egotism of being God's exclusive preoccupation in creation. So he wallows in the belief that his evil-doing is something singular, which can crucify God:

> God hears me, it is God I am deafening, and that is enough for me, for He is the only enemy worthy of my talents. There is only one God, the phantoms and myself. . . . This city will go up in flames. God knows that. At this moment, He is afraid. I can feel it. . . . I shall dare. In a few moments, I will march in His fear and His anger. The city shall blaze; the soul of the Lord is a corridor of mirrors, the fire will see itself reflected in a thousand glasses. Then, I shall know that I am a monster in all purity.
>
> (p. 54)

He is sharply disillusioned by the renegade priest, Heinrich, who tells him that good on earth is impossible, that a man can only do evil, that God Himself has made it so:

HEINRICH: If you want to deserve Hell, you need only remain in bed. The world itself is iniquity; if you accept the world, you are equally iniquitous. If you should try and change it, then you become an executioner. [*He laughs*] The stench of the world puts out the stars. . . . We are all equally guilty, bastard, we are all equally deserving of hell-fire, but the Lord forgives us when it pleases Him to forgive.

GOETZ: He will never forgive me against my will.

HEINRICH: Miserable wretch, how can you struggle against His mercy? How can you exhaust His infinite patience? He will take you up between His fingers if He pleases, raise you to the level of His paradise; with the tip of His finger He will make you overflow with His goodwill, and you will find yourself becoming good despite yourself. Go! Burn Worms. Go to pillage, go to massacre—you're wasting your time; one of these days you'll wake up in Purgatory like everyone else.

(p. 61)

The realization that everyone is doing evil destroys the uniqueness in evil which was Goetz's aim, and compels him to throw his inordinate pride into being singular in the opposite way, that is to say, by doing only good—something which, according to Heinrich, is against God's will and which therefore cannot fail to challenge Goetz's ambition. He at once makes a wager that from then on, he will only do good, and in order to compel God to decide whether good or evil should be Goetz's future, he puts the decision to a throw of dice, after having taken the precaution of weighting them; in that way, he is sure that God will give the answer he wants Him to give, which is to try to be absolutely good in a society riddled with evil.

The attempt is, of course, doomed to failure. Goetz's goodness is an insult to his peers and a source of hatred to those who benefit from it, each one construing his deeds as means to satisfy his own egoism. The barons get hold of him and beat him; Nasti, the Lutheran prophet, the head of the peasants' rebellion, tells him that his duty is not to do good but "to administer your fortune and to watch it grow. That is the task to fill up a life time." Goetz refuses to believe that good could engender evil, or that it should be unfolded in instalments; he says that "it suffices for one man to love all men with undivided love for that love to spread from one to another throughout humanity". But he realizes more and more that good is more difficult than evil; his efforts are more and more thwarted; pure goodness is easily misunderstood by a populace terrified by the idea of the Devil and completely in the hands of the Church, which exploits its superstitions. Goetz realizes more and more that what has been once is beyond change, that "nothing can efface nothing", that "no-one ever expiates a sin", and he has to confess that "whether I live by Evil or by Righteousness, I always find myself detested". He realizes that love is a kind of grace; one is loved straight away or never. He accepts the fact that God helps those who help themselves; that is why he weights the dice, and produces his own stigmata with his dagger. But he realizes also that the loneliness of good is perhaps worse than the loneliness of evil; his good deeds are always explained away as trickery, and in the end the people who have followed him and the community which he has created are destroyed, and only Hilda remains alive amongst the smoky ruins. He still continues to accept the blows which rain upon him, he continues to fast and to abase himself, until the appointed day when Heinrich arrives. Stung by the slighting remarks of Heinrich, who tells him that "in one day of virtue you killed more people than in thirty-five years of malice!" he first acknowledges his pride:

Listen, priest; I had betrayed everyone, including my own brother, but my appetite for betrayal was not yet fulfilled; so, one night, before the ramparts of Worms, I invented a way to betray Evil, that's the whole story. Only Evil doesn't let itself be betrayed quite so easily; it wasn't Good that jumped out of the dice-box; it was the worst of Evil. What does it matter, anyway; monster or saint, I didn't give a damn, I wanted to be inhuman. Say it, Heinrich, say I was mad with shame, and that I wanted to amaze Heaven to escape the scorn of men.

(p. 130)

The Contemporary French Theatre

Then, after Heinrich's reply:

> Torture the weak, or martyrize yourself, kiss the lips of a
> harlot or a leper, die of privation or excesses; God doesn't
> give a damn.
>
> (p. 132)

Goetz's dormant pride awakens, and he flings back the answer
that there is no God:

> The silence is God. The absence is God. God is the loneliness
> of man. There was no one but myself; I alone decided on
> Evil; and I alone invented God. It was I who cheated, I who
> worked miracles, I who accuse myself today, I alone who can
> absolve myself; I, the man. If God exists, man is nothing; if
> man exists. . . . Where are you going?
>
> (p. 133)

Heinrich, outraged, tries to kill him, but Goetz reacts, and it is
Heinrich who is killed. After that, Goetz decides to throw in his
lot again with men and with their struggles:

> Men of today are born criminals. I must demand my share
> in their crimes if I desire my share of their love and their
> virtue. I wanted love in all its purity; ridiculous nonsense;
> to love a man is to hate the same enemy; therefore I will
> embrace your hatred. I wanted to do Good: foolishness: on
> this earth and at this time, Good and Evil are inseparable; I
> accept my share of Evil to inherit my share of Good.
>
> (p. 137)

Nasti, in the name of the peasants, asks him to take his place in
the struggle in the position for which he is suited, the position
which, according to Nasti, he should never have relinquished,
that of General. Goetz pleads that leaders are alone, and that he
wants men around him, but Nasti soon shows him that he, the
prophet, has been even more alone than Goetz claims to have
been, and that one cannot participate in human affairs and

maintain ideals of uncompromising purity. Like everybody else, he has to compromise and submit himself to mummeries in which he does not believe. The desperate plight of the rebels moves Goetz, who agrees to be their leader and to enforce the ruthlessness which such a task demands; his first gesture of authority is to stab a captain who insults him. After that, he makes a declaration of his tactics, which are simple and effective; they consist in making his men more terrified by him than by the enemy. As for himself:

> I shall remain alone with this empty sky above me, since I have no other way of being among men. There is this war to fight, and I will fight it.
>
> (p. 141)

This is undeniably Sartre's most ambitious work, and to my mind his major achievement. It is a complex, panoramic creation, certainly difficult to stage, though not half as difficult as Claudel's *Soulier de Satin*, which it unfailingly brings to mind as being the dark side of the diptych of creation—a creation which, in spite of Sartre's professed atheism, has obviously not forgotten God. It is Heinrich, the renegade apostate priest, who says: "An elect is a man the finger of God has driven into a corner." There is here and there a slight flavour of melodrama born from the very theme of the play and the startling oscillations of the main character; there are above all serious *longueurs* in scenes vii, viii and ix of Act III, which slow up the pace and blunt the tension through unnecessary prolixity and elaboration of incidents which to my mind could be reduced to the minimum required to convey the Hilda-Goetz relationship and Goetz's final break with the rebel peasants; I feel that the play would gain by some trimming in these three scenes, and by reducing their bulk by half. But that is not a major flaw. The dramatic tension, even if it sags at the points mentioned, is maintained throughout; it rises to great excitement in the magnificent third scene of the first act, which reveals Goetz's terrifying ruthlessness, and it is maintained at a high level right to the end of the second act; there it slackens, to rise again in the last two scenes.

The character of Goetz is extremely well-drawn, in fact the best drawn of Sartre's characters. His historicity is irrelevant, his human reality is undeniable. He has in him the demonic pride to challenge God's sole attention, and as he does not get it, for obvious reasons which he himself confesses—"I have made the gestures of love, but love did not follow"[1]—he answers for God when God probably does not deem him fit to receive an answer, and he ends in echoing Nietzsche's cry: "God is dead." Goetz is, of course, a kind of superman, but Sartre, besides investing him with the ruthlessness which a superman requires in order to carry out his task of leadership, endows him with such an urgency in his search for love that although we know that search to be motivated above all by pride, we are at times moved, as Hilda is moved, and profoundly interested in his fate, which has something of the Promethean adventure. He is ruthless—at least he is described as such—but on the whole he is more so in words than in deeds, for he only kills in self-defence or in the exercise of his functions. His fearful threats to Nasti, Heinrich and Catherine are not put to the test, and the society against which he is pitted is such that, although he looks the most prominent in evil, he is not the least attractive. His peers, who reproach him with his bastardy, or the Church, which uses him and trades in corruption, do not come up to his level of goodness and daring, whether or not his goodness is only meant to test God, as when he emulates St. Francis or kisses the leper. The priests, whether in the Church or out of the Church as Heinrich is, are rather abject characters; the Lutheran prophet has grandeur in his rugged faith, but he is too engrossed in the materialism of this world, something which probably is one of the flaws of Lutheranism. Goetz may be a first-class showman, as when he cheats for a wager or when he wounds himself, yet that last deed is not entirely without value, for although it is merely a redemptory gesture on the part of a man who has done

[1] p. 106.

great harm to the woman who implores him, it elicits nevertheless a certain amount of sympathy for having complied, even by
cheat, with such a piteous and moving request.

There is in this study of blackness a certain tragic grandeur
which is impressive and makes this play a moving experience,
something which transcends adhesion to philosophical or religious
beliefs and leaves us face to face with a world which, though
repellent and terrifying, is fascinating in its psychological truth
and in its aesthetic coherence. This is obviously an important play
which one ought to face without making the sign of the cross or
sprinkling holy water all round; it is to my mind a much greater
homage to God than one generally thinks, certainly much greater
than many homilizing praises of saints who do not need our human
praise; it is a play which shows us in tortuous ways, reminiscent
of the proverb quoted at the beginning of Claudel's *Le Soulier de
Satin*, "God writes straight with crooked lines", the magnitude
of evil, the anxiety for God's attention and the majesty and range
of creation which is no more altered by Goetz's venom than a
battleship by a bee's sting. Sartre's philosophy, that existence
precedes essence and that it is pointless to govern one's actions by
any religious or ethical conventions, finds here its justification.
No man can foresee the results of his actions. "Call no man
happy", said Sophocles in *Oedipus Rex*. Therefore the only sen-
sible thing to do is to act in accordance with one's nature, keeping
to one's station (Eliot said something similar in *The Confidential
Clerk*), and not to try to be something else or to act according to
a priori principles.

CHAPTER 9

Jean Anouilh

SARTRE brings to the theatre a philosophical mind which, if it at times overweighs the plays, can throw a most disquieting light on many aspects of human life. Giraudoux has not only the fantasy with which Anouilh has been so abundantly graced, but also a sense of tragedy and of the nobility of human suffering. But of all the playwrights I know of in our modern times, Anouilh has the surest sense of the stage. His skill is breathtaking, and one cannot withhold admiration. Within the bounds of the genre—fantastic comedy—I know of nothing more accomplished in range and dramatic skill than the first act of *Léocadia* (*Time Remembered*); and that skill is evidenced even in the difference which exists between the reading and the stage effect of the play. Owing to the fact that the old Duchess, a key character in the play, has to unfold at the beginning the elements of the plot which make the play plausible, the reading might be a trifle slow, but with the characters on the stage this first act becomes a bewildering display of moods in the course of which the audience is tossed about between fantasy, amazement, wild laughter and sheer pathos at the extravagant love of the old Duchess for her nephew or at the plight of young Amanda having landed in what undeniably looks like a mad-house.

Of course, Anouilh's theatrical skill is widely recognized, and people fall back for denigration on questions of ethics and generally end in describing him as a nihilist, a pessimist, or, even worse, an amoralist. These strictures may have some validity if his characters are judged not from the auditorium but from the study or the drawing-room. It is true indeed that Antigone is a thorough nihilist, a little girl obsessed with the idea of death; it is true that Thérèse, Jeannette, Eurydice, etc., are promiscuous to a degree and have begun to have lovers from the age of fifteen; it is true also that practically every character in *Ardèle*, with the exception of the two hunchbacks, is committed to an idea of love which is positively obscene, and preaches and practises a revolting amoralism. But what of it? What if all these weaknesses were true in life also? What if it were true that unfortunate young girls lose their virginity at fifteen, or that one could meet in life blasé society ladies going from lover to lover trying to find in each of them an ever-receding youth? The nihilism of Antigone or of Eurydice is more symbolic than realistic; it is more the expression of a belief or an attitude towards life than an attempt at projecting life objectively on the stage. Besides that, Antigone has an element of topicality or of historical truth which cannot be dissociated from the characters and the actions of the play. But for the rest, for amoralism and promiscuity, these things exist, and our problem is surely not to condemn them as aspects of behaviour which we regret in life but as elements which are part of a dramatic picture meant to produce, through acceptance or rejection of what happens on the stage, a rewarding aesthetic experience. Is not Emma Bovary amoral? Is not Marguerite Gauthier both promiscuous and amoral? Is not Ophelia immoral from the point of view of Church precepts? Yet who cares about such aspects of those characters' behaviour? What counts surely is not that Emma Bovary passes from Rodolphe to Léon and then into death, but the final effect left upon us by the life and death of that character as part of a pattern of actions which form a whole and take place not in real life but on the plane of the imagination. Emma Bovary's carnal lapses are both part of the revelation of her character to herself and to others and also the means to create the ever-growing disgust which transforms her wishy-washy idealism and her incapacity to discriminate between the dream and the real, into death. Rodolphe and Léon are landmarks on the road which, given her background and make-up, she is bound to tread. The cruel expulsion of Ophelia from Hamlet's life could not be so cruel, so mentally disrupting if her ties to him were not something more than platonic. True, Ophelia's physical surrender is based on a kind of idealism and belief in true love unknown to any one of Anouilh's heroines, but from the strict point of view of morality she is immoral too, and although one could not say that death is the punishment meted out for that crime, she nevertheless dies for having allowed a crazed head to rest on her maiden lap. Anouilh's heroines flaunt their promiscuousness because they are living in an age in which faith and idealism have been replaced by hedonism and the search for gross, material pleasures. Thérèse, Eurydice and Jeannette are sisters of Marguerite Gauthier; they believe, as she did, that the body is unimportant and that one can trade it time and again on the steps of the temple while keeping one's soul pure in order to offer it to the divinity inside. They separate body from spirit, they believe that one can hold purity like a candle in one's cupped hands and brave with it the surrounding filth and stench; but they soon come to realize that it cannot be so, that a flame cannot burn on air alone but ever requires some substance to feed it or to project it, and in the end that substance may have been so affected by soiling contact that it poisons and kills the flame. Thérèse cannot accept happiness, her past prevents her from doing so; Jeannette and Eurydice try to burn themselves out in a few brief moments, knowing that they will not last and that life is far more difficult to face than death; so that when they emerge from their murky past, when they meet at last the dream longed for, the contrast between what can only be for a brief moment, and what has been and would irrevocably be if they went on living, is too much for them and they plunge into death in order to avoid what they cannot stand. Eurydice, Antigone and Jeannette know that happiness, what they call "le sale bonheur", is not of this world.

Who, unless he were a nihilistic, suicidal case, would choose such ways of life ever strewn with misery and crowned with death? Who could find in these characters' behaviour an encouragement to repeat their failures? We may shriek and groan at the degradation of most of the characters in *Ardèle*, as many of us shrieked at the horror of Orwell's *1984*, but these things exist, or will certainly exist if we allow certain of our inclinations to develop or some looming failures to take place. Can we fling upon Anouilh the reproach which was flung by smug, self-satisfied bourgeois and courtiers upon Molière when *Le Misanthrope* was described as having given "un tour agréable au vice et une austérité ridicule à la vertu"? Flaubert, writing to Maupassant, had something to say on this subject when the latter, like Baudelaire and Flaubert himself, was threatened with proceedings for "outrage aux moeurs et à la morale publique". "Denounce to them", says Flaubert, "*all* the ancients from Aristophanes to Horace and Virgil, then the moderns, Shakespeare, Goethe, Byron, Cervantes, Rabelais, Chateaubriand, Molière, Corneille, etc." People will say, continues Flaubert, that "votre histoire pousse à la conjonction des sexes", and he comments: "D'abord, ça n'y pousse pas, et quand cela serait, par ce temps de goûts anormaux il n'est pas mal de prêcher le culte de la femme." This is as true in every respect in 1950 as it was in 1880.

Anouilh's heroines are wilful sinners, that is true indeed; but does he crown them with laurels, does he reward them with marriage, numerous children and happiness ever after? He never does so. The wage of their behaviour is generally death, as is the case in most widely-praised morality plays or merely moral plays. Does he make them attractive, sympathetic and moving to the point that one might feel like taking up their lives as models or that one might set about to emulate them? Certainly not, if one is in one's senses; who indeed would choose Thérèse's, Monime's or Eurydice's fate? None of these heroines behaves like a normal, well-brought-up young lady; but then, normality is not a subject of narration or characterization on the stage. It is the abnormal which is matter for art; the artist looks for the singular, for what tends towards the archetype, source of certain dominant traits which are permanent in mankind and therefore form universals. These heroines of Anouilh are undeniably rather strange characters; they are all in some ways kind, sweet, attractive, but they are all intent upon head-on collisions with life; they are in rebellion against it, and they wilfully take the hard road. They are mostly drawn from the bohemian world and brought up not in good schools or convents but amidst the promiscuity, the graft and corruption of strolling players or of completely degraded parents who are used to selling their daughters in order to make money or to get on in life. Why such an outcry, when such things are unfortunately true, and at more levels of society than one would like to believe? It is not merely in the world of the Tardes or the Vincents that young women have to sell their bodies for money or some other favour! The fact is that these young women, in spite of their dream about purity, never recover from the stain of their youth, or never succeed in liberating themselves from the soul-destroying influence of their family or the society in which they live; from the beginning they are condemned either to die or to live on in misery.

There are plays, and they are not the best or the greatest, in which the didactic or the moralizing elements are explicit; they illustrate beliefs or ideas passionately held. As far as one can see, Anouilh holds no religious or philosophical belief which he tries to put forward in his theatre. His plays are not, like Sartre's, above all a means to illustrate certain beliefs; they are rather the direct projection of his amused, detached or aggrieved observation of the comic or sad human saraband which is life. The morality is part of the aesthetic experience. When this experience is aesthetically satisfactory, as it is in *Ardèle*, we come out of the performance chastened of any urge to emulate any one of the characters of the play. When on the contrary the play is not satisfying as an artistic creation, as is the case with *Roméo et Jeannette*, one cannot help being struck by the improbability of the characters, by their lack of coherence or the absence of human interest; and as for the promiscuousness and the volatility of

Jeannette, they are too crude to suggest emulation or to confer any pathos on her death. She seems to be as wilfully promiscuous as her brother Lucien is wilfully cynical and savagely intent on revenging his cuckoldry upon the whole world. Here the conscious didacticism of the author bent upon his demonstration overwhelms the play, which by the end of the second act disintegrates and dissolves from the reader's attention. In my view we have the same wilfulness in Antigone's and Eurydice's nihilism, and it is that which makes nihilism not a moral flaw but an aesthetic flaw which seriously mars these two plays. But on the whole Anouilh does not censure, approve or condemn; at his best he tells a story or relates experiences. He may obviously sympathize with some of his amoral characters—Thérèse, for instance—but he does not reward them with happiness.

Anouilh seems to be haunted by the kind of idealism which kept for a long while "la jeune Parque" wondering whether she should not prefer the pure, boundless world of non-being to the finite, sorrowful world of life and death. Anouilh does not opt for non-being, since he starts from being in the world, but it is obvious that the purity of which he dreams is not of this world and that death and silence are the only possible aims of anybody longing for ideals so opposed to life. Death, of course, becomes for him not another aspect of Being, but non-being or a kind of ideal Platonic world in which only purity exists and in which the particulars, categories or universals regain the transcendence and immutable fixity of ideas. In that world Orpheus and Eurydice will be for ever the same, without impresarios or other human impediments to disturb their fixed happiness.

One might feel that by now Anouilh has overstated or is labouring his theme; yet it is obvious that there is at the very core of his dramatic work a real experience of soiled idealism and of absurd cruelty imposed by life on purity, and it is that experience which confers imaginative truth upon his attractive or repulsive characters. One feels that he loves Thérèse as much as he hates all the filthy, degrading ways of her parents, who render her happiness impossible. By now the dream of disillusionment threatens to become a stifling nightmare, the mocking wit, the brilliant satire of the early plays seem to be tapering off into sheer savagery, as in *Ardèle, Colombe* or *La Valse des Toréadors*, and one might at times feel inclined to repress a polite yawn or a sigh of impatience at the prolonged family resemblance of his characters; yet one could never say that he has lost his humanity or that his dramatic skill has degenerated into mechanicalness. Admittedly, the machinery is at times slightly shrill, as in *Colombe* or *La Valse des Toréadors*, yet in spite of that, the old General's plight and his desperate attempts to find a way out of his limitations remain very real, and so does the broken happiness of the two lovers in *Colombe*.

For Anouilh, as for many other writers and thinkers from Molière to Rousseau, power corrupts, money corrupts, society corrupts. Man is born good, says Rousseau, society corrupts him. For Anouilh man's natural purity, the state of grace from the Garden of Eden, is ever thwarted, soiled, distorted or destroyed by the family and by society. Both are simply means of destroying the inner reality of the individual, of bullying him and crushing him under compromises and hollow conventions and rules made to uphold the power of the rulers and vested interests. His approach to social problems is singularly indirect, remote for instance from the Shavian way, for although he brings out conflicts of interests, these conflicts are generally confined to encounters and struggles between individuals. Money is both a means of corruption, as in *La Sauvage* and *L'Invitation au Château*, and a necessary implement for happiness, as in *L'Hermine*; though even in that play the importance of money is secondary to the need for self-assertion and for the growth of personality of the main character, Frantz.

The pessimism of Anouilh is no put-up romantic attitude of wearing one's heart on one's sleeve, or of crying to the waves and to the winds wondering why one cries or why one feels miserable; it is the revolt of a sensitive being appalled and wounded by the cruelty of life and expressing man's despair at never being able to know his true self or to meet another self in a state of purity. It is the regret of the lost Eden, but it is something taking place in a man who is obviously endowed with a capacity for poetry, which manages to flower at times on the very ruins of destroyed hearts or in the grey dawns of hopeless mornings. His heroes and heroines are alone, and when they hope to escape from their loneliness through another they generally realize that there is no escape, that life soils everything and that unless they choose to live a lie, death is the only solution—or failing death, the acceptance of suffering as a refining fire which will consume the dross into the ashes of a life devoted to an ideal. Such is the path chosen by Thérèse, who can neither shake off the stifling grip of her father's sloth and graft and her mother's corruption, nor shatter the placid self-confidence of her lover, nor succeed in maintaining in his heart a wound which could teach him the true price of tears and the worth of an ever-reconquered happiness. He is rich in money and talents, but poor in that kind of human experience which his gipsy lover has acquired through the grinding of her very soul; he has money, but money is nothing to her except a reminder of the slavery it can create; and so, with a savage gesture, she tears bank notes to pieces in the same way as Isabelle in *Ring round the Moon*, and she brings to mind memories of Giraudoux's rag-picker in *La Folle de Chaillot* or of Pagnol in *Topaze*. With these heroines we have moved away from the jeremiads of Frantz in *L'Hermine*, who feels not only poor but "stained with the dirt of honest work" into the bargain.

The degradation of being without money and of being compelled to reckon all aspects of human life and above all of human happiness in terms of money is what seems to haunt Anouilh's early dramatic career and is the theme of his early plays. In *L'Hermine*, his first serious play, produced in 1932, the hero Frantz loves a young heiress, who loves him but cannot secure the consent of her rich old aunt, a duchess, to marry him. The only possible solution seems to be to find the necessary money and to elope; but every one of Frantz's attempts proves vain, and in the end his repeated failures and his hatred of the obstacle to his happiness crystallize into the contemplation of the deed which might redeem his much weakened ego and remove the barrier to his happiness: that deed is the murder of the old duchess. "Our love," he says, "is too beautiful a thing, I expect too much from it for me to risk its being sullied by poverty; I am going to build round it a barrier of money." Like Raskolnikov, he persuades himself that his true liberation and the assertion of his own self require this rejection of human and divine laws. He argues coldly that alive, the duchess is no good to anybody, and he performs the deed with clear-eyed and unruffled logic. But his lover Monime, who had calmly given herself to him so as to show him how much she trusted him, shatters his pathological egotism by shouting her horror at his crime and by refusing to connive with him. So in the end Frantz, who has completely defeated the police, quietly confesses his crime and accepts to pay the price with the hope that through expiation he will regain Monime's love. The whole thing is rather melodramatic, laborious and unmoving. The fate of the protagonists of the drama in spite of their profuse rhetoric, leaves one cold and with a strange impression of unreality. One cannot take them seriously, for they look more like the instruments of a demonstration than real human beings. Still, they set the ball rolling, and from then on money will play a prominent part in Anouilh's work.

Jézabel, which follows *L'Hermine*, offers a similar problem. Again we have a young man in love with an heiress and he too, like Frantz, is unable to marry her because of his poverty. But this time we have other complications. Certain ingredients which will become part of Anouilh's stage property make their appearance: they are the paragons of filth, dirt and crime which every one of his pure heroes or heroines seems to drag behind as parents. Marc's parents could give points in degradation to any: the father is a lecherous drunkard, the mother is a sex-obsessed criminal. The young woman, Jacqueline, could not but be shattered by such a picture; Frédéric will experience the same shock when he meets Julia's relations in *Roméo et Jeannette*. Marc takes a road which will become well trodden before the end of Anouilh's dramatic career; afflicted with a profound sense of guilt which drives him to masochism, the kind of masochism which afflicts Thérèse, Marc flaunts his mother's and father's vices, wallows in his degradation and his sordid love for a venal, criminal maid and turns down Jacqueline's entreaties to leave "the filth to which he belongs". He claims to have coldly helped in the poisoning of his father, and at the end of the play he chases Jacqueline away while he remains prostrate between the blackmailing maid and the criminal mother. The next play, though it turns us away from melodrama, continues to deal with money and poverty, but this time in a fantastic, light-hearted vein: it is *Le Bal des Voleurs*. The whole play is interwoven with music and dance, and certainly is brilliant entertainment.

In 1934 Anouilh wrote *La Sauvage*, one of his most moving and one of his best plays, with *Ardèle* and *Le Voyageur sans Bagage*. The character of Thérèse leaves far behind Antigone, Eurydice, Colombe and all the heroines who drag along Anouilh's stage, the weight of their purity and the sorrows of their wounded hearts. Unlike the first two, Thérèse does not seek refuge in death; like Giraudoux's Judith, she consents to live, knowing that it is more difficult to do so than to die; and her humanity and her plight are far more heartrending than those of any other character in Anouilh's work. There she is, a girl born with a thirst for purity and with love for her fellow-beings, and she has been condemned to spend her youth in an atmosphere of degradation and poverty. Her father is a weak, low and vulgar sybarite, a fifth-rate musician like Orpheus's father, and a completely unscrupulous character. Her mother is worse, and is capable of any kind of villainous action; indeed, when she is in fear of losing her lover, she unhesitatingly offers him her young daughter, who of course will never forget such a soul-destroying experience. When at last Thérèse meets love and possible happiness in

Florent, her past imprisons her and the memory of her vileness pursues her; besides that, her parents prey on her and once more want to make use of her love so as to live on it and to acquire through it money and comfort. The vulgarity and venality of her parents cling to her and weigh much more heavily upon her than any mythological doom on Antigone. Besides that, her fiancé's past life of comfort, success and happiness has insulated him against pain, and he is unable to break through the barrier of suffering, humiliation and disgust which surrounds Thérèse. In his home, with his love bestowed upon her like an orchid on a wedding-dress, she feels adorned, decorative but terribly unhappy and alone. Her family, who have not the faintest clue about the meaning of love and purity, simply look upon her as a chip off the old block; they merely think that she has succeeded in marrying for money, they hope to share the spoils and they crowd around her like crows round carrion. Jeannette, her former colleague, urges her to make "him" buy diamonds because "they always fetch a good price afterwards". Her mother makes private arrangements with a jeweller from whom Thérèse is supposed to be buying her engagement ring, and her father wants a good-bye concert where Florent might lend his reputation and his services to make a lot of money for the lazy, lean days to come.

Thérèse realizes, at least as vividly as Sartre's victims in *Huis Clos*, that "hell is other people" and that a family can be hell. She is horrified, in fact half-destroyed, by the awareness of the unbridgeable gap which exists between what an individual may think or feel and the way this is looked upon by his fellow-beings. She knows that her love will always have this dark side and that it will always be threatened by these indelible stains, just as her present is constantly threatened by her past. Besides that, she is aware that she has no means of awakening her fiancé to her plight. He is happy, and he thinks that Thérèse, under his protection and with his love, cannot but be happy too. But things are otherwise; Thérèse is eaten up by a sense of guilt born from her fallen condition and from the awareness of the misery through which she has lived and which still surrounds her. She wants to shatter Florent out of his complacency, she wants to make him see what her life has been and thus enable him to realize her plight; she brings her father to her fiancé's house and encourages all his displays of vulgarity. She wants to hurt Florent:

Vous me dégôutez tous avec votre bonheur! On dirait qu'il n'y a que le bonheur sur la terre. Hé bien, oui, je veux me sauver devant lui. Hé bien, oui, moi, je ne veux pas me laisser prendre par lui toute vivante. Je veux continuer à avoir mal et à souffrir, à crier, moi! C'est extraordinaire, n'est-ce pas? Vous ne pouvez pas comprendre, n'est-ce pas?

(Pièces Noires, p. 159)

She sends for Jeannette so that she might tell Florent about her past lovers, and as he still remains unmoved, she wallows in filth, giving him all the details of a lengthy and terrifying abortion; yet when she is about to leave him, she sees tears in Florent's eyes, and they are like dew on drought-parched plants or divine grace on sin-ridden souls; they speak to her heart: "But . . . you are crying, you! Are you crying because of me? So you *can* cry? . . . Oh, you must need me, Florent, then I shan't suffer too much." So she changes her mind, and instead of going away she dismisses her father, the symbol of her past, and she decides to stay. But not for long; she has to struggle very hard and relentlessly in order to accept the happiness which seems so natural to her surroundings and to try to forget that there are suffering and misery in the rest of the world. Suddenly her father and Gosta, the pianist, reappear, Gosta completely drunk and threatening to kill Florent; Thérèse takes away the revolver from him and persuades him to go away. But after a few moments' reflection, Thérèse, who hears Florent playing the piano, realizes that he has settled down again into a comfortable happiness of which she is only a part. As he comes in at that moment, she wistfully talks to him about their honeymoon; when he goes out, she says: "It is no use trying to cheat and to shut my eyes. . . . There will always be a

stray dog somewhere in the world to stop me from being happy";
and with these words, as the piano resumes its playing, she quietly
slips out into the night and returns to the world to which she
belongs.

This is the nearest Anouilh has ever come to tragedy, and in
spite of the fact that there is no death, the feelings of pathos and
pity which emerge from the play are practically as pure as in any
true tragedy. Thérèse is the most moving of Anouilh's characters,
and she is as close as possible to a tragic character; pride, or if one
wishes to be more precise one could say the self-consciousness of
what she truly is, is the very cause of her plight. She finds herself
torn between the consciousness of her worth, the strong sense of
purity which has enabled her to survive all aspects of human
degradation, and the memories of past degradations which she
cannot shed off. She is locked in a sense of inner destiny based
on compulsions which are as unavoidable as fate in the Greek
world. Anouilh's wisdom consists in presenting to us a character
whose central purity has been her salvation in the past, and is
bound to be her undoing in the present and in the future, unless
she succeeds in finding in transcended suffering the kind of joy
which characterizes great souls. That conclusion is the more likely
one, for Florent himself, realizing that suffering is incommunic-
able and can only be shared through sympathy and by a heart
which has endured it, says: "Tonight I have come to understand
that suffering too is a privilege that everybody is not fortunate
enough to have." Happiness, the kind of happiness he lives in,
is a form of inferiority unworthy of a great soul; he himself is
enclosed in it like a tortoise in its shell, and he cannot get out of it
to meet Thérèse who has always lived unprotected and exposed
to all the hazards of life.

Most human beings who have experienced the life that she has
experienced would jump at the chance offered to them and would
consent to survey at last the human struggle from the vantage-
point of wealth and comfort; yet those who did so could not
possibly have endured Thérèse's ordeals and maintained purity of

mind and soul, for if such a purity had survived, it ought to make it possible, as it does with Thérèse, to sink into a night of Capuan delights and to forget about the past and about the rest of the world. Thérèse's behaviour is perfectly consistent throughout; she knows instinctively what to do and what she is meant for; like Antigone, she is meant to refuse, but this time with consistency, humanity, and out of a background which the audience fully grasps and contemplates with undisguised sympathy. At the normal level of living, she could have accepted marriage and happiness with Florent, and the audience would have been satisfied; yet not for long, and not after reflection. Thérèse, well aware that she is not born for this kind of humdrum happiness, chooses to remain faithful to her purity of ideals and to seek happiness by accepting to confront her faith in herself and her worth with the conflicts and the stains of life. Only true love, a kind of Franciscan love which would have looked upon riches and worldliness with the eyes of innocence, could have saved her. Florent is not of that nature, the true nakedness of giving is unknown to him, so although a few people might exclaim that she is a silly girl not to accept her gilded chains, those who have any insight into her character will readily approve, with compassionate pity for a human being who can show so much sensitiveness and courage in the midst of a dull and cruel world. One could say about her what has been said about Racine's Phèdre: "une juste à qui la grâce a manqué". And when she walks away into the night, or without angry words bitterness, we feel the poignancy of her situation and we know in our deeper selves, torn between pity and admiration, that she has taken the only road which she could take, the road towards greatness.

Antigone was first produced in February 1944; compared with Thérèse, Antigone who, like her, says "no" to "le sale bonheur" lacks the human reality which could give her refusal consistency and bring true pathos to her death. She is not a human being but a symbol of revolt which, in the climate of a France occupied by the Germans or just liberated from them, could obviously crystallize powerful emotions round her uncompromising attitude, an attitude which is bound to look rather cold and mental now that the emotions that she called forth have subsided. Her gratuitous nihilism, her refusal to compromise or to believe in facts, when facts and compromise were destroying the very soul of France, were bound to find resonances in the hearts of many Frenchmen who in the dark days of defeat refused to believe that France could die. Then, many of them said "no" in a way which to so-called realists looked as mad as Antigone's way, and therefore these uncompromising Frenchmen would naturally find in that frail figure, who in the grey dawn scrapes up the earth with a child's shovel, a powerful symbol of their faith. Like hers, their refusal, though apparently illogical, came from deep sources which link men with the past and with the belief that though the body may die, the spirit never does. But what is, in Anouilh's play, the basis of Antigone's refusal? Why does she say "no", except out of the sheer obstinacy of saying "no"? In Sophocles, Antigone's behaviour is part of a pattern of beliefs which held together an ancient civilization. The dead had to be buried; it was not quite sacrilege not to do so, but one could feel that the reverence due to them as lares would make it impossible for any of their relatives to rest until they had been buried. We have no such feelings in Anouilh's play. The atmosphere is modern, the characters look like puppets playing a part, and the mixture of realism and fantasy contributes to the already existing artificiality which sets in from the very start of the play. A chorus is a lyrical instrument, but not an announcer or a sports commentator; the up-to-date jargon of the guards is clever work, but completely out of place in a play which ought to have some unity of atmosphere. It is not because they create comedy: Thérèse's relations are certainly comic, yet they do not destroy the atmosphere of tragedy; they are truly part of its climate. The guards in *Antigone* are not; they are French soldiers talking about or to a girl who was born at least 2,500 years before; and indeed, she must either be of that age, in spite of the fact that she is dressed by Parisian *couturiers*, or as a modern French girl she has no meaning except a symbolical one in the climate mentioned before. So the talk of "les moutards qui veulent pisser", "Grossis un peu, plutôt, pour faire un gros garçon à Hémon", or the mention of "fleur de cotillon", "fêtard", "joueur", or of Polynice "ricanant, qui allumait une cigarette", by the same Creon, ruler of Thebes in the year 3000 B.C., is like a firework display in a musical comedy or a brilliant farce about the past, but out of place in a play which ends with three corpses and general wailings. Antigone is merely afraid of growing old, therefore she prefers death; she has the right to do so as an individual, but she cannot expect an audience to take seriously this kind of Peter Pan attitude:

> Je veux être sure de tout aujourd'hui et que cela soit aussi beau que quand j'étais petite—ou mourir. . . . Nous sommes de ceux qui lui sautent dessus quand nous le rencontrons, votre espoir, votre cher espoir, votre sale espoir!
>
> (*Nouvelles Pièces Noires*, p. 193)

The final quarrel between Creon and Antigone sounds hollow, rhetorical and bearing the imprint of futility. The reaction of the crowd is unprepared, its arrival unannounced, and one cannot understand why Creon, with all the means at his disposal, could not put this silly little girl in her place. Antigone's dictation to the guard is to my mind sheer piffling sentimentality in a play which has nowhere tragic seriousness, in spite of brilliant and moving passages, chiefly in the part of Creon.

Eurydice

Eurydice has the same obsession with death as Antigone:

> On n'a jamais mal pour mourir, Mademoiselle. La mort ne fait jamais mal. La mort est douce. . . . Ce qui fait souffrir avec certains poisons, certaines blessures maladroites, c'est la vie. C'est le reste de vie. Il faut se confier franchement à la mort comme à une amie. Une amie à la main délicate et forte.
>
> (*Pièces Noires*, p. 338)

Life is sordid and futile; love cannot stand the test of reality. Orpheus must not look Eurydice in the face, for if he does, she vanishes into the shades, in our times as well as in Greek mythology. Orpheus fails to accept the necessity of the mystery in love, and in Anouilh as well as in the past, his curiosity is the undoing of Eurydice. This is one of the most beautiful and lasting myths of mankind; it tells of man ever visited by aspirations that cannot be satisfied, and in Anouilh's world certainly less than anywhere else, for here, absolute idealism can accept no compromise. Orpheus and Eurydice are each saddled with parents whose sordidness and amorality render them fit to be with those of Thérèse, Julia, Gaston, etc.—in fact, they are parents as Anouilh generally conceives of them, and once more the hero and the heroine have to renounce them and their friends in order to be happy. Both Orpheus and Eurydice find themselves up against a problem which Thérèse has already faced: they would like to rewrite or to forget the past, but this cannot be done. Unfortunately, Eurydice's past is a particularly shady one, and it soon catches up with her in the person of the touring company manager whose mistress she has been for the last year. The manager enjoins her to leave Orpheus; she tries to run away from both, and she is killed in a road accident. She is subsequently allowed to return to earth in order to tell Orpheus the truth, and she begs him to leave things as they are, under a protecting veil; but Orpheus wants the truth, the whole truth, he cannot accept compromise:

> Vivre, vivre! Comme ta mère et son amant, peut-être, avec des attendrissements, des sourires, des indulgences et puis de bons repas, après lesquels on fait l'amour et tout s'arrange. Ah! non. Je t'aime trop pour vivre!
>
> (p. 383)

After these words he turns round to look at her; and she fades back into the shades. Then comes Monsieur Henri, a kind of chorus or omniscient person, who tells Orpheus what to do if he really wants to find Eurydice and, with her, the purity of love:

Tu es injuste. Pourquoi hais-tu la mort? La mort est belle.
Elle seule donne à l'amour son vrai climat. Tu as écouté ton
père te parler de la vie tout à l'heure. C'était grotesque,
n'est-ce pas, c'était lamentable? Hé bien, c'était cela. . . .
Cette pitrerie, ce mélo absurde, c'est la vie. . . . Je t'offre une
Eurydice intacte, une Eurydice au vrai visage que la vie ne
t'aurait jamais donnée. La veux-tu?

(p. 409)

Orpheus accepts, and chooses death.

In spite of very beautiful, moving scenes in which Anouilh
skilfully blends oratory and whimsicality, comedy and poignancy
as he alone can do it, the fate of the two protagonists of this
drama fails to be moving. They lack humanity, they are out-
weighed by the mythological framework of the play, and they
are more symbolical than real human beings. We do not see them
as twentieth-century persons but as manifestations of a great myth
or story, and we follow their actions as we read a legend. The
realism of the subsidiary characters, their speeches, the setting of
the action are not enough to bring the myth into reality; they
merely progress side by side, without blending into a powerful
whole. In fact, the parallelism ends at times in collisions; the
symbolic aspect of the two main characters keeps us uneasy, ever
wondering about the true meaning of their actions and at what
level one ought to accept them. In the end, the mixture of reality
and unreality, myth and modernity, and the easy transitions
between death and life are such that they cannot be accepted as
part of a valid attempt to portray the plight of impossible love.

L'Alouette[1]

The Lark, Anouilh's latest play,[2] dealing with the life and death
of St. Joan, confirms once more the fact that he is incapable of

---

[1] The break in the chronological order is merely in order to try to exhaust the examination of a theme which has presented Anouilh with difficulties which, in spite of the change
of subject, he has not been able to overcome.
[2] Since this study was completed Anouilh has written two more plays: *Ornifle* and
Pauvre Bitos.

understanding tragedy and that whenever he deals with myth, legend or history he unfailingly reverts to a pattern which is all too well known by now. To read Shaw's play on the same subject is to be made fully aware of the vast scaling-down process which has taken place in Anouilh's work and has reduced one of the greatest subjects of tragedy to a blend of suggestiveness, petulance and nihilism. Shaw's critics, overlooking the fact that there exists a fanaticism of ideas, and that Shaw was passionately attached to them, have often enough blamed him wrongly for lack of feelings, confusing the absence of emotional origin in the feelings, for the feelings themselves; they forget that Robespierre was not moved by the same causes as Mirabeau, but his attachment to what he believed was just as great and of lasting import in history. *Saint Joan* is, with *Heartbreak House*, Shaw's masterpiece, and there are extremely few scenes in the modern theatre which carry more emotion and pathos than the trial scene and the final tearing up of the recantation which Joan signs.

Gide and many others of similar views have tried to argue that tragedy is pagan and cannot exist within the context of Christianity. They say that the hero of a Christian tragedy, instead of being the victim of an ineluctable and hopeless fate as in Greek tragedy, is on the contrary sure of a happy ending. This might be a very limited view of tragedy, it certainly credits man with a kind of knowledge of God's purpose which no man can have. Joan of Arc has strong beliefs and faith, but she cannot be sure that she is right and that the Church against her is wrong. She can only do what she does: she stakes her life here and for ever on the worth of her truth, but not without terrors, fears and human agonies. Besides that, such a limitation of tragedy to the pagan world denies pathos and truth to the most moving of all tragic events known to man—the death of Christ, the essence and symbol of purity sacrificed so as to end man's ignorance and brutality and to bring to him anew the awareness of his ties with his Creator. Joan of Arc has become a saint, one of God's elect, but her plight on earth and her trial are neither rendered unreal or dehumanized, nor abolished by her final triumph. We may or may not have notions of sainthood, but in her case we know her and apprehend her reality as that of a young girl still in her teens. Her trial and ordeal by fire are facts of this world which are apprehensible to flesh and mind, and which no *a posteriori* heavenly reward makes any the less harrowing or piteous.

Joan of Arc's trial is certainly the most moving of the human trials. Socrates was in his full maturity, and his wit and wisdom still roll on along the pages of history; Mary Queen of Scots was adult, and she trailed behind her memories which rendered her fate less excruciating than that of the young girl from Lorraine. Joan of Arc was all purity, and to realize the hopelessness of the odds which faced her when she pitted her simple wit against the shrewdest brains of her time, or to watch her innocence irrevocably dragging her down in spite of the attempts of those who wanted to save her, is to apprehend to the full the meaning of tragedy as a merciless progression towards the light of an unavoidable death. Shaw has understood all that, and although his play has some slight flaws, it seems to me as final on the trial of St. Joan as Shakespeare's Lear is on the foolishness of old age and on the unnaturalness of his daughters' behaviour. Mr. Ustinov might think that he can still add to the theme or suggest Lear by making a doddery old man walk across the stage with the body of his dead daughter in his arms; M. Anouilh might think that with a few touches bearing his hallmark he could give us a St. Joan which could stand the test of Shaw's light: these are to my mind only illusions and attempts to strain talents in wrong directions.

Once more grandeur and nobility of theme are here replaced by a kind of simpering pathos and wishy-washy homeliness which Anouilh might possibly describe as a humanization of the main character, but which are merely attempts to introduce a form of realism which belongs to bourgeois comedy and drama, and which is completely out of place in this context and has no relevance to the theme. Anouilh's attempts at humanization and modernization are suggested by the use of slang, up-to-date colloquialisms and other similar samples of speech which are as blatantly alien to the period to which they are applied as any sample of modern technology is bound to be in a mythological setting. We are even led to believe that, whether in Bourges or Paris, with or without Dior and Balmain as dressmakers, French-women have always been the best-dressed women in the world, and Charles is pleadingly asked by his wife and mistress to foot the clothes bill so that they may give one in the eye to their English rivals in fashion!

Here Anouilh follows once more the pattern of *Antigone*. To begin with, all the main characters involved in the life of St. Joan are on the stage from the start, and they come forth in turn in order to perform their appointed parts in a pageant in which the dramatic tension and pathos of this most famous trial are dispersed and thrown away in attempts at bringing a most ill-advised realism into what should remain a very unadorned and purified historical theme. In order, probably, to give an all-round view of the main characters, and also in order to link up past and present, we have Joan getting a beating from her father as any naughty girl in her social background might, and we have the romp with La Hire, the foul-mouthed, kind-hearted trooper, with all the elements of barracks language and behaviour which Anouilh loves to throw into all kinds of situations, and which are perfect examples of poor or rank bad taste. La Hire even addresses Joan as "Madame Jeanne", as if she was the proprietress of a doubtful establishment; then he gives us a disquisition on the value of onions, garlic and wine as tactical ingredients, while Joan talks about the joys of war, in particular that of inhaling the fresh scent of dawn and of feeling "la vraie chaleur du copain contre la cuisse"! One can easily detect the dubious aim of this dexterous and obviously ambiguous language, and if one adds to it the inordinate stress on the idea of Joan's virginity, one becomes at once aware of a wilfully suggested pseudo-Rabelaisian atmosphere which is here in poor taste and out of place. Warwick announces at the beginning: "Je l'ai ma pucelle"; Baudricourt thinks at first that Joan has come with the intention of sleeping with him, and his immediate reaction is to haggle about the price! Charles declares that he is not virile and does not like virgins.

After all this preparation one begins to know what to expect from the heroine; the shades of Antigone, an obvious elder sister of Joan, are looming nearer and nearer, we begin to realize that she too has come to say "no", and after her private conversation with her patron saints and the visit of Warwick, the perfect public school boy, who comes to shake hands with the loser of the match and exalt once more the virtue of virginity, Joan realizes that her recantation has robbed her of the chance of singularizing herself by a striking death. Warwick explains in vain that a well-born person only dies when it is necessary and not for the sake of dying and shouting insults all round; Joan, like Antigone, cannot contemplate the idea of growing old and following the common road:

> Vous voyez Jeanne fardée, en hennin, empêtrée dans ses robes, s'occupant de son petit chien ou avec un homme à ses trousses, qui sait, Jeanne mariée? . . . Mais je ne veux pas faire une fin! Et en tout cas, pas celle-là. Pas une fin heureuse, pas une fin qui n'en finit plus. . . .
>
> (p. 215)

That cannot be, she cannot consent to die of old age; she realizes what her saints, "Monseigneur" St. Michel, "Mesdames" Catherine and Marguerite, meant by their silence; she must therefore assume her part, and she shouts for liberating, transfiguring death with the joy with which one would welcome the choirs of heaven. She might have used a less patronizing language towards Warwick, who suddenly becomes "mon petit gars", and she could have been less suggestive of fish-market coarseness in calling for the "goddams" and the priests; but she certainly gets what she is after, her stake and her death by fire. Yet not quite; there is only just enough singeing to make our flesh creep and to wring out a few tears, for the audience must not be left with a sad impression and must not forget that Joan's true story is that of "l'alouette en plein ciel, c'est Jeanne à Reims dans toute sa gloire . . . Jeanne d'Arc, c'est une histoire qui finit bien!"[1] So Baudricourt, out of breath, erupts on to the stage, shouting that they have forgotten the coronation ceremony; the play ends—with guns firing and bells ringing—as a fashion parade with Joan's father much impressed by his daughter's future, and we are left with the happy Voltairian or Leibnitzean feeling that, in spite of death or earthquakes, all is for the good in the best of possible worlds.

It is obvious that Anouilh can blend fantasy and realism with perfect skill and can easily transport us into realms where anything can happen. He can do what Sean O'Casey did so wonderfully well in his early creations, he can give us idealized, moving characters and offset them with samples of striking realism and irrepressible fun which could be called Joxer or Fluthergood instead of Vincent Tarde; but he cannot emulate Synge or W. B. Yeats in creating tragic characters. He lacks the depth of vision and the imagination to realize that the tragic character, the hero or the being who embodies myth, is something essentialized and something which cannot be entangled in a trivial form of petty, homely realism which must not be confused with tragic irony or the grotesque element, which, in the great Shakespearian plays, is only used in order to render more vividly poignant the stark contrast of certain moods and situations. The porter's song in *Macbeth* is no more "realism" in the normal meaning of the word than are the discoveries and the talk of the grave-diggers in *Hamlet*. They are bare facts, stark facts, not artfully processed to fit into a pattern of carefully suggested modernity; they are actions of perennial worth, part of the life of mankind. Singing and dying, agony and laughter can take place at the same time, in the same room, and a funeral can start at times the most gruesome form of hilarity; but Shakespeare, Racine, Dante, Villon or any other great poet produce these stark events in their

---

[1] p. 227.

bare reality; they do not use them as a rhetorical means to suggest similarities transcending historical time, but as an integral part of a picture seen by an eye which does not transform in order to obey mental concepts. The eye merely sees and records, the comments emerge by themselves and they have at times an unbearable intensity. The remarks of Lear's fool on the heath have the kind of realism with which Rembrandt transfixes the wrinkled skin of a hand or face and transports us to the very source which gives that skin its intensity and its immutable glow; they are the shadows which make light all the more striking and awe inspiring, and nobody has used shadows with more telling effect than Rembrandt. This is realism as form-pervaded matter or as phenomenon objectifying essence; it has nothing to do with the jigsaw-puzzle system employed by Anouilh and others in order to give historical characters a flavour of timelessness by adding to them bits of colour which belong to the present. The daubs of paint, the many-coloured coat merely jar on sensibility, and do not hide the nakedness.

The grotesque as an element of universality and fully rounded human life cannot be replaced by a form of realism which consists in transposing trivial details or peculiarities of daily life from one age to another. Such an operation merely affords the maximum of interference with the true nature of the work, for it is essentially a mental process imposed on reality; besides that, the grotesque is heroic, while this kind of realism is confined to trivialities which are not heroic and have nothing to do with tragedy. True realism, the realism of Vermeer, Breughel, Rembrandt, and not that of Poussin, is the result of intense observation; it consists in rendering without distortions or transpositions each detail in its proper, normal setting, and by so doing endowing it with the true life of poetry. The emotions which arise in the onlooker or listener are not prompted or prepared by any conceptualization which may have presided over the composition of the picture or poem; they spring from the direct contemplation of concrete elements which have not been used by the creative mind in order to exteriorize emotions or notions which he wishes to convey. In such a case the attitude towards creation has been that of "negative capability", and intuitive revelation emanating from the intense contemplation of the phenomenal world in its diversity and from its confrontation with the subject, but not an attitude of intellectual construction. Hemingway, for instance, in *Death in the Afternoon*, has an admirable example of how to suggest without comments the poignant irony between the glory and servitude, the brilliance and greyness which compose the life of a matador. He allows things to speak by themselves and without interference, he merely presents the reader with two striking images which are all he sees of the gored matador—the whiteness of the bone laid bare and the grey dirt of the underclothing.

The theme of St. Joan and that of Antigone are themes of tragedy, and a tragedy is a kind of ritual like a bull-fight—a ceremony overshadowed by the great wings of death, which needs a victim and therefore may strike man or the animal. But who has ever heard of one of the Fratellini or some similar clowns, elements of comedy or of realism in the bull-ring at the moment when the matador is about to strike down the bull? This kind of realism takes place when the bulls are driven through the streets towards the arena; then one has comedy, in spite of wounds and sometimes even in spite of death. But once one is in the arena, the acknowledged style must dominate a ceremony in which every gesture has its meaning and its reverberation through human sensibility and history. In order that death may acquire a transfiguring force, a kind of cathartic power illuminating the onlookers, revealing to them the true majesty of the most ominous moment of human life, it must have a certain setting, a certain purity of form; if not, it is stained with vulgarity. Who has ever heard of jesters or clowns at the foot of the Cross at the moment when the world rent itself in an eternal wound? Clowning and tumbling can certainly be moving homages to God, but they cannot take place at the foot of Calvary. The death of a saint, a hero or a myth-maker is part of the revelatory process of the very essence of life through death, and in order to be effective it can only take place in a setting of austere grandeur, which may include irony but not snivelling or tearful jocularity. A tragedy must have a style, a form or ritual which cannot include barracks life.

Le Voyageur sans Bagage

Anouilh's attack upon the family and society as organizations which fetter the individual reaches its climax in *Le Voyageur sans Bagage* (written in 1936), which is undeniably one of his major plays. Giraudoux had dealt with a similar theme in *Siegfried*, and Pirandello makes use of madness as a means to escape from reality. Anouilh's work is harsh and merciless, but has a coherence and a dramatic force which carry the play from beginning to end through revelations which leave us terrified and deeply moved. In spite of the fact that there is no death, this is a play with a much greater emotional impact than many of Anouilh's plays which end with death. There is of course the symbolic "killing" of a young man or of his past "so that a man may at last live his own life". The action moves with a relentless force and tempo which have a tragic inevitability; one is vaguely reminded of that brilliant, lightning play of Yeats in which an old beggar stabs his son to death "so as to put an end to the suffering of a dear shade and to terminate the possible spread of rot". We cannot in this case give our sympathy to the murderer, even in spite of the fact that he wants to avenge his mother's suffering, but we have sympathy for the murdered boy and a possibility of forgiveness and sorrow for the crazed gesture; the characters are not tragic, but there is tragic grandeur attached to this short play.

There is something similar, though in a lesser degree, in the play of Anouilh. Gaston has been a turbulent, reckless character, but we easily understand that he should wish to escape from the stifling atmosphere in which he has spent his youth. His mother is not Clytemnestra, but she has some of her unrelenting ferocity, and we can understand Gaston's revulsion when he meets her again after eighteen years' separation during which, in spite of war and suffering, her anger does not seem to have abated. Gaston must kill Jacques Renaud in order to live. He has been given a chance which Thérèse did not have, that of freeing himself from his past and his family. The character of Jacques is revealed progressively from the memories of the other people who knew him, until we reach the certitude that Gaston and Jacques are one and the same person, and we then wonder what is going to happen, for we feel sure that Gaston cannot return to the Renaud family. The only moment when that could happen is when Georges in the morning talks to Gaston in his bath and shows us clear signs of understanding, of forgiveness and of brotherly affection. But Gaston, who has a unique chance of being what he wishes to be, refuses to link up with Jacques and with the family; he prefers the childhood which he has built for himself, and he is appalled at the discovery that he was in fact the contrary of what he dreamt he was. His horror is shared by the audience which has given Gaston all the sympathy which his loneliness, his plight and his desperate search for liberation deserve. Happily the little boy from England saves the situation and brings relief to the hero and to the audience. This little boy is uncommonly wise in every respect—speech and behaviour; he is perfectly free from parents, and he is provided with a will which requires the existence of a nephew, so that Gaston is as necessary to preserve the house and the riding ponies in Sussex as the little boy in the Eton suit is necessary to him. Therefore all is well; Gaston's only relative is a ten-year-old uncle, and we can relax and move from anxiety to quiet laughter and, naturally, to a diminution of our sympathy towards Gaston, who has once again succeeded in pulling a fast one on his family quite as well as, if not better than Jacques would have done.

The plays discussed up till now come under the heading of *Pièces Noires*; let us now consider the *Pièces Roses*. Anouilh is certainly an outstanding master of fantastic comedy, or rather of a kind of comedy poised between laughter and poignancy, as is quite often the case in some of the works of Synge or of Sean O'Casey.

L'Invitation au Château (*Ring Round the Moon*), is well-known in Great Britain, and is a *comédie d'intrigue*. The plot is slightly contrived, but there are moments of exhilarating fun, with satire and even genuine emotions. Two aristocratic twins, identical in looks, but opposites in temperament, live in a château with their aunt, Madame Desmermortes. Hugo, one of the twins, is in love with a rich girl called Diana, who is in love with him, but who has accepted to marry his brother Frédéric out of pique, following a rebuff. Hugo is furious with his brother, and he brings to the engagement ball a young, penniless, beautiful dancer called Isabelle, in order to have her steal the limelight by her beauty and through an atmosphere of mystery which he will weave around her presence. Isabelle is not quite as pliable as Hugo had anticipated, and she is not without wits either. Diana having discovered that she is not a real guest makes a scene, and as Frédéric appears at that moment, Isabelle thinks that he is Hugo, and pours out to him all her distress; Frédéric is touched and becomes interested in her. Diana's rich father, Messirschmann offers Isabelle a fortune if she will leave at once. Isabelle refuses and both set about tearing up Messirschmann's bank notes and to do away with his fortune. The latter telephones his various bankers and tells them to sell out; but money is not easily got rid of and when he thinks that he is as poor as Job, he learns that his various agents have sold and bought again and they present him with a fortune even bigger than he had before. After a few fantastic complications, Isabelle and Frédéric pair off together, and Diana, at last, turns to Hugo.

This is an enchanting entertainment with brilliant dialogue, among scenes and fleeting moments of bitterness. It is the typical Anouilh mixture of all the characters we already know—injured innocence, a boisterous dowager, a hopeless mother, plus a lunatic lepidopterist, a priceless butler, a melancholy millionaire, and a crazy confidante, all interweaving in scenes of glittering fun.

Léocadia is one of Anouilh's best plays and deserves a greater reputation than it has yet achieved. The first act is a masterpiece of dramatic skill, and though the other two acts fall below this high level and even have one or two slightly dull moments, there is throughout a poetic sweep, a pervading tenderness and a power of rhetoric which make it a true dramatic achievement. The theme is the same as usual, the dream confronting life, but this time it succeeds in imposing itself upon reality. The stage properties are well known; once more we have an extravagant old Duchess, an obvious relation of Madame Desmermortes, of Gaston's patron or of Lady Hurf in *Le Bal des Voleurs*; the young prince is in love with his memories and refuses to face reality, reality being in the event young Amanda, whose materiality at first repels the dreamer, yet she ends in persuading him that there is more in her youth than in the ghost of Léocadia.

Le Rendez-vous de Senlis (*Dinner with the Family*), another *Pièce Rose* has the same happy ending as *Léocadia* and again a masterly first act. The main character of the play, Georges, like Gaston, is revolted by his family, and he leaves it in order to create one of his own and to live at last his dreams, but not without great difficulties. For Georges' situation is not unlike that of Thérèse, with the difference that he is much less pure than she is. He is not only married to a wife whom he loathes, but he is also surrounded by sordid, unscrupulous relations and a mistress who loves the lowest aspects of his character. His redeeming feature, his salvation, is Isabelle whom he loves, and through that love he is ashamed of his past and determined to achieve liberation and to reach the dream, even for only five minutes if a lifetime is impossible. Isabelle is so innocent, so pure that nothing can stain her or change her, and when Robert, one of the villains of the play, meets her, he is completely ineffective. The play oscillates continually between dream and stark reality, between brilliant comedy provided by the real and the unreal relations of Georges, and the pathos of his and Isabelle's situation. In the end Isabelle's purity, confidence and readiness to accept anything for Georges' sake win; Georges leaves his family and goes to her and to happiness. For Isabelle's sake more than for Georges', one hopes that their love might last, yet one has some doubts. Georges is only partially like Thérèse; that is why he can accept turning his back on life, while she could not; yet the purity that is missing in him is supplied by Isabelle, who is truly moving while, on the contrary, Florent was not; so one understands why she wins and why she helps us to forget Georges' past and his refusal to face life.

Before returning to the *Pièces Noires*, one ought to mention a transition between *roses* and *noires*, the best play of the volume entitled *Pièces brillantes*: *La répétition ou l'amour puni*, which is possibly the most technically accomplished play of Anouilh's. The theme is again purity destroyed by a corrupt society which cannot tolerate its existence. The play is most skilfully interwoven with Marivaux's *La double inconstance*, and the nimble wit, the freshness of the style, the caperings and the exquisite fencing displays of the characters are such as to make it very difficult to distinguish between Marivaux and Anouilh. But the fourth act, the most varied in affective range and the most moving of the play, breaks the spell, and smiles and ironic laughter turn into wry contortions which end in tears. Lucile, a sister of Thérèse, Eurydice, Antigone and all the white-robed heroines of Anouilh, has angered by her purity the cynical heartless people which surround her, and she is at last pitted against a minor Iago, who, after a masterly display of wiles and cunning, succeeds in breaking her down in a climate of intense pathos. The gay frills and frolics of Marivaux are forgotten, the pink and white colours of the beginning are trampled down and they fade away into a greyness with which we are, by now, familiar.

Ardèle

In *Ardèle*, the darkest and most powerful of Anouilh's plays, there is no way out. The dream tries in vain to batter its weak wings against the iron bars of life; it never succeeds in breaking out of the cage, and it ends in destruction. The only two idealist lovers of this sombre play are a couple of hunchbacks, and they are so cornered that they commit suicide before the end of the play. Through them one sees clearly the plight to which love is reduced. It is difficult to find a more scathing, more ferocious onslaught on the idea of love; and the yells of the maddened woman, the animal couplings of the General and the maid, the chess-like exchanges between the Count, the Countess and her lover and the abject confession of Nathalie, are enough to send anybody away raving with anger at the very mention of the word "love". This is a terrifying play, and something unique of its kind, in the modern theatre. The world which it presents is a nightmare world in which the characters, much more surely than in *Huis Clos* are enclosed in their own hell and cannot break out of it; tortured by love, they all end in depravity, madness, abjection or suicide. "It is Love itself which is on trial", says the Count.

> Aunt Ardèle has the demon of love hidden in her hump like a malignant spirit, stark love exploding in her twisted form, under her wrinkled skin. And we, who since we can remember have played Blind Man's Buff with Love, come suddenly face to face with him at last. What a meeting!
>
> (pp. 42-3)

Love cannot stand its arch-enemy, life, and in each case it is turned into a haunting parody whose stark reality revolts and destroys the heart. The General married for love, the Countess married for love, Nathalie dreamt of love, Ardèle found love—and where are they all? The General mechanically allays his lust and keeps some contact with the material order of things through the maid who accepts his embraces with the indifference of a machine. The General's wife has gone mad and lives tormented and terrified by the multifarious aspects of sexuality which surround her, whether in the vegetable or animal world. She cannot get out of it, and the description of her plight and of the obsessions which besiege her demented mind at the end of the play is certainly one of the most powerful and most pathetic moments lived on the stage. The agonized cry, echoed by the peacock's screech, which every ten minutes stabs the General, is a kind of torture compared with which most of Hell's circles are benign peace. The life of the Count, between his suicidal seamstress, his jealous wife and her obstreperous lover, is hardly better than the General's. The Countess herself, an egomaniac who uses love to bolster up her morale or as a mirror to console her for her absent youth, shares comedy and pathos with her alternately down-trodden and irascible lover. Nathalie, the pure, like Isabelle or Monime, has sunk into complete abjection, having prostituted not her body but something much more important—her soul. Thérèse and Eurydice had lovers, but their soul remained pure because they submitted their bodies to men in the same way as Ada, the maid, submits herself to the General; but Nathalie falls from the angelic state of purity into the furred, four-footed animal world which is unable to resist the seasonal or nocturnal rut.

In this play, love is only lust, and when it survives, it is only in a couple of hunchbacks whom society condemns to death. They die not with the pathos and grandeur which surround Romeo and Juliet, but in an atmosphere of sarcasm, bitterness and strident farce caused by the three men breaking down Ardèle's bedroom door and tumbling helter-skelter into her room. After that, the two little children, as if to show us that the seeds of distorted love and perversion will not be lost, pick up the love theme, play it once more with all the gusto which their mimetic gifts have en-abled them to borrow from their parents' example, and end up, as the animals do, on the floor or on the ground, with naked claws, shrieks and ferocious moans. This is savage satire in which laughter turns into a bitter grin or a sneer, and in which comedy tapers off into poignancy and pathos. Each character has his cross to bear, he must walk to his Calvary alone, and lust or love are both the opiate which each tries to take in order to forget loneliness and also the arsenic which makes him retch. The style is brilliant, and the passionate sincerity and dismay of the author at the realization that love is doomed to madness, savage behaviour or death, lift the play on to a high artistic plane where man finds, if not comfort and optimism, at least a stern demonstration and a warning that nobody can be saved or reach a modicum of satisfaction on earth without another or other human beings.

After *Ardèle, La Valse des Toréadors*, which is a continuation of the General's story, is rather pathetic and mellow, in spite of its bitter moments and its lack of hope, for it is obvious that the General's situation is brought about by his own personality and by his attempts to compromise between his impulses and his desire to understand others. We have here less savagery and a growing awareness that small betrayals and meanness can turn life into unrelieved misery. This is practically every man's plight, for far from being heroes, men are compounds of petty betrayals and pathetic attempts at happiness, and they are sources of pity or laughter according to the angle from which one looks at them. Anouilh does not make them so, he merely sees them as they are, as Molière saw them before him, and he might well answer the criticism of nihilism levelled at him with the well-known words: "The fault, dear Brutus, is not in our stars, but in ourselves." Anouilh's violent attacks on human weaknesses are undeniably disturbing, but they should and they are meant to stimulate reactions towards less cowardice, less self-centredness and less grossness of passions.

Anouilh excels in fantastic comedy, a genre which enables him to give free rein to his inventiveness. He is never hampered by realism, which he uses skilfully in order to build up character. Whenever necessary, as in *Le Voyageur sans Bagage* or *La Valse des Toréadors*, he brings about an ending merely to fit the characters, in the same way as Molière did at the end of *Tartuffe* when he brought in the king's power. He is keenly aware that the theatre is not a photograph of life or a place to display pedestrian realism, but a place where, behind the footlights, conventions preside and acting is what counts. His characters, his main ones at least, are both real and unreal, sophisticated *personae* or masks standing for certain human traits and miserable wretches plagued with all the weaknesses of men. The blend of reality and fantasy enables him to convey, midst laughter or a frozen grin, the most startling ideas and the strangest freaks of human behaviour. Although he is not strictly speaking a poet, there are in his plays beautiful moments expressed in true poetic language which rises beyond character into a world of its own. His language, less poetical, less rich, less precious, has a greater range than that of Giraudoux, and is certainly a subtler and more pointed instrument in satire and biting comments against vulgarity or social weaknesses. Both Anouilh and Giraudoux are obsessed by innocence which experience generally destroys; their visions of mankind are similar. Helen in *La Guerre de Troie*, talking to Andromache, divided the world into two groups; so does Monsieur Henri in *Eurydice*:

> Mon cher, il y a deux races d'êtres. Une race nombreuse, féconde, heureuse, une grosse pâte à pétrir, qui mange son saucisson, fait ses enfants, pousse ses outils, compte ses sous, bon an mal an, malgré les épidémies et les guerres, jusqu'à la limite d'âge; des gens pour vivre, des gens pour tous les jours, des gens qu'on n'imagine pas morts. Et puis il y a les autres, les nobles, les héros. Ceux qu'on imagine très bien étendus, pâles, un trou rouge dans la tête, une minute triomphants avec une garde d'honneur ou entre deux gendarmes selon: le gratin.
>
> (*Pièces Noires*, p. 360)

The noble hearts, the chosen few, are not born for happiness, they are born for disappointments and suffering, and some of them, unable to or refusing to accept a kind of Christian or pagan stoicism which transcends suffering without being over-whelmed by it, prefer the pure white world of death. Loneliness is the human lot, and is beyond remedy. Our personalities, our past, our families or society imprison us, and the only hope of achieving some form of liberation midst suffering and tears is by being what one is meant to be, as Thérèse is, and not by trying to stifle one's own nature and thus causing more harm by irresolution than by one single cruel deed. General St.-Pé proves such a truth before Goetz, and by doing so he shows that Anouilh has dealt with problems which are now part of Sartre's existentialism and which are in fact problems as old as man. It is the human reality and not systems or concepts which Anouilh is after, and that is why his characters, full of human contradictions, are emotionally alive. It is in fact not what they think, but above all what they feel which is the main factor and the link between a family of characters all involved in similar problems. They are neither revolutionary bomb-throwers nor politicians nor Utopians, they are idealists in search of love—the ideal which they cannot find. Whether young or old, they show that idealism cannot reconcile itself with life; however, there are signs with *Colombe*, *Médée* and *La Valse des Toréadors* that somehow some kind of compromise must be found. Yet, whether Anouilh modifies his philosophy or continues with it, one can remain confident that his vitality, his unpredictability and his dramatic skill will fuse again into new and rewarding works.

CHAPTER 10

Henry de Montherlant

MONTHERLANT wrote his first play, *L'Exil*, in 1914; in 1928 he wrote *Pasiphaë*, a "poème dramatique" of no great import. He had to wait until he was forty-six years of age to write, with *La Reine Morte*, his first great dramatic success. *La Reine Morte*, produced at the Comédie Française, in 1942, is, it seems to me a tragedy, and one of the very few plays examined in this study which qualifies for greatness. As the problem of tragedy has already been briefly touched upon in connection with Giraudoux and Anouilh, a few preliminary remarks about it might be useful.

Our fundamental views of tragedy are primarily drawn from the Greeks; its aim was, according to Aristotle, to purify and to temper passions like terror and pity by a stage representation which is moving, and therefore removes from them what is excessive and vicious and renders them controllable by reason. The hero must not be a criterion of virtue nor a completely evil man, he must be something in between, and he must be somebody of considerable rank who, through his fault, falls into great misery. He may be actuated by some inner flaw, or he may be, and he generally is, the plaything of the gods who compel him to purge some terrible original sin afflicting families like the Atrides or the Labacides. The original sin of the family may be pride; the hero, intent on avoiding some fearful prediction, commits some unspeakable deed and then discovers what he has done. Aristotle does not mention transcendence, but the Greek world is both immanent and transcendent, and Greek tragedy implies divine law and order.

The doom which overtakes the tragic hero is due neither to chance nor to perverse will for suicide, as is the case with Anouilh's Antigone; it must be foreseen and accepted as unavoidable. Misfortune or death by itself is not enough; it only matters in relation to the knowledge that it imparts and the climate in which it takes place. In tragedy truth must provoke the catastrophe; tragic knowledge reveals with it, unavoidable death; it is a form of knowledge which resolves itself in song which has a universal and not a private meaning, and which can be worked out, not through all, but through the few individuals who are the symbols or beacons of mankind.

Shakespearian necessity is not Greek fatalism, since the springs of the actions of Macbeth or Lear are internal, but their necessity is as inexorable as any fatalistic force; the characters are as much tied down to their inherent and clearly detected causations as if the compulsion were external and announced at the beginning of the play.

Shakespearian man lives in a world in which time, immanence and transcendence are no longer in communion through faith and divine grace. He is alone, without any means of understanding or accepting the unnaturalness of things which surround him, and without the immanent will which confers upon the Renaissance hero all the attributes of divinity with the exception of eternity. He is naked and helpless in the face of an incomprehensible nature, and he is endowed with a vision and a conscience which ceaselessly show him what separates him from the way things should be if the world were truly attuned to the beauty of his soul. He has vision and sensibility in a world which he could only ignore or dominate through pride, self-centredness or indifference, and being incapable of such attitudes, he has no alternative but madness or death which reconcile and restore him to where he belongs. Ophelia is not what she should be, Hamlet's mother and his people are living with the wrong man, while he, the true king, therefore his mother's son and husband, is in the wilderness seeing horrors which only the ghost sees. Poet or saint, he has a vision which pierces beyond the mask or the appearances, to the true reality, and in accordance with the truth of the most perennial myth, embodied in Christ Himself, he can only transform life by his death, for he knows that man can only reach plenitude in a realm where "all is silence".

The tragic hero has, like the saint, a desire for liberation from the self and a sense of destiny and dedication to transcendental truth which leads him to death and eternal becoming. Phèdre, Hamlet and Lear are tragic characters. They all die for their truth, as Christ, the saints and Joan of Arc did before or after them, and they die without leaving behind signs that they are marked for Heaven or for a sacred shrine, source of blessing for a city. The force which compels them to their doom may be more explicitly religious, as in the case of Phèdre, or more unspecifiedly transcendental and part of the search for truth and fulfilment of destiny, as in the case of Hamlet or Lear; but they are not God-willed, and the last act takes place not in Heaven, as in the case of didactic plays, whether the didacticism is philosophical as in *Faust* or Christian as in Corneille or Claudel, but on earth and in utter nakedness and despair.

The experience of tragedy implies the cognizance and the acceptance of all the implications of the conflict between cosmic and human forces involved, and their resolution into the ineluct-ability of death which is accepted as a kind of supreme joy. The joy of tragedy resides in the fact that once the theme and the protagonists of the conflict have been introduced, we follow this harrowing experience with mounting terror and pity until the end, which like the final movement of a symphony, could not be altered without destroying the whole and without engendering a feeling of overwhelming frustration. This kind of joy or catharsis is therefore not ethical, but aesthetic; it is not due to any sublima-tion of fears or longings, or to any vicarious liberation from passions, but to the final relief and joy of having lived through intense emotions and thoughts shaped into an experience whose structure is such as to satisfy our more or less developed innate sense of perfect harmony. The experience of tragedy suggests, therefore, the maximum of intensity of feelings within a pattern such as to seem organic and the best that could be conceived on the human plane. Let us now return to Montherlant.

La Reine Morte is in three acts. The first act opens with the Infanta of Navarre talking to Ferrante, King of Portugal, in Lisbon, where she has been invited in view of a possible marriage with the King's son, Pedro. The Infanta relates that Pedro has told her that he is in love with another woman, Inès de Castro. The Infanta is furious at the humiliation which has been inflicted upon her and she sums up her haughty pride in one phrase: "Si Dieu voulait me donner le Ciel, mais qu'il me le différât, je préférerais me jeter en enfer à devoir attendre le bon plaisir de Dieu." Following the information received from the Infanta, the King summons his son to tell him how much he has disliked him since he has passed the age of thirteen, and that now the best thing he can do is to marry the Infanta and to retain Inès as his mistress. After this talk Pedro goes to see Inès, and here we realize that he has behaved like a coward for he has not dared to tell the King, his father, that he and Inès are married and that the latter is expecting a child. It is clear that the task of defending her love and her child will fall upon Inès, and she is soon put to the test. The King summons her and gives her a sample of his formidable lucidity and cynicism; he speaks as if he were the father of Anouilh's Antigone, "Encore le bonheur comme l'autre! C'est une obsession! Est-ce que je me soucie d'être Heureux, moi?" He shows clearly that he hates the very name of happiness and he wants to make sure that such a thing is not part of his climate; that is why for instance he entrusts the task of arresting Pedro to his former tutor, Don Christoval. In the second act, Ferrante is with his counsellors and he continues to unfold his very complex character. He says he hates violence; "Je préfère le style doucereux" but he indicates that he cannot resist the lure of evil: "J'ai conscience d'une grande faute; pourtant je suis porté invinciblement à la faire. Je vois l'abîme et j'y vais." What he wishes to avoid is to appear as what he truly is—weak. His Counsellors know it and they try to play on this fear of his; but of course, as he does not wish to appear weak, he refuses to follow Egar Coelho's advice to kill Inès. He has her brought to his presence and confesses to her his solitude and his loathing of the corruption which surrounds him; he even tells her that his counsellors want her death. When she thanks him profusely, he shows once more his sinister lucidity with the words: "Il me passe quelquefois sur l'âme un souffle de bonté, mais cela est toujours court. Je ne suis pas bon, mettez-vous cela dans la tête." Inès is deluded by the King's deceptive confessions and she believes that he is genuinely good and generous, but compelled by circumstances to take cruel decisions. Pedro, whom she is allowed to see briefly, knows his father better and says aptly: "Vouloir définir le roi, c'est vouloir sculpter une statue avec l'eau de la mer." At that very moment the Infanta arrives on the scene, and she shows what extraordinary lucidity, wisdom and courage she possesses. She says about Ferrante: "Mon père dit du roi Ferrante qu'il joue avec sa perfidie comme un bébé joue avec son pied". And further: "Il est naturellement incertain et son art consiste à faire passer incertitude pour politique." Everything she says or does is imprint with nobility, she moves with the proud bearing of an eagle in flight. She says to Inès: "La nature m'ordonne de vous haïr mais je fais peu de cas de la nature." And in an extraordinary scene, one of the most luminous and moving ever written, she confronts her nobility and generosity with the devotion and purity of feelings of Inès whom she tries to save by persuading her to follow her to Navarre. Image follows image in a style whose poetic beauty matches the emotions involved; but in vain, Inès is caught in her devotion to her love and to her altruistic feelings, and she accepts her fate.

In the third act, Ferrante has again summoned Inès and he continues to unburden himself of his disgust of the world and his solitude. A brief moment of absence leaves Inès alone with the page who describes Ferrante as a glow-worm, dark and bright in turns. Then the King returns to receive, in the presence of Inès, the First Sea Lord, who relates an incident which requires ruthless punishment. Ferrante of course, the moment he is asked, refuses, and talks like Giraudoux's Gods who believe not in discriminating punishment, but in random blows on men who are, in principle, all guilty. After that he continues to confess himself to Inès in a way which thickens the atmosphere of doom and shows that she cannot come out of this alive. The King is obviously in a state of moral disintegration, he is merely an appearance without substance, and he is no longer centred upon his functions; he no longer knows what to do or where to go. Only a violent action or deed, unprepared yet necessary can crystallize him out of indecision and incoherence and tell him who he is and where he is, and that will be the death of Inès. He has become entangled in a strange mesh of sympathy and hatred towards her—that of the murderer for his victim—and up to a point responds to it, but the awareness of this sympathy shows him that he is weak, perhaps mediocre like his son; this provokes the reaction which must enable him to prove to himself that he is not so, and this reaction is swelled by the feeling that he has to kill somebody whom he vaguely likes and recognizes as part of himself. Inès, in her innocence, makes the mistake of thinking that he is logical and coherent, and that his professed detachment for his function can stand, or might even be compensated by, the announcement that he is going to be a grandfather. She fails to realize that he is merely incoherent, and that her confession summons the memory of his lost childhood, and that of his son, and this load of regretted memories jerks him up at once into action: "Un enfant! Encore un enfant! ce ne sera donc jamais fini!" He is suddenly like the beggar in Yeat's play, *Purgatory*; he realizes that the curse which weighs upon the family must be brought to an end and that can be done by the death of the unborn child. Inès has not understood that Ferrante has no positive will, that therefore he can only react against something, and the reaction has been brought about by her somewhat exaggerated praise of childhood, of maternal and paternal feelings, and of optimism about life. Ferrante becomes then acutely aware, and makes her feel aware, that her life is in his hands, and this awareness of power enables him to assume control over himself and to act. He undeniably loves her sweetness, her trust and the dream of what she thinks he is, or might have liked to be, though he knows he is not, and he hates her violently for compelling him to act, for having shaken him out of his apathy and forced him to put an end to his sadistic and masochistic feelings. Inès has not understood that the last thing to do with a ruthless and undecided character like the King is to stir up his emotions; for emotions cause actions. He tells her: "Vous m'avez étalé vos entrailles et vous avez été chercher les miennes. Vous vous êtes servie de votre enfant pour remuer mon passé, vous avez cru habile de faire connaître votre maternité en ce moment et vous avez été malhabile." Inès has been indeed singularly clumsy here, perhaps even a little too much for sympathy, for it is this clumsiness which sets into action the mechanism which leads to her death. This clumsiness remarked upon by Ferrante himself, diminishes the pathos one feels for her and replaces it by the pity one feels towards a woman who has proved herself to be slightly foolish. She immediately tries to redeem herself by saying that she was clear-eyed and that she did what she did consciously, trusting in his generosity or in God's mercy, but it is too late, Ferrante has been knocked into internal cohesion and readiness for action by the realization that her trust in him rests upon the notion that he is weak and in need of feminine solace. The moment he realizes that he is what he is, that is to say, an undecided character, he must rush into action: "Un remords," he says, "vaut mieux qu'une hésitation qui se prolonge." Practically the very last words which Ferrante speaks, sum up his character: "O mon Dieu! Dans ce répit qui me reste avant que le sabre repasse et m'écrase, faites qu'il tranche ce noeud épouvantable de contradictions qui sont en moi, de sorte que, un instant au moins avant de cesser d'être, je sâche enfin qui je suis." Ferrante talks and behaves like a true existentialist; he makes himself through his actions which are not reasoned, but intuitive, spontaneous; he does not know what he truly is, only his death will transform him into "Tel qu'en lui-même enfin, l'éternité le change." At this point, existentialism meets the ancient wisdom of Sophocles, embodied in the words of the chorus at the end of *King Oedipus*: "Learn that mortal man must always look to his ending, and none can be called happy until that day when he carries his happiness down to the grave in peace."

The construction of *La Reine Morte* has a classical purity; it is like a tree which has been shorn of its leaves and dead branches and is waiting for the final stroke of lightning which will bring it down. The first two acts are a relentless progress in the exposition of character towards the final high ground where the final contest and denouement will take place. This is a play which shows the austerity, and the ritualistic, streamlined gestures of the bull-ring: the characters are introduced, paraded round the arena, then the banderillas are planted and finally the two main protagonists of the drama are left alone. At this point, the analogy partly breaks down, for Ferrante is not a matador running risks against a still strong and wild animal, he is on the contrary a huge spider who has enticed a fly into his web and cunningly, and at times aimlessly, plays with it for the sake of playing and enjoying the pleasure that he derives from the interplay of power and pity, until he finally decides to deliver the death-blow.

The main characters involved in this play, whether their deeds are noble or ignoble, bear all the imprint of tragic grandeur. Whatever they do, they do it on a scale above the average, and whether in cruelty or in goodness, there is never in them anything common, vulgar and stamping them as average individuals whom one could meet in plain everyday life. Every one of them overflows the mould of the category to which he belongs. The Infanta is certainly not the kind of young woman one could meet on the top of a bus, or travelling strap-hanging in the tube, and her magnificent pride and sense of unique dignity flow into words which no tape recording of the average millions could produce. Inès is a tragic character; she is in love with the absolute, and subconsciously, she prefers death to anything less than perfection; therefore she is in love with death, the supreme absolute, as the Infanta tells her in their first meeting and in the third act when she comes to her as a shade. Ferrante is a kind of sinister crowned head, who, without having the cruelty of Timon of Athens, is a monstrous force which has lost its orientation and which grinds upon itself. For a brief moment, soon hated, he allows a woman to hear his moans and to witness his weaknesses, but he soon reasserts his existence and coherence through a bloody action which is Inès's death.

The style of this play is sinewy, compact, laden with direct, telling images and carrying more poetry than most pseudo-poetic plays.

Fils de Personne, which follows *La Reine Morte*, was written and produced in 1943, and is again a tragedy of sacrifice. It is not so much the sacrifice of a son by his father, although this actually takes place in a sequel to this play written in 1949, as a suicide of the father, who, with ineluctable lucidity, becomes more and more aware that his son is not truly his son but "Fils de la femme? Non, fils de Personne, comme les autres." The woman, a mediocre woman, whom he must have known in a moment of lust, wants her son to be like her, and not like him. The word tragedy, with regard to this play is mentioned advisedly, for it seems to me that *mutatis mutandis*, that is to say bearing in mind the fact that the main characters command all the pity and pathos one finds in tragedy but lack the grandeur which commands terror, this play is both in theme and structure a kind of bourgeois tragedy.

The theme could be summed up by Oscar Wilde's tag phrase from the *Ballad of Reading Gaol*: "We always kill the thing we love." In this case, a father sacrifices what he holds most dear—the love of his son, to the absolute of ideals with which he cannot compromise. He is, in this respect like Alvaro in *Le Maître de*

Santiago, or better still, he is like Ferrante, except that the latter seeks to delude everybody, but cannot delude himself, while George Carrion does not try to delude himself, but is on the contrary, so obsessed by the vision of what he thinks his son should be that he does not realize it is above all himself and his own failings which he vicariously hates and condemns in his son. This son, who is without individuality, is the image of the mediocre woman who is his mother and he stands as a living reproach of his failings, for a man of his principles and ideals, had it not been for certain flaws of character, should have had nothing to do with such a woman. He sees himself about to lapse again into the same acceptance of mediocrity and he realizes that unless he reacts, he too, will be like them, so he strikes with the violence of a man who feels poison creeping along his veins, the kind of poison which awoke revulsion in Ferrante, making him destroy the image which was coming closer and closer to himself, and for which he was feeling a growing liking. This liking, one must remember, is shared by all those who know Inès and is not stopped by her death, and in the end it conquers all, including the young page who had stood longest by Ferrante. In both cases, we have a father against a coalition of woman and son, and in each case, the father is the loser. Both fathers are in search of themselves; the difference is that George Carrion knows what he should like to find, and he is a victim of the obsessions and inner laws which compel his destruction. He pays the price which any singular, misunderstood man has to pay whenever he comes into conflict with the sentimentalism of the average man who condemns him as a ruthless individual who disowns his son and his mistress. Yet only those who misconstrue Montherlant can entertain such notions and confuse this play with the *drame larmoyant* of Diderot, or with various melodramatic plays which have dealt with similar themes. Montherlant is always after emotions totally different from these. One can generalize and say that his characters, whether evil or good, or half way between, like most men, are never vulgar, sentimental, or prone to indulge in facile attitudes. They all have the imprint of nobility; they may break and cry but their tears fall from eyes which not only command pity and sympathy but always some form of admiration.

The structure of this play has been once more pared to the essentials. There are no tricks in dramatic construction or characterization, there is only what is absolutely necessary, and the play has the tautness and bareness of Montherlant's best work in which truth is pitilessly revealed amidst poignant pathos.

Malatesta, written in 1947, is an historical play, and it stands in marked contrast to *Le Maître de Santiago*, which follows it. *Malatesta* has a rich, fully rounded plot, and it offers a splendid picture of Renaissance life with its love of sensuous experiences, its scheming, ambitions, surface glitters, and ruthlessness. The hero, Malatesta, is the perfect embodiment of this world and his speech is as exuberant as his actions.

The principal weakness of this play seems to be that the main characters are all striking types, representing aptly the categories they stand for, but drawn in too heavy lines and exhibiting a certain mechanicalness in their gestures which makes them appear stagey and over-exuberant in speech. The result is that one watches them with interest, but this interest is simply intellectual and not affective. Although they are fully recognizable human types, they all lack, including Isotta, the essentially human complexities of emotions and the particularlizations which could engage our deep sympathy or our antipathy. This play is for me a splendid pageant, and a kind of epic, but it lacks the human elements which can generate dramatic or tragic catharsis.

Le Maître de Santiago was written in 1947, and is one of the three *Autos Sacramentales*, or plays on Catholic subjects, the others being *La Ville dont le Prince est un enfant* and *Port-Royal*. *Le Maître de Santiago* has an austere classical purity, and the action which takes place in Castille in 1519, centres upon the figure of Alvaro who, after a glorious but short military career, is sickened by the ways of the world, and decides to withdraw from it and to enter holy orders, taking with him his daughter Mariana, aged eighteen. Montherlant himself describes *Le Maître de Santiago* as "une piece dénouée . . . très claire et évidente". This is perfectly true and it is probably what keeps the play in a minor key. If Ferrante makes himself, and therefore only knows himself through actions, whose tortuous unfolding excite our interest and emotions, Alvaro has a clean-cut image of his character and of what he is and wants to be. "Je ne tolère que la perfection," he says, and he longs to be out of the world, for in the world everything one does is corrupt; purity is always vanquished and action is useless; therefore he hates action. His views on purity are not unlike those of some of Anouilh's characters, except of course that he has a dignity and a kind of aloofness which one does not find in Anouilh's theatre. He is already practically out of the world, and he resents any obstacle or commitment which delays his progression towards pure contemplation and God: "Tout être est un obstacle pour celui qui tend à Dieu." His friend Bernal says of him to his daughter Mariana: "Votre père est un saint, ou peu s'en faut. Toutefois je commence à comprendre que les saints devaient être un peu agaçants pour leur entourage." Saints in the making are excellent material for drama, but a practically fully evolved saint or a saint who has almost left the earth, is not good material for drama, although he could be good material for a mystery play provided the actions he has to go through are significant enough. Whether Alvaro is a saint or not is another matter, though one might mention in passing that a character who is so concerned with himself as to say, "Périsse l'univers, si je fais mon salut," could hardly offer such an egotistical and exclusive concentration on his own salvation as a prerequisite for sainthood. Still, what interests us here, is Alvaro as a dramatic and/or tragic character, and he seems to me to be in a minor key on both planes and for the following reasons. As dramatic characters, both he and his daughter are taken too near their final goal— monastic silence—to have room to develop and to generate dramatic interest. They are so set in their course and are so near the end of their journey that they barely stir the plot, which has only a mild flutter or peripeteia caused by Mariana's fleeting lapse, before it comes to a standstill at the gates of *Todo* and *Nada* which they have practically reached. The tragic element suffers from the same limitation which is lack of scope for the unfolding of the human element. Alvaro, whatever he is, is not a tragic character, he is all of his own making, a single-minded block rolling on to its appointed end, irrespective of who aches or squeals. Therefore he could even be in spite of his lofty ideals, faintly unpleasant or he might only be admired like a magnificent palace of ice, at a distance. He shares with Ferrante the same disgust for children and continuity of life, but for different reasons. He is a mystic, intent on the absolute, a Buddhist tired of metempsychoses and he therefore hates anything transient—the body and the senses. He feels that his daughter is his own flesh, and he hates the thought that she could be polluted or manhandled by a male. This does not indicate incestuous desires on his part, but on the contrary a total revulsion from the contingent and a desperate longing for the absolute and nothingness. His daughter is himself and he wants her to remain pure and to die with him as he wants to die to the world. Throughout the whole play, white is the dominant colour, and the white mountains of Avila tower over the scene, and in the end, snow covers all; Mariana says: "Neige . . . neige . . . la Castille s'enfonce sous la neige comme un navire sous les eaux. . . . Elle va disparaître. Elle disparaît. De l'Aragon n'apparaît plus que la haute cime de la sierra de Utiel. La neige engloutit toute l'Espagne. Il n'y a plus d'Espagne?"

Mariana is worthy of her father; she approves whatever he does and will never do anything which might displease him. Only once does she agree to plot against her father so that he may be persuaded to go to the Indies under the pretence that the King himself has made the appointment, but at the point when Alvaro is going to say yes, she can't stand it and she breaks in with the truth. She has had a sudden moment of illumination; the crucified had taken on the resemblance of her father, and she can't consent to have him cheated. Alvaro who before considered her more as an impediment than a help, now truly cares for her and asks her to follow the same path as his. If Mariana was going to be a little more than an innocuous ingredient in the plot, and reach to the level of a truly tragic character, she should have been given more human reality than she has so that she could interest and move an audience. Her faint aspirations towards the young man whom she might have married are easily swept aside at the first faint breath of her father's words. She is worthy of his noble ideals of earthly detachment and unsullied purity, but she has no true life of her own; she is merely a projection from Alvaro's soul, a final glimmer of a kind of dialogue, or the last backward glance before he sinks into the silence of God; she has not enough individual existence about her to wrench tears and to make us pity her undeserved plight as we do for Inès de Castro, so that in my view, this superb play is not quite on the same level as *La Reine Morte*.

After *Le Maître de Santiago*, Montherlant wrote *Demain il fera jour, Celles qu'on prend dans ses Bras*, and in 1951 *La Ville dont le Prince est un enfant*. The theme of this play is of a very delicate nature and it lends itself all too easily to sensationalism, sentimentality and coarse or obscene gestures and tricks in order to deal with a problem which calls for psychological insight and a full imaginative grasp of the experience conveyed. There is no doubt that Montherlant has both, and he shows once more in this play the nobility and distinction of feelings which make of him a tragic author. If one compares this play with various attempts made in order to come to grips with this theme—ranging from *Tea and Sympathy* in which the hero has to be provided with a kindly headmaster's wife willing to take him to bed so as to give him a proof of his virility, to various other plays in which a male character has to be kissed on the lips by another man so as to make it clear to the girl who wishes to marry him, that he is really a pansy—one can appreciate here the merciless austerity and the compassionate attitude which are worthy of

Montherlant's best plays. The play is set in a Catholic school, and the action, extremely simple, revolves round three main characters—the Abbé de Pradts who is the senior master of the school, André Servais, senior and prize pupil of the school, and Serge Sandrier, a junior boy who is loved by the Abbé and by Servais in slightly different ways, and who responds accordingly to both. The two boys share a complex platonic passion which is as extreme as youthful passions involving people of the same sex can be, and the author analyses it and suggests its strength with subtle expressions and gestures. The relationship between the young boy and the teacher is similar but complicated by the fact that one of the protagonists is a much older man than the other, and a Catholic who ought to be fully aware of the implications of his behaviour. There is no doubt that the handling of the Abbé's part calls for great dexterity in order that he may avoid the odium which he nearly incurs in the course of his unjust treatment of Servais, and in order that he may retain the sympathy and compassion of the audience. He does so, after Servais has sacrificed himself to his ideal, and after young Sandrier has responded to the best of his ability, and he does it in the course of a final scene with his superior, the head of the College, who compels him to strip himself bare of all pretences and egoism and to accept his surrender with devoted humility. This final resolution of a difficult theme, explored to its innermost recesses by the compassionate eye of a surgeon who knows all that is involved, and what he is doing, and yet retains a mastery which precludes sentimentality or playing for the gallery, is the measure of the excellence of this play. Love, whatever it is in this case, must be a way to individual sacrifice and to the higher love of God. The stumble into darkness of l'Abbé de Pradts and his despair will, one hopes, lead him to God. His superior speaks to him words which trail behind them the light of coming dawn at the end of night. "Il y a un autre amour Monsieur de Pradts, même envers la créature. Quand il atteint un certain degré dans l'absolu, par l'intensité, la pérennité et l'oubli de soi, il est si proche de l'amour de Dieu qu'on dirait alors que la créature n'a été conçue que pour nous faire déboucher sur le créateur . . . un tel amour puissiez-vous le connaître. Et puisse-t-il vous mener à force de s'épanouir, jusqu'à ce dernier et prodigieux amour auprès duquel tout le reste n'est rien?"

Port-Royal is the last play of Montherlant; it was produced and published in 1954. I hold no brief for what Montherlant himself calls "le théâtre d'action". I share his admiration for the Greek theatre, which he describes as static, and I share his contempt for a great deal of buffoonery, trickery, disguises and posturings which take the place of internal action and merely impel the theatre towards the circus or the cinema. This does not mean that physical action on the stage can be considered, *ipso facto* as reprehensible and detrimental to the possible greatness of a play. It depends on the play and on the aims and creative processes of the playwright. The austere dramatic patterns of Racine cannot, by any means, be made to coincide with those of Shakespeare, and neither can their respective aims and styles; they are part and parcel of two different concepts of tragedy and the various physical actions which are part of *Hamlet* are as relevant to the main character's development and to the social climate of the play as they would be irrelevant to *Phèdre* and to the highly mannered and convention-ridden society in which Racine lived. It is not the lack of kinetic action which is the main weakness of *Port-Royal*, considered as drama or tragedy. In fact the arrival of the Archbishop and the men-at-arms, and the dispersal of the rebellious nuns provide sufficient action for a normal play. What is principally deficient here is the absence of plot and the insufficient particularization of the theme which is strong and moving, into human beings whose thoughts and actions should generate either dramatic tension or pathos. These two emotions are present when we read the play or watch it in performance, but they are too diffuse and too widely distributed among the various characters involved to produce the strong and exclusively affective reactions expected from a dramatic action. This is neither an Ibsenian, nor, for that matter, a Racinian type of play, in which the characters must bear the imprint of verisimilitude and truth to known norms; neither is it a Shakespearian poetic drama in which imagination has fused characterization and plot into an organic poetic entity which defies clear-cut categorizations. It is a play in which the characters are a team, and those who speak most are the mouthpieces of the trends of feelings and thoughts which are those of their community, but they are not fully particularized creations meant to carry over a plot which does not exist. This play is a dramatization of a striking historical event and it bears the mark of the great stylistic gifts, intellectual subtlety and compassionate feelings of the author. It is as entrancing to read as it is to watch; it is in every respect a rewarding experience, yet, without getting lost in an artificial form of nominalism and futile attempts at categorizing it still remains difficult to decide whether this kind of play could be produced successfully in translation, or, for that matter, outside the climate of an intellectual centre like Paris. Nevertheless, this is merely a passing consideration which cannot be given much weight in the final judgment of the value of *Port-Royal* which is in every respect worthy of the high standards of its author.

Port-Royal is supposed to be Montherlant's swan song, Montherlant has decided to write no more for the theatre and to publish little, leaving his writings to be published posthumously. He will, he says, continue to write as long as he feels the urge to do so, but with him, "il ne s'agit pas de guider le public; il ne s'agit même pas d'obtenir une réaction de lui". This is a perfect devotion to aesthetic truth, free from any desire to preach religious or anti-religious, political or social creeds or "pour épater le bourgeois" like so many masters of gimmicks. There are many reasonably good playwrights who feel compelled to deal with subjects beyond their means, because these subjects are supposedly great or topical, such as homosexuality or Lesbianism which provoke "le frisson de la boue" and have for a certain public, the value of an X certificate on a film. Unfortunately these authors, lacking the imaginative power and the psychological insight required for such subjects are often compelled to fall back on cheap tricks and devices in order to sustain the dramatic interest or to suggest what in fact they themselves have not grasped. They hope that a certain vagueness will pass for profundity, and so they muffle great themes. On the purely dramatic plane, Montherlant is the most gifted playwright alive, that is to say he is the one who has the power to grapple with a great theme and to produce a great play. He knows what he can do and what he cannot do; he is like Picasso, who has both the genius and the confidence which enable him to paint under the glare of arc lights and surrounded by film technicians. Montherlant knows what he can do with themes which are within his imaginative experience and, as he is an artist of great integrity, he confines himself to them. He meets his audience, not like a cheap conjuror who clouds by tricks and words the limitations of his trickery, but like a perfect athlete who has scrupulously trained for his performances, or like a medieval knight spiritually and physically prepared to fight a deadly duel, or better still—to use a simile more akin to Montherlant's temperament—like a bullfighter who stands in the arena, in the glare of light, knowing that when "the moment of truth" comes, he can only rely on his skill and courage to face the creative instant which turns death into a work of art.

Conclusion

THE artistic sensibility which underlies the arts of our time acquired its most distinctive traits at the end of the nineteenth century, and, in spite of the ups and downs of two world wars and the great progress of scientific discoveries, it still retains them. Science has added to its failure to bring about the expected millennium a greater and greater anxiety brought about by its potentially lethal discoveries. Nature and anything pertaining to it have proved uncontrollable and murderous, therefore artists tend to feel that the best is to abstract Nature, that is to say phenomenal reality, or to transmute it. Such is not of course the point of view of Marxists or of true Christians. The Marxists trust in scientific materialism and they believe that the determinism of history works in their favour. There is, and there has been, no Marxist theatre in France. Sartre is the only important playwright who has shown affinities with Marxism, and his play *Les Mains sales* which deals with Marxist ideology, was not received with applause by the party. Brecht has been a success in Paris, not because of his rather unorthodox Marxism, but because he has written good plays. His theatre is the opposite of naturalism, his characters are no photographs of reality; they embody it in a magnified way which makes every trait perceptible from the auditorium. The actors keep at a distance from the part they are playing, and the audience is kept at a distance from the actors, so that there is no possible room here for any identification of actors with parts, or actors with audience. The cleavage between nature and art is rigorously maintained.

Christianity from Thomas Aquinas onwards has regained some of the materialism of Jewish thought and has reasserted the Augustinian aspect of realism and existentialism, which is the true foundation of Christianity shorn of Platonic and neo-Platonic accretions. For true Christianity, the real actualizes the analogical diversities of being reflecting the immanence and transcendence of the subsistent Being. What we call the real, in everyday life, is the world of phenomenal appearances which are used in art by the imagination as means to compose organic entities which symbolize or stand for experiences of perceptual apprehensions or of emotions which have been imaginatively lived. Imagination is not anti-realistic; on the contrary, it works directly from perceptual reality towards the revelation of the essential structures of reality which it apprehends in moments of apperception and which it represents in symbols. Great art is always realistic, not in the sense that it is perceptually the same for all, something which is not possible, but in the sense that the phenomenal appearances used, are perceptually recognizable as in Rembrandt's paintings, or imaginatively recognizable as embodiments of truth, in Milton, Shakespeare or Dante. They are not unreal shapes from the world of fantasy, they are imaginative representations of relationships between existents themselves and also between them and the transcendent Being which informs existence. The realism of Rembrandt or of Breughel is precise and without any intellectual distortions; the imagery of Dante and Shakespeare always conforms to perceptual reality, even when it purports to suggest the impression of fleeting emotions or visions. The best poetry of Yeats is that of his later years and it is taut, precise and realistic. It is the same for Eliot and Claudel, who although they are described as post-symbolists, convey their experiences through precise images or symbolizations of the phenomenal world.

The examination of the work of Sartre, Anouilh, Montherlant, and Claudel has shown that these writers displayed at times, taut, stark realism, fully integrated by the imagination. As a staunch Catholic convinced that creation was God's work, Claudel had the greatest regard for reality and, together with other Catholic artists like Ghéon and Copeau, he played an important part in the flight from naturalism, and in restoring drama to its pristine function of religious art without ever confusing it with religion itself.

Naturalism in art is not the copying or the mirroring of nature, for every copy or reflection distorts and is not the real thing, but the lifting up of lumps of nature through senses as mechanical as cameras or tele-recorders, and their use without any imaginative transmutation. This is plain reporting and functionalism, but not art, and it can only be the refuge of the small talent, for none of the important originators of the naturalistic movement at the end of the nineteenth century applied his preachings to the letter. Flaubert used to spend days in rolling his phrases through his *gueuloir*, and his dialogue was certainly not the kind that could be obtained by tele-recording from everyday life the characters he sought to portray. Yet this is the kind of naturalism, which some critics, as intent on discovering genius as Columbus's sailors were in discovering land, have hailed as the new theatre. They say that this is the age of the plain man and therefore the setting of plays must be a plain man's home, so that when he goes to the theatre and looks at such a setting from the other side of the proscenium, he will feel in his own climate while the characters on the stage will behave and talk in a way which will enable him to think that it is he himself who is on the stage. Copeau's dream of communion between actor and audience in a religious theatre is in this case fully realized, and it enables the audience not to worship God but to worship itself. The aim of this kind of naturalistic theatre is not aesthetic pleasure, but satisfaction of the craving for sensationalism for the political and sociological topicality which one finds in the daily Press; it is a kind of naturalism which, much as its authors profess to despise it, rejoins the naturalism of the bedroom farce and kitchen comedy which are the usual post-prandial forms of entertainment or jollifications of the commercial theatre. The names of these playwrights are not worth mentioning at this juncture, but there is one playwright who sails very close to naturalism which he mingles with abstractionism and who has also been hailed as a new light by professional discoverers of talents and snobs intent in being "cultured": Ionesco. In some of his plays he uses a form of flat naturalism made up of dull iterations of platitudes and banalities, which Flaubert had already listed in his "dictionnaire des idées reçues". The result is unbearable banality and dullness, and characters who sound like mechanical parrots. In other plays he uses surrealistic fantasy, expressionism and explorations of the subconscious in a manner which could be exploited in novels or films, but which is totally unsuited to drama. The result is that none of his full-length plays are worth a serious examination and his success, which is entirely out of proportion with his achievement, rests for the moment on two or three moderately good one-act plays.

In the same line of country we find Beckett whose reputation has also been much inflated, but with far more reason and evidence of talent than in the case of Ionesco. *Waiting for Godot* is not, in my view, a masterpiece, but it is in parts an original play and quite an achievement. The first act is truly brilliant and the author has sustained throughout a masterly dialogue laden with suggestiveness and conveying admirably the boredom and hopelessness of the two tramps, representative of the human condition, and whose plight draws our sympathy. Unfortunately the second act labours the first, is fully repetitious and over stresses a very obvious symbolism. This play is technically a dead end, but it is also a commendable *tour de force* and it is interesting to watch and see what Beckett will do next.

There are no such doubts about Montherlant who is now with T. S. Eliot, the only writer in the world who could write a tragedy, that is to say who has proved that he is capable of approaching the highest summits of drama. Anouilh remains the most versatile and accomplished playwright of our time. His last plays, which have not been discussed, continue to show him as a master of wry pathos—which is not of course, the pathos of tragedy, which must remain pure of any Chaplinesque or little man's comedy which dilutes it, and must be only shot through with the grotesque and irony which heighten it. In spite of certain failings, such as lack of unity of style and the absence of a truly tragic character, I am inclined to think that O'Casey's masterly play *Juno and the Paycock* comes closer to tragedy than any of Anouilh's plays, and for that matter, than those of Arthur Miller. My previous restrictive remark about one of his plays, should not be construed as a lack of admiration for his achievements which are, in my opinion, unsurpassed in the American theatre of to-day. Yet in spite of his praiseworthy intentions to write what he calls a tragedy of the common man, I am not convinced that he has as yet fully succeeded. Reading or watching the performance of his best plays, one is brought face to face with aspects of characters, events, situations which partially shatter the atmosphere of tragedy. The melodramatic flaunting of the dead airman's letter, at the end of *All my Sons*, is such an event and the paltriness, sentimentality and mushy suicide of Willy Loman, together with the sociologico-psychological ambiguities inherent to the theme, mar the tragic atmosphere of *Death of a Salesman*. On the contrary, Eddie Carbone, in *A View from the Bridge* shows none of these defects. He is like a dumb animal consumed by elemental force which he does not understand, but which leads him to destruction. He is, all in all, the most accomplished tragic character Miller has created. Tragic emotions whatever they are, must not be flawed by self-consciousness or compromises which could suggest vulgarity, sensationalism or insignificance. The tragic hero need not necessarily be cast in a heroic mould, but he must not be stained by any of the petty defects that have been mentioned above, or anything similar, for, if so, the pity which he draws from the audience will lack terror and could well induce in it conscious or subconscious strains of contempt and condescension. Similarily the speech of tragedy, whether prose or verse, and whatever its level, must always be concise, avoiding throughout, pseudo-poetical vagueness suggestive of sentimentality or incoherence of vision, and baroque adornments which are empty rhetoric. One could never stress enough the fact that imagination is not day-dreaming but creativity, and that poetry, whether direct or indirect, is, when it is good, an art of rigorous precision.

Sartre is only in his middle life and he has shown that he can compensate by mind and psychological insight what he lacks in dramatic skill. There is no doubt that he still has plenty to say. The name of Sartre has often been linked with that of a man who shares some of his philosophical beliefs, and this man is Albert Camus. To date, he has written four plays—*Le Malentendu, Caligula, Les Justes* and *l'Etat de Siège*. It seems to me that Camus has not yet resolved the problem of giving dramatic reality to the ideas and problems which preoccupy him, and I have too great an admiration for his other imaginative works to take up what still seems to me a secondary aspect of his creative activities and to submit it to a rigorous analysis and evaluation. This seems to me both unreasonable and unwise. On the one hand Camus's dramatic works do not yet warrant a full assessment of his dramatic abilities, on the other he is still young; in fact he has not yet reached the age when for instance both Giraudoux and Montherlant produced their first dramatic successes, therefore it seems wise to postpone judgment.

Sartre is well-known as an existentialist; up to a point, Montherlant and Anouilh have a similar attitude. For them as for Sartre, man is alone; he is the sum of his actions; he makes his life and its meaning (as we have seen for Ferrante) can only be known once he is dead. These writers are part of a climate which includes Camus, who believes with them that life is absurd and does not imply any essence, and also writers like Bernanos, who was a believer, or Malraux and Montherlant who have a religious attitude. All these writers accept the notion of some kind of plight or despair which, whether it is called original sin or the absurdity of the human condition in a hostile, timeless world, can elicit only one response from man: a noble stoicism which refuses to be deluded by pharisaism or false values, and which seeks refuge, not in passivity or in the ivory tower, but in action towards all those who endure the same plight and who accept all—death and even wars—with a noble dispassionateness. Leaving out questions about the Primal cause and the meaning of evil, the Promethean revolt of all these atheists against suffering and despair meets Christ's love and accepted suffering for his fellow beings.

Together with these playwrights, there are excellent producers who have maintained in Paris a style of production which is both inspired and free from sensationalism. Foremost among these producers is Jean-Louis Barrault, who has had the courage to produce plays which no commercial management would have undertaken. With him there are Pierre Dux, and Jean Meyer, who produces regularly at the Comédie Française. The dowager of the theatre has not been unwilling to open its doors to living playwrights, and there is no doubt that Paris remains the town which can still claim the most lively theatre in the world.

SELECTED LIST OF WORKS

MAURICE MAETERLINCK
(All works published by Fasquelle)
La Princesse Maleine (1889)
L'Intruse (1890)
Les Aveugles (1890)
Les Sept Princesses (1891)
Pelléas et Mélisande (1892)
Alladine et Palomides (1894)
Intérieur (1894)
La Mort de Tintagiles (1894)
Aglavaine et Sélysette (1896)
Ariane et Barbe Bleue (1901)
Sœur Béatrice (1901)
Monna Vanna (1902)
Joyzelle (1903)
L'Oiseau bleu (1908)
La Tragédie de Macbeth (from Shakespeare, 1909)
Marie Magdeleine (1913)
Le Bourgmestre de Stilmonde (1919)
Le Miracle de Saint Antoine (1919)
Les Fiançailles (1922)
La Puissance des Morts (1926)
Marie-Victoire (1927)
Judas de Kérioth (1929)

EDMOND ROSTAND
Les deux Pierrots ou le Souper blanc (Fasquelle, 1890)
Les Romanesques (Charpentier, 1894)
La Princesse lointaine (Charpentier, 1895)
La Samaritaine (Fasquelle, 1897)
Cyrano de Bergerac (Fasquelle, 1897)

L'Aiglon (Fasquelle, 1900)
Chantecler (Fasquelle, 1910)
La dernière Nuit de Don Juan (Fasquelle, 1914)

HENRI GHÉON
Le Pain (N.R.F., 1911)
Les Trois Miracles de Sainte Cécile (Rombaldi, 1924)
Le Triomphe de Saint-Thomas d'Aquin (La Vie spirituelle, 1924)
Le bon Voyage ou la Mort à Cheval (Le Correspondant, 1920)
La Farce du Pendu dépendu (Stock, 1920)
Le Pauvre sous l'Escalier (N.R.F., 1921)
La Bergère au Pays des Loups (La Revue générale, 1925)
Le Comédien et la Grâce (Plon, 1925)
La Vie profonde de Saint-François (Cahiers du Théâtre chrétien, 1925)

JULES SUPERVIELLE
(*All works published by Gallimard*)
La Belle au Bois (1932)
Comme il vous plaira (adapted from Shakespeare) (1935)
Bolivar (1935)
La première Famille (1935)
Robinson (1948)
Schéhérazade (1949)
Le Voleur d'Enfants (1949)

PAUL CLAUDEL
(*All works published by Gallimard*)
L'Endormie (1882)
Tête d'Or (1889)
La Ville (1890)
La jeune fille Violaine (1892)
L'Echange (1894)
Le Repos du Septième Jour (1896)

Partage de Midi (1905)
L'Otage (1911)
L'Annonce faite à Marie (1912)
Protée (1913)
Le Pain dur (1914)
La Nuit de Noël (1915)
Le Père humilié (1915)
L'Ours et la Lune (1917)
L'Homme et son désir (1917)
Le Soulier de Satin (1924)
Le livre de Christophe Colomb (1927)
Sous les Remparts d'Athènes (1927)
La Sagesse ou la Parabole du Festin (1933)
Jeanne au Bûcher (1935)
L'Agamemnon d'Eschyle (translation) (1896)

JACQUES COPEAU
(All works published by N.R.F.)
Les Frères Karamazof (1911)
La Maison natale (1923)
Le petit Pauvre—François d'Assise (1946)

JEAN COCTEAU
Parade (Marguerat, Lausanne, 1919)
Le Bœuf sur le Toit (Marguerat, Lausanne, 1920)
Les Mariés de la Tour Eiffel (Marguerat, Lausanne, 1924)
Roméo et Juliette (Marguerat, Lausanne, 1926)
Orphée (Marguerat, Lausanne, 1927)
Oedipe-Roi (Marguerat, Lausanne, 1928)
Antigone (N.R.F., 1928)
La Voix humaine (Marguerat, Lausanne, 1930)
La Machine infernale (Marguerat, Lausanne, 1934)
Les Chevaliers de la Table ronde (N.R.F., 1937)
Les Parents terribles (N.R.F., 1938)
Les Monstres sacrés (N.R.F., 1940)

La Machine à écrire (N.R.F., 1940)
Renaud et Armide (N.R.F., 1943)
L'Aigle à deux têtes (N.R.F., 1945)

JEAN GIRAUDOUX

(All works published by Bernard Grasset)
Siegfried (1928)
Judith (1931)
Intermezzo (1933)
Tessa (after The Constant Nymph by Margaret Kennedy and Basil Dean, 1934)
La Fin de Siegfried (1934)
Sodome et Gomorrhe (1934)
La Guerre de Troie n'aura pas lieu (1935)
Supplément au Voyage de Cook (1935)
Electre (1937)
L'Impromptu de Paris (1937)
Le Cantique des Cantiques (1938)
Pour ce onze novembre (1938)
Amphitryon 38 (1939)
Ondine (1939)
La Folle de Chaillot (1944)
L'Apollon de Bellac (1948)
Pour Lucrèce (1953)

JEAN-PAUL SARTRE

(All works published by Gallimard)
Les Mouches (1943)
Huis Clos (1944)
La Putain respectueuse (1946)
Morts sans sépulture (1947)
Les Mains sales (1949)
Le Diable et le Bon Dieu (1951)
Kean (from Alexandre Dumas, 1954)
Nekrassov (1956)

JEAN ANOUILH

Humulus le Muet (Calmann Lévy, 1929)
L'Hermine (Calmann Lévy, 1931)
Jézabel (Calmann Lévy, 1932)
Le Bal des Voleurs (Calmann Lévy, 1932)
La Sauvage (Calmann Lévy, 1934)
Y avait un Prisonnier (Calmann Lévy, 1934)
Le Voyageur sans Bagage (Calmann Lévy, 1936)
Le Rendez-Vous de Senlis (Calmann Lévy, 1937)
Léocadia (Calmann Lévy, 1939)
Euridice (Calmann Lévy, 1941)
Antigone (La Table Ronde, 1942)
Roméo et Jeannette (La Table Ronde, 1945)
Médée (La Table Ronde, 1946)
L'Invitation au Château (La Table Ronde, 1947)
Ardèle (La Table Ronde, 1948)
L'Ecole des Pères (La Table Ronde, 1949)
La Répétition (La Table Ronde, 1950)
Colombe (La Table Ronde, 1950)
La Valse des Toréadors (La Table Ronde, 1951)
L'Alouette (La Table Ronde, 1953)
Ornifle (La Table Ronde, 1955)
Pauvre Bitos (La Table Ronde, 1957)

HENRY DE MONTHERLANT

(All works published by Gallimard)
L'Exil (1929)
La Reine Morte (1942)
Fils de Personne (1944)
Un Incompris (1944)
Malatesta (1946)
Le Maître de Santiago (1947)
Demain il fera jour (1949)
Pasiphaë (1949)
Celles qu'on prend dans ses Bras (1951)

La Ville dont le Prince est un enfant (1951)
Port-Royal (1954)

Some useful critical works

Dorothy Knowles: La Réaction idéaliste au Théâtre depuis 1890 (Droz, 1934)

Henri Peyre: Hommes et Oeuvres du vingtième siècle (Paris, 1938)

Pierre Brisson: Le Théâtre des années folles (Genève, 1943)

Jacques Copeau: Critiques d'un autre Temps (N.R.F., 1923)

André Antoine: Le Théâtre (Paris, 1932)

Antonin Artaud: Le Théâtre et son Double (N.R.F., 1938)

Harold Hobson: The French Theatre of Today (Harrap, 1953)

Index

237

241